TRANSCRIBING ORAL HISTORY

Transcribing Oral History offers a comprehensive guide to the transcription of qualitative interviews, an often richly debated practice within oral history. Beginning with an introduction to the field and an overview of the many disciplines that conduct and transcribe interviews, the book goes on to offer practical advice to those looking to use transcription within their own projects. A helpful how-to section covers technology, style guides, ways to format transcripts and troubleshoot the many problems that can arise. In addition to the practicalities of transcription itself, the book encourages the reader to consider legal and ethical issues, and the effects of troubling audio on the transcriptionist. It explains how scholars can turn recorded interviews and transcripts into books, films and museum exhibits, enabling the reader to understand the wider concerns surrounding transcription as well as the practical uses to which it can be put.

Based upon the author's personal experience as a freelance transcriptionist and interviews with more than 30 professionals working around the world in the oral history and qualitative research fields, this is an indispensable guide for those involved in interviews and transcription at any level of an oral history project, including historians, transcriptionists, interviewers, project administrators, archivists, researchers and students.

Teresa Bergen is a freelance writer and transcriptionist based in Portland, Oregon. She has transcribed, indexed and edited qualitative interviews for more than 20 years, and is a member of the Oral History Association. Her articles appear in many consumer magazines and websites.

PRACTICING ORAL HISTORY

Series editor, Nancy MacKay

Museums, historical societies, libraries, classrooms, cultural centers, refugee organizations, elder care centers, and neighborhood groups are among the organizations that use oral history both to document their own communities and to foster social change. The *Practicing Oral History* series addresses the needs of these professionals with concise, instructive books about applying oral history best practices within the context of their professional goals.

Titles fall into one of three areas of applied oral history. The first format addresses a specific stage or skill within the oral history process. The second addresses the needs of professional communities who use oral history in their field. The third approach addresses the way oral history can be used to make an impact. Each title provides practical tools, ethical guidelines and best practices for conducting, preserving, and using oral histories within the framework of acknowledged standards and best practices.

Readers across a wide array of disciplines will find the books useful, including education, public history, local history, family history, communication and media, cultural studies, gerontology, documentary studies, museum & heritage studies, and migration studies.

Recent titles in the series

Practicing Oral History to Improve Public Policies and Programs
Marella Hoffman

Practicing Critical Oral History
Connecting School and Community
Christine K. Lemley

Practicing Oral History to Connect University to Community
Beverly B. Allen and Fawn-Amber Montoya

Transcribing Oral History
Teresa Bergen

For more information, or to place orders visit Routledge, Practicing Oral History, https://www.routledge.com/Practicing-Oral-History/book-series/POHLCP

TRANSCRIBING ORAL HISTORY

Teresa Bergen

Routledge
Taylor & Francis Group

NEW YORK AND LONDON

First published 2020
by Routledge
52 Vanderbilt Avenue, New York, NY 10017

and by Routledge
2 Park Square, Milton Park, Abingdon, Oxon OX14 4RN

Routledge is an imprint of the Taylor & Francis Group, an informa business

Library of Congress Cataloging-in-Publication Data
Names: Bergen, Teresa, author.
Title: Transcribing oral history / Teresa Bergen.
Description: New York, NY : Routledge, 2019. |
Series: Practicing oral history | Includes bibliographical references and index. |
Identifiers: LCCN 2019010525 (print) | LCCN 2019016615 (ebook) | ISBN 9781351142007 (Ebook) | ISBN 9780815350903 (hardback : alk. paper) | ISBN 9780815350934 (pbk. : alk. paper) | ISBN 9781351142007 (ebk)
Subjects: LCSH: Oral history--Methodology. | Oral history--Handbooks, manuals, etc. | Transcription.
Classification: LCC D16.14 (ebook) | LCC D16.14 .B47 2019 (print) | DDC 907.2--dc23
LC record available at https://lccn.loc.gov/2019010525

ISBN: 978-0-8153-5090-3 (hbk)
ISBN: 978-0-8153-5093-4 (pbk)
ISBN: 978-1-351-14200-7 (ebk)

Typeset in Bembo
by Taylor & Francis Books

To all the transcriptionists, unsung heroines who work behind the scenes to help preserve history and other important data. Also, to Thomas Medina, my eighth grade typing teacher at Dana Junior High School in San Diego, California.

CONTENTS

ILLUSTRATIONS

FOREWORD

The transcribing of oral histories has been one of the most persistent debates among my colleagues over the thirty years I've been working in the field. Though the argument swings back and forth, and the evolving digital environment nudges the dial further towards the "nay" side, there remain strong arguments, pro and con. I am on the "yea" side of the argument: I believe that a thoughtfully created transcript will always have a place in the historical record. In *Transcribing Oral History*, author Teresa Bergen begins by raising some of the questions that underpin this debate, arguing that the answer cannot be reduced to a "yea" or "nay," but rather, "it depends." Citing opinions from creators, curators, and users of oral histories, she finds a spectrum of answers, based on both theory (such as the loss of narrator's voice), and practical matters (such as the high cost of creating a transcript). The bottom line, she concludes, is that "transcription is widely favored in oral history practice. If a project has a budget, it usually produces transcripts."

Despite acknowledged favor of the transcript as a research tool, neither the *act of transcribing* nor *the role of the transcriptionist* have gained the same respect. Transcribing is commonly considered a clerical job to be dealt with in the final stages of an oral history project, assigned to student assistants, outsourced to an agency, or postponed to a mythical future when money and time are plentiful. Transcription decisions are often made by busy administrators and done by ill-informed students or volunteers if they find some spare time at the end of the day. It is all too easy for the transcribing task to slip through the cracks and not be done at all. So, if transcription is considered so important and is one of the most expensive and time-consuming steps of an oral history project, why it is so often neglected? How can such an important step be treated so lightly?

In theory, I understand. I've worked as an oral history program administrator trying to move a project along to meet deadlines and budget limits, hoping the execution of good transcripts will take care of itself. I've also done my share of transcribing, understanding the temptation to skip over foreign words or not to verify the spelling of proper names—the time-consuming details that add so much value to a transcript. But it wasn't until I started brainstorming with Teresa on this book that I understood quite how underappreciated both the process of transcription and the role of the transcriptionist are.

As Teresa mentions in the Preface, this book was born in an aquarium during a reception at an Oral History Association conference. Our very first discussion took place in the presence of the marine life from the Pacific Ocean so dear to our hearts (we are both Left Coasters). What Teresa did not know is that I had long hoped for a book on transcribing oral histories for this series and had thought of her as the logical author. When I broached the idea, Teresa looked dumbfounded: "A whole book on transcribing? You just listen to the recording and type; I could say it all in 500 words!" I figured she would find a lot more to say but I didn't realize at the time quite how much. Those 500 words grew to an encyclopedia of knowledge on everything you could possibly want to know about transcribing, beginning with an overview of oral history and transcribing, and ending with a chapter on how transcripts are used in research. In between is a wealth of information on technology for transcribing, editing transcripts, legal and ethical issues, and the human side of working as a transcriptionist. The content is based on Teresa's personal experience as a freelance transcriptionist and a wide range of interviews with transcriptionists, administrators, and librarians from around the world, whose stories come to life on these pages. This is probably the only technical book you will read this year that will have you laughing out loud.

Transcribing Oral History will be useful to anyone involved at any stage of oral history or interviewing. In particular,

- *Interviewers, project planners and administrators* will enjoy the overview of oral history and transcribing (Chapter 1), how to choose a transcriptionist and prepare recordings for transcription (Chapter 2), legal, ethical and regulatory issues (Chapter 8), and how transcripts are used in research (Chapter 10).
- *Transcriptionists*, experienced or aspiring, will enjoy the entire book, and especially the practical tips on choosing technology and equipment (Chapter 4), setting up the document and doing the transcription (Chapter 5), editing transcripts (Chapter 7), confidentiality and liability issues (Chapter 8). Transcriptionists will be most excited to read about the rarely discussed hard decisions that inevitably arise in transcribing (Chapter 6), and a whole chapter on the human side (Chapter 9).
- *Family historians, community oral historians,* authors using interviews for a book, students, and anyone else doing a one-time-only transcription project will find the clear instructions and easy organization of the book a help to go straight to the information they need. See especially tips on technology and equipment (Chapter 4), a step-by-step sequence of transcription (Chapter 5), and editing and polishing transcripts (Chapter 7).

- *Librarians and archivists* who have oral histories come into their care, knowingly or not, transcribed or not, will gain the tools to understand and evaluate their collections and make decisions about the transcripts they already have in their collection or need to create. Begin with an overview (Chapter 1), then how to choose and work with a transcriptionist (Chapter 2), alternatives to transcription (Chapter 3), and legal, confidentiality and restrictions with transcripts (Chapter 8).
- *Researchers* using transcripts, Chapter 10 is written especially for you, but don't neglect the rest of the book, including an overview of oral history and transcription (Chapter 1), and all you need to know about legal and regulatory issues (Chapter 8).

I have learned a great deal working with Teresa over the past months, and the point that sticks with me most is how underutilized and underappreciated are the transcriptionist's skills. I hope this book will raise the consciousness of both transcriptionists and those who employ them, and that the transcriptionist will come to be regarded as a professional member of the oral history team, whose judgment and skills will be utilized to the fullest, and that she will gain a rightful position on the oral history team.

I am pleased to bring *Transcribing Oral History* into the series so that readers and transcriptionists around the world can gain a deep and broad understanding of the field. This is the first book on transcription since oral history pioneer Willa Baum published *Transcribing and Editing Oral History* in 1978, reprinted in 1991, all before the digital age. I think you will agree that this book is a long time coming and will be useful for a long time to come. Enjoy!

Nancy MacKay
Berkeley, California
February 2019

PREFACE

The biggest surprise writing this book was that when I finished my first draft, it was 20,000 words over the size required by my book contract. I'd been more worried about filling the space than having to cut a quarter of the manuscript. When oral historian and "Practicing Oral History" series editor Nancy MacKay approached me about writing this book—in the Aquarium of the Pacific in Long Beach during the presidential reception of an Oral History Association meeting— I thought writing a hundred pages would be a stretch. Who knew there was so much to say about transcription? Some of these topics, especially interpreting transcripts, organizing them for research and developing them into other projects, could fill their own books.

Qualitative research is alive and well around the world, in a surprising number of disciplines, and many researchers need transcription. It was enlightening to explore how widely qualitative research is used—from oral history kept in archives to oral testimony of refugees that hopefully will help set government policy, to tourism applications, such as walking tours and roadside exhibits.

I've written this book for a few different groups of readers. The main two groups consist of people who are doing their own transcription, and people overseeing a project, managers who may never transcribe and are figuring out how to find and interact with a transcriptionist. This first group includes freelance transcriptionists, one-person oral history projects, graduate students, family historians, and other types of qualitative researchers. Note while the word "transcriber" is also widely—and accurately—used, I favor "transcriptionist" because it sounds more like a person and less like a machine. I must also include a note on gender. While men make fine transcriptionists, I have mostly encountered women in this role. So I use female pronouns in this book. Guys, please don't take offense. I'm not trying to exclude you, I just want to avoid the clunky he/she and him/her construct.

Many oral historians are now recording their interviews on video. In this book I usually talk about audio, because even if I'm transcribing from video I'm mostly relying on information coming through my ears. Please keep in mind that most of the same principles apply to transcribing from either audio or video. Occasionally I'll mention something specific about one format or the other.

I've mostly focused on recent research, and conducted many interviews myself for this book. But several times I quote the late oral historian Willa Baum, who published the first edition of her similarly titled *Transcribing and Editing Oral History* in 1977. While technology has rendered much of her book outdated, it's still an excellent read and offers good advice on editing and transcription. I want to especially acknowledge her work in spreading transcription standards to a wider audience.

My work in oral history transcription and editing has been based in my home country of the USA for twenty years. I've transcribed a couple of UK and Europe-based projects, and worked for an NGO that interviewed people all over the world, but most of my contacts have been American. In my attempt to get international perspectives for this book, I corresponded with people in Germany, Singapore, Australia, China, Spain and many other places. It's been a joy to establish contact with oral historians and other kinds of qualitative researchers internationally. I'm grateful for the accessibility of many busy authors, scholars, history center personnel and educators who took the time to answer my questions, either via phone or email. If you wish to share a transcription issue you face in your part of the world, feel free to contact me. Maybe there will be a second edition.

ACKNOWLEDGMENTS

This book would never have existed without Nancy MacKay, world's best editor, who convinced me I had enough to say about transcription to fill these pages.

I would not be half the typist I am today without the tutelage of Mr. Thomas Medina, my junior high school typing teacher. He was a mysterious figure who wore a black leather jacket and rode a motorcycle. He fostered a competitive atmosphere that spurred us to stay after school typing for extra credit—a system I thought unfair at the time but which ultimately paid off. Good thing he taught me touch typing, because I type so much I wear the letters off my keyboards.

Oral historian Pamela Dean gave me my first consistent transcription job during my initial semester of graduate school at Louisiana State University. Thanks, Pamela, for all the instruction on oral history in general and transcription in particular.

Thanks to the Oral History Association, which has helped me increase my contacts, expand my knowledge, and develop friendships since I first joined more than 15 years ago.

The biggest joy of this book was interviewing oral historians, transcriptionists and qualitative researchers around the world. Some were already close personal friends, some acquaintances, and some I've never met in person but they graciously shared their insights with me via phone or email. These include: Maija Anderson, Lindsey Annable, Jenna Bain, David Beorlegui, Heather Bidzinski, Doug Boyd, Jennifer Campbell, Indira Chowdhury, Jeff Corrigan, Jennifer Cramer, Skye Doney, Jodi Giesbrecht, Lois Glewwe, Francis Good, Mary Contini Gordon, Reagan Grau, Victoria Greene, Kim Heikkila, Neal Ross Holtan, Susan Hutton, Barb Jardee, David Katz, Sharon Kruse, Almut Leh, Carol McKirdy, Sarah Milligan, Susan Nicholls, Juliana Nykolaiszyn, Troy Reeves, Carol Roberts, Jami Roskamp, John Sheehy, Steven Sielaff, Grant Stoner, Trần Thị Minh Phước, Linda Valois, Alexis Waldron, Mark Wong and Sun Yi.

Thanks to everybody at Routledge for seeing this book to fruition, especially Eve Setch, publisher in modern history, and Zoe Thomson, the editorial assistant who answered all my picky little pre-publication questions. Thank you Susan Dunsmore for carefully copy editing this book, and Abbie Chilton for help with marketing.

My dear friend and talented photographer Jennifer Kapnek took the cover image. Thanks, Jen.

I appreciate the many people who've entrusted their interviews to me over the years, trusting me to accurately turn voice into text.

And thank goodness for a lifetime of support from my parents and sisters, and more recently from my beloved husband, Gideon Parque. Also, my dearest companions Rudy the Keeshond, who reminded me to get up and walk him, and Lucifer the black cat, who forced breaks by sitting in front of my computer monitor.

1

ABOUT ORAL HISTORY AND TRANSCRIPTION

My earliest recollections of history consist of the dates of wars and lists of presidents I had to memorize for school tests, most of which I promptly forgot after taking the exam. This is an all-too-typical experience for students, leading them to believe that history is boring. How much richer my education would have been to hear a veteran recall a medic leaving him for dead on D-Day, making him spitting mad and even more determined to live. Or a politician telling the story of winning a state election and moving into the governor's mansion, then finding it dilapidated and infested with bats. For most of us, stories are more memorable—and more interesting—than dates. We can empathize and identify with a person's triumphs and losses, joy and humiliation, while dates are just numbers. Oral history puts the "story" back in history.

About Oral History

The Oral History Association (OHA), the professional organization in the United States, offers us this definition:

> Oral history is a field of study and a method of gathering, preserving and interpreting the voices and memories of people, communities, and participants in past events. Oral history is both the oldest type of historical inquiry, pre-dating the written word, and one of the most modern, initiated with tape recorders in the 1940s and now using 21st-century digital technologies.[1]

When the OHA mentions that oral history is the oldest type of historical inquiry, it is referring to what is often called "oral tradition." The terms "oral history" and "oral tradition" are often used interchangeably, and they do overlap. But "oral tradition" usually refers to the preservation of history, stories, songs, folklore, and poems from one generation to another. This was especially important in societies without written language, or where many people weren't literate. For example, oral tradition preserved Homer's *Iliad, Beowulf,* African folktales and Native American origin stories so we can still know them today.

"Oral history" is usually used to describe recorded audio interviews. We know a collection is oral history rather than oral tradition if it meets the following criteria:

- Must be in interview format (Q&A).
- Must be recorded.
- Must be grounded in history.
- Narrator's wishes are respected.
- Narrator is considered the primary author.
- Archived for long-term future use.
- Follows professional standards.

In this book I will use the term "project" to refer to any oral history endeavor. The size and scope of a project dictate how oral history work is organized. An independent scholar may have a focused research question, such as assessing the Yakima Brewing Company's contributions to the development of craft beer in the United States. Or the topic could be very broad and involve multiple staff members, such as the Commonwealth Oral History Project, which aims to produce a resource on the oral history of the British Commonwealth since 1965. Oral history methodology can be used to document anything that people remember and wish to talk about in a recorded interview. Some projects require researchers to act quickly, targeting the oldest people who are still alive and able to tell a story, such as recording the last survivors of World War II. Other projects gather more recent history, such as the Arab Spring or the unfolding of Brexit. Not all oral history consists of high-profile topics. The methodology is used to document family history, the history of a neighborhood, or even a classroom project where students interview each other.

Projects are usually organized either as life histories or community histories, though there is plenty of overlap. A life history consists of any number of interviews documenting someone's life, usually in chronological order. I've transcribed more than a dozen interviews with a single person for a historian writing a biography. Life histories can also include interviews by other people who knew that person, such as the oral history collections of US presidents housed in presidential libraries.

Another way to organize an oral history project is around a topic. For example, a project might collect interviews with many people involved in a local activity, such as ecologists working in urban communities, participants in a bus boycott or scientists who worked on the atom bomb. Oral history projects can also focus on a certain place or an event, such as a university, a town centennial anniversary, or a national park. While the narrators are sometimes famous or highly esteemed, oral history more frequently chronicles the lives of everyday people.

Oral history can often fill gaps in historical accounts. As Stephen H. Paschen explains in *Catching Stories: A Practical Guide to Oral History*:

> Oral history provides sources beyond the traditional kinds of information found in books, articles and primary sources. It illuminates environments, perceptions, and feelings of individuals able to paint verbal pictures of all sorts of experiences such as workplace conditions, aspects of institutional living or foster care, and leisure activities.[2]

Oral history can challenge existing historical accounts, and bring emotions to centerstage. Sometimes interviews are cathartic and sprinkled with both tears and laughter. Often the narrators haven't publicly told their stories before. These stories might be at odds with widely accepted ideas about the way things were, especially if they rain on the parade of somebody else's good old days.

About Transcription

Oral history interviews are, by definition, recorded. The recording is considered the primary source and is kept in a repository (these days, usually an online repository) to preserve the historical record. But recordings are clumsy and inconvenient, so researchers are less likely to use them. People usually prefer print for research purposes, so recorded interviews are often transcribed. The transcript is one important access point.

I define transcription very simply: the process of transferring the spoken word into written form. But this seemingly simple job description requires a surprising amount of skill.

The role of a transcriptionist includes the following components:

- *Careful listening.* This profession requires patience, focus, and an above-average attention span to accurately capture every word.
- *Good grasp of language.* The transcriptionist faces constant decisions about how to represent spoken word as text, using punctuation and paragraphing to render a natural-sounding interview. The reader should feel as if he or she is hearing a real conversation when looking at the page.
- *Research skills.* Patience and diligence are required to track down correct spellings and facts.
- *Accurate typing.*
- *Technology.* A transcriptionist must handle multiple audio and video formats and navigate transcription software. Nowadays new recordings are usually digital, but recordings on older formats—such as reel-to-reel, audiocassette, and mini-cassettes—still need to be transcribed and usually require special attention. Proficiency in word processing, search engines, and email is also necessary.
- *Subject expertise.* Often this is gained on the job while transcribing a set of interviews with common language. The more interviews a transcriptionist

types involving a certain place, time period, profession or activity, the easier it will be to accurately render future interviews in the same area.

- *Humility.* Transcription is the ultimate fly-on-the-wall experience. While the transcriptionist may feel like she gets to intimately know the narrator, the narrator is focused on the interviewer and may never know the transcriptionist exists. Try this exercise: Name one famous transcriptionist.

What Is Special about Oral History Transcription?

Accuracy is crucial for all types of transcription. Inaccurate medical transcription could compromise medical treatment. Poor legal transcription could endanger an innocent person's freedom. The oral history transcriptionist will probably not face such life-threatening pressure. But she bears responsibility for a whole different animal: the historical record. Future generations—including those who have not yet been born—will count on the accuracy of our transcripts to provide an authoritative record of past events. This is important to remember on those days when typing seems tedious and the mind wants to wander. Transcribing oral histories is more than a secretarial job to pay the bills. It's a gift to the future.

Transcription is widely favored in oral history practice. If a project has sufficient budget, it usually produces transcripts. Most oral historians consider the recording the primary document, and the written transcript as a research tool and preservation format. Even with this in mind, many researchers prefer the ease of working from an accurate transcript and may never listen to the recordings. Here's why:

- Regional dialects, heavy accents or other difficult speech patterns are made accessible in the transcript.
- Proper names and spellings of difficult words are clarified.
- Electronic versions can be searched by keyword.
- Many people report better comprehension and retention via print than sound.
- At this point, paper is the most reliable preservation format.
- It's faster and easier to scan visually than to listen to a recording.

It takes a certain type of person to transcribe well. She must be conscientious about preserving history, and take that duty seriously. She must have respect for archives, and scholars, and stacks of old paper that may or may not ever be read. She must be able to sit in a chair for a long period of time while maintaining mental focus and paying attention to detail. A successful transcriptionist requires a fluent grasp of punctuation, sentence structure and paragraphing. She must be patient and committed enough to research hard-to-find words, whether it be the correct spelling of a town in Vietnam or the name of a cancer medicine. "Transcribing involves listening carefully to each word in the interview," Barbara W. Sommer and Mary Kay Quinlan write. "This is intense work and can be tiring. The possibility of making mistakes or mishearing words or phrases increases as the ability to concentrate decreases."[3] Transcription looks deceptively simple, but involves more than mere typing.

Current Debates about Transcription

Despite the usefulness of transcriptions, some oral historians frown upon transcription. Their reasons include that transcription:

- discourages listening or viewing;
- is the most expensive step in oral history work;
- cannot capture sarcasm, irony and other nuances of speech;
- is less necessary as alternative access tools are emerging.

So there's a tension between the ideal world—where researchers would listen to the audio and hear the narrator's every inflection, or watch body language on a video—and the more text-dependent real world. Historian Michael Frisch, famously critical of transcription, points out that "to work with texts in a transcript is to encounter them in a form once-removed from the original."[4]

Even the best transcript loses something in translation. A transcriptionist can't capture the tones and nuances of a voice, nor indicate the exact nature of a pause, laugh or gasp. And when they try, the text can be hard to read. Historian Donna DeBlasio wrote:

> There are essentially two extremes in the transcription universe. There are the transcripts so polished and heavily edited that they are easily readable but lack character and liveliness. Then there are transcripts that try to preserve as much of the original interview as possible, down to gurgles, burps, coughs, and other assorted vocal expressions. The ideal transcript, then, reflects the tenor, flavor and character of the interview yet is still readable. In producing a transcript, good transcribers will determine what is essential to keep and what may possibly be eliminated.[5]

And when you send those transcripts to the narrator for review, I can pretty much guarantee she will be relieved to see her unconscious vocal expressions excluded.

Sherna Berger Gluck became involved in oral history through feminist studies in the 1970s. She and her colleagues were tired of feeling like women's voices were drowned out. They wanted

> not just their words on the printed page, but their unmediated voices. In other words, we wanted to preserve the complex performance of our oral history narrators with their inflections, pitch, pace and rhythm instead of flattening these to a monotone in a transcript.[6]

Nyssa Chow explained her concern for the loss of "orality" on the Columbia Oral History Master of Arts Blog:

> Spoken language is not prose. Unlike prose, it utilizes more than punctuation, vocabulary and juxtaposition to convey meaning. Oral communication also

uses intonation, emphasis, loudness, whispers, silences and pauses—both intentionally (as in volume and quickened speech used consciously to build suspense) or unintentionally (such as the hesitant pause before saying something difficult).[7]

A transcript cannot fully convey these nuances.

Francis Good, who managed the Northern Territory Archive's Oral History Unit for more than 20 years, has noted a shift away from transcription in Australia. "The nation's premier program at the National Library of Australia now transcribes only a select number of interviews," he told me in an email. While he doesn't think transcription will disappear entirely, he said many oral historians consider it an obstacle to avoid or overcome and that there's a sense of distrust in the end product.

> Doubts about the veracity of the process—distance between spoken word and written text—soon loom large if they ever attempt it on any large scale. I know it took me years of practice to evolve consistent strategies that I felt were valid solutions to cope with things like: broken or re-started sentences, hesitations, pauses, how to punctuate for clarity while retaining accurate reflection of meaning and speech style—the list goes on. Even then, I always included a disclaimer at the beginning of every transcript that for any critical content, readers should listen to the original recording.[8]

Advent of Recording Technology

Since the recorded interview is the core product of oral history, the evolution of oral history goes hand in hand with the evolution of recording technology. Magnetic recording technology was first pioneered in the late 1800s, but was not available in a user-friendly form until the 1930s. The German company AEG introduced the Magnetophon brand reel-to-reel tape recorder in 1935. In its first few years, this new recorder produced dreadfully distorted recordings. But by 1939, tape manufacturing had improved enough that people could recognize the Magnetophon's potential. What started out as a German secret would soon lay the groundwork for the field of oral history.

According to the Museum of Magnetic Sound Recording website, the early Magnetophon recorders were a closely guarded secret—widely used in German radio broadcasts during World War II, but details of its construction and operation were shrouded in mystery until the Allied invasion of Germany during 1944–45.[9]

In 1945, American soldier and audio engineer John "Jack" T. Mullin acquired two Magnetophons and 50 reels of magnetic tape from a radio station near Frankfurt. Mullin brought these back to the US, where he spent two years tweaking and modifying the machines. The machine caught the interest of celebrities like Bing Crosby, who found that recording in a studio provided a nice break from the pressure of live audiences.

Historians were also quick to see the possibilities.

The Influence of Nevins

American oral historians generally trace the origin of oral history as an academic discipline to the work of historian Allan Nevins of Columbia University. When Nevins was researching his biography of President Grover Cleveland, the written record disappointed him. To access more intimate details, Nevins decided to record interviews with those who knew Cleveland. This was in 1948, the same year the first US-made Ampex Model 200 tape recorders hit the market. What sets Nevins' work apart from other people with a tape recorder and a list of questions was his attempt to standardize practices and carefully archive his interviews.[10]

Nevins also believed in oral history's superiority over autobiography. "To produce a truthful record of a man's acts, thoughts, and motives, two qualities are obviously essential: self-knowledge and a fair amount of candor," he said. However, many people, he believed, are deficient in one or both of these traits.

> But in the hands of an earnest, courageous interviewer who has mastered a background of facts and who has the nerve to press his scalpel tactfully and with some knowledge of psychology into delicate tissues and even bleeding wounds, deficiencies can be exposed; and oral history can get at more of the truth than a man will present about himself in a written autobiography.[11]

Other historians eagerly adopted this new methodology. T. Harry Williams, an Illinois-born history professor, was teaching at Louisiana State University when he became interested in using the new tape recording machines. Williams dragged his cumbersome reel-to-reel recorder around Louisiana in the 1950s, collecting interviews for his biography of Louisiana politician Huey Long. He recognized oral history as a way to access stories that otherwise left no paper trail. "Trained researchers using a tape recorder ought to interview people to get the information that is in their heads and no place else," Williams said.[12] When I worked at Louisiana State University's (LSU) oral history center, which is named for Williams, we proudly displayed this recorder. It sure looked heavy! But since it had the feel of a sacred relic, I never touched the recorder, let alone tried to lift it.

Meanwhile, researchers around the globe were placing tape recorders in front of narrators. The Welshman George Ewart Evans, a frustrated writer and teacher, discovered his life's work would be recording stories of everyday rural life throughout the UK. The British Library houses 254 of his recordings made between 1956 and 1977, documenting agricultural work, folk beliefs and songs.[13] The London-based publisher Faber & Faber still offers 14 of Evans' oral history-based books for sale, starting with *Ask the Fellows Who Cut the Hay,* published in 1965.[14]

Hazel De Berg, born in 1913 in New South Wales, began using a tape recorder in 1957 while doing volunteer work for the Blind Book Society. She quickly saw the potential for recording life histories and turned her attention to interviewing writers, artists and other creative and influential people around Australia and abroad. She recorded 1,290 narrators over a 27-year span.[15]

The Nehru Memorial Museum and Library in New Delhi, India, began laying plans for its oral history program in 1966, and has since recorded more than 1,350 people connected with Indian political movements and events. The Oral History Centre in the National Archives of Singapore began its collection in 1979 and now contains more than 4,000 interviews from all walks of life, including everything from street hawkers to medical professionals.[16] These are just a few examples of the burgeoning popularity of oral history around the world, beginning in the 1950s and 1960s.[17]

Transcripts were vital in early days, as it was much easier for researchers to read manuscripts than to struggle with delicate tapes strung through cumbersome reel-to-reel recorders. In the early years, the transcript was considered the primary document, and, appallingly, oral historians often erased and reused expensive tapes as a cost-saving measure. As a result, a great many of the early oral history interviews exist in transcript form only.

Birth of Oral History Organizations

Nevins' emphasis on shaping best practices is crucial to oral history as a field. Unlike many other academic disciplines—say, chemistry, mathematics, music and engineering—oral history has a very low barrier to entry. Nearly everybody in the world participates in the basic foundation of oral history—dialogue—and it's not difficult to record a conversation. Even within the field of history, the work of oral historians is sometimes belittled by other historians who question the reliability of memory and the general credibility of the sources. Sometimes oral historians feel like underdogs crusading to add the common man and woman's voice to the historical record.

Oral historians began to identify as a group, perhaps due to a slight feeling of being outside the mainstream, and started to form professional oral history associations. In the US, a group of oral historians met in Lake Arrowhead, California, in 1966 to discuss developments in and the direction of their field. This meeting led to the founding of the Oral History Association. In 1968, the new organization published its first set of statements outlining principles and obligations of those using the oral history methodology. The 1968 statements specified that interviews be transcribed, and that transcripts would be presented to narrators for approval. Once the narrator approved the transcript, the tape and transcript could be deposited in an archive.[18]

In fact, from the very beginning, transcribing and archiving the interviews were defined as essential steps in this new field. That the early oral history programs found homes at major university libraries in the US, Columbia University (1948),

UC Berkeley (1954) and UCLA (1959), is testimony to the importance early oral historians placed on the role of interviews in scholarly communities.

The Oral History Society (OHS) in the United Kingdom began in a similarly casual way as its US counterpart. In 1969, an informal day conference at the British Institute of Recorded Sound planted the seed for the society's founding in 1973.[19] The Oral History Association of Australia (now Oral History Australia) credits one woman for its founding—dynamic social worker turned oral historian Jean Teasdale, who began canvasing for support for a national organization in 1978.[20] These are some of the earliest national oral history associations. But around the world, more associations formed, and continue to form today.

Fifty years after the inception of the Oral History Association, the International Oral History Association (IOHA) unites scholars worldwide. Many countries have their own associations, such as the National Center for Documentation and Research in the United Arab Emirates, Colombia's Colectivo de Historia Oral, the Japan Oral History Association, the Oral History Association of South Africa and the National Oral History Association of New Zealand, to name just a few.[21]

The Rise of Community Oral History

In their early years, the academic oral history programs founded by Allan Nevins and other historians emphasized collecting the stories of well-known people in politics, business and entertainment. As these programs matured, a grassroots oral history revolution was underway.

In the 1960s, British researchers in the emerging field of labor history recognized the value of oral sources. As described on the UK's Oral History Society's website, "Information was difficult to find about the past domestic and working lives of the majority of the population. And there were large parts of British working class history that were simply absent from surviving documentary evidence." So lives of the "laboring classes" became a focus of collecting. John Saville, a leading labor historian at this time, became the first chair of the Oral History Society.[22]

In 1976, the US bicentennial inspired many Americans to contemplate history—especially that of ordinary folks. This look backwards, coupled with the 1970s consciousness of social history and the availability of inexpensive cassette tapes and recorders, launched many community history projects.

As defined in *The Community Oral History Toolkit,* community oral history encompasses projects "undertaken by any group unaffiliated with an academic institution. Such groups could be neighborhood associations, historical societies, museums, libraries, professional associations, clubs, or any of the myriad ways people organize themselves to accomplish particular ends." [23]

Community history is priceless, and many projects succeed in documenting groups that would otherwise remain voiceless in the historical record. These efforts are especially successful if interviews are preserved in a reliable repository. But community history projects face a different set of challenges than those housed in academic institutions. They generally lack institutional and financial support and rely heavily, if not entirely, on volunteers. Often they spring up around an anniversary or other event important to that community. These oral history projects usually scramble for funds, equipment and expertise, and face uneven staffing and a lack of infrastructure.

In their excitement to start a project, community historians often skip over the important planning steps, underestimate their budgets, and overestimate the commitment and availability of volunteers. I've transcribed for community projects that finally admitted their volunteer transcriptionists had disappeared for good, or that eventually got funding to transcribe mystery boxes of tapes left behind—sometimes for decades—by a previous incarnation of the project.

Newer Technology and Digitization

The field of oral history is constantly evolving, and technology has led to some of the most significant changes. Reel-to-reel tape recorders gave way to cassette tapes in the late 1960s and early 1970s. The pace of change accelerated with the rise of digital technology, and the quick succession of laser disks, CDs, DVDs, memory sticks and other storage media. How durable were all these formats? How would they be migrated to new formats that would be invented in the future? Nobody knows for sure. However, we do know that without proper conservation and close attention to migrating audio to newer forms of media, the original recording degrades. In addition, some interviews become obsolete because playback devices are hard to find.[24]

When I first encountered digitized oral history interviews, I hoped it was a passing fad. I was used to transcribing cassette tapes, and perfectly comfortable with my cumbersome transcription machine. But when Maxell, TDK, Sony and Memorex all stopped manufacturing cassette tapes in the first decade of the twenty-first century, I had to admit digitization wasn't going away anytime soon. Today, the biggest surviving cassette manufacturer, National Audio in Springfield, Missouri, mostly markets to nostalgic consumers seeking retro trends.[25]

Of course, most of us now live in a digital world. The digital revolution changed the way we practice oral history, from the way interviews are recorded to the ways they are transcribed, cataloged, stored and accessed. A scholar in China can electronically send an audio or video file to a researcher in Canada within seconds. Online collections can be accessed from anywhere. Transcriptionists no longer have to figure out where to store padded envelopes bulging with cassette tapes awaiting transcription.

As archives began to post interview transcripts and recordings online, huge new ethical areas opened up, especially about access. Earlier oral historians couldn't see into the future and predict the need to have narrators sign an all-encompassing waiver. Oral historians at universities also knocked heads with institutional review boards. Did narrators of oral histories fall into the same "human subjects" category as patients in medical experiments? The ethical, legal and administrative aspects of oral history are endlessly debated.

Oral History Today

Worldwide, people now use oral history to reevaluate or discredit governments and colonial regimes, whether it is former Soviet countries looking at communism or South Americans recording the testimony of those victimized by state terrorism.[26] In China, oral history is slowly gaining traction. Di Yin Lu, who conducted oral history interviews in China about the delicate topic of the government appropriating art during the Cultural Revolution, described the importance of the methodology:

> Since the 1980s, a quiet revolution has been brewing in the field of Chinese studies. It started when scholars like David Faure and Emily Honig talked to Jiangsu migrants about work and identity, and when Chinese writers, such as Liao Yiwu and Feng Jicai, collected stories about ordinary indignities in Chengdu and Ningbo. These oral histories juxtaposed interviews with archival data, using personal memories to supplement and even contradict official narratives. The studies' wealth of township and district-level data have transformed our conception of twentieth-century China, as well as the methodological boundaries of Chinese historical research.[27]

However, according to documentary filmmaker Sun Yi, China is still ironing out many questions of ethics, intellectual property and oral history access.[28]

In Spain, much of the early oral history work was related to Francoist repression, and the political dimension continues to be important to oral historians, according to David Beorlegui, a researcher and oral historian at University of the Basque Country. He told me in an email:

> Oral history is not very popular due to our recent violent past. Our government is not interested at all in promoting oral history, because it is considered something "dangerous" to the status quo. Some testimonies have been collected, but the lack of interest is huge. We also have problems in the past trying to publish some results or getting access to archives (our law is quite restrictive).

Instead of any association that serves as a gathering point, Beorlegui said historians using oral history tend to work in small, interdisciplinary groups.[29]

Oral history programs and archives are housed in universities, historical societies and libraries around the world. Some large corporations and organizations also collect oral histories to preserve their history and institutional knowledge. I've worked with many cultural and ethnic groups that collect histories from their elders, such as Native Americans documenting basketry traditions, nuns recalling the evolution of their order, and musical history for the Friends of Negro Spirituals. There seems to be an oral history project—or the potential for a project—on just about any topic.

Many people unaffiliated with oral history associations or archives also adapt oral history methodologies to their own work. Graduate students record oral history interviews for theses and dissertations on myriad topics. Documentary filmmakers do video oral histories. Qualitative researchers in anthropology, sociology, public health and other fields borrow oral history methodology and make it their own.

Recording technology has grown more accessible over the last 50 years. Prices of audio and video recorders have dropped while quality has improved, putting audio and video recorders into the price range of most users. Smartphones, with a recording app that provides decent quality recording, place the ability to audio- or video-record interviews in the hands of pretty much everyone, especially youth around the world, further democratizing the field of oral history. While most folks are busy filming their cat or their sandwich, some will rise to the calling to record people telling their true, significant and heartfelt stories.

Add up all these sources of recordings and you have an insurmountable amount of data to organize. And there is a sense of urgency. Already people are forgetting the words of the old Negro spirituals. Memories of the lonesome silence of the novitiate are lost as old nuns die and few young women join orders. Without the narratives of Native Americans, future generations will think of their baskets as stagnant museum displays, rather than useful, spirit-filled items meant to carry, dance, and eventually return to the earth. All of these precious stories need collecting. The world needs finding aids, such as indexes and abstracts. The world needs transcripts, and well-trained transcriptionists to produce them. And transcriptionists need guidance and best practices so that we can do these narratives justice.

Who Needs Transcription?

Oral history brought me into the transcription field. But I've learned that myriad professions rely on and benefit from accurate interview transcription. Here are some of the main ones, with examples and mini case studies about how transcription fits into their work. If you're an oral historian or qualitative researcher, this will give you a bigger picture of the uses of transcription. If you're a transcriptionist, these are some of the industries and disciplines you might work in.

University Oral History Programs

Many universities around the world sponsor oral history programs, usually housed in their libraries. Whether researchers are studying Manitoba food history at the University of Winnipeg's Oral History Centre, or Ireland's notorious Magdalene laundries at Maynooth University in County Kildare, they count on universities to preserve oral history and make it accessible. Older university collections are extensive, such as the Columbia [University] Center for Oral History (CCOH), founded in 1948 by Allan Nevins, which holds more than 10,000 interviews in its archives.[30]

Baylor University in Waco, Texas, is home to the Baylor University Institute for Oral History (BUIOH). The collection includes 4,000 interview transcripts and 2,000 audio files of interviews in its digital collection.[31] Strong proponents of transcription, staff aim to transcribe all their interviews.

Not all university programs prioritize transcription. The Oral History Program at the University of Wisconsin, Madison, has limited transcription funds, according to Troy Reeves, program director. He describes himself as a one-person shop. Despite staffing and budget limitations, Reeves is responsible for an impressive collection of more than 1,650 interviews totaling around 4,500 audio hours. Reeves estimates that 15–20 percent of the total collection has been transcribed. While transcription was a high priority in the early years of Madison's program, which started in 1971, directors in the 1980s prioritized collecting over transcription, Reeves said. Nowadays, with limited funding, Reeves would like to transcribe more but must be very selective about which interviews get transcribed.[32]

Administrators of Archives and Library Collections

All kinds of libraries and archives serve as repositories for oral history collections, ranging from national archives to university libraries down to neighborhood public libraries. Sometimes library personnel are involved in collecting these oral histories. Other times, oral history collections are donated and the librarians must process them for the public use. People might try to donate only recordings, in the form of cassette tapes, digital files, or even reel-to-reel tapes, without transcripts or even much accompanying information. Libraries seldom have the resources to transcribe such collections, or even to process them at all. Note that libraries are not obligated to accept such "gifts," which could be difficult and time-consuming to process. The best practice is for the donor to find a logical repository for a collection and to make an agreement with the library ahead of time and deliver complete packages, along with metadata.

The Oral History Centre at the National Archives of Singapore's collections include projects on sports personalities, performing arts and the occupation by Japanese soldiers during World War II. Oral historian Mark Wong told me that about 30 percent of their interviews are transcribed:

> This strikes a balance between the immense value that transcripts give and the high costs of producing them. We regard the recorded audio as the primary source and transcripts as metadata, but as it is faster to read through transcripts than to listen in real time, researchers generally prefer to consult transcripts over the audio. That said, we encourage researchers to listen to the audio (to be able to better interpret the material) and we help researchers by putting the majority of open-access recordings for streaming online.[33]

For library administrators, running an oral history program may be only one task of many in a large agenda. At Oregon Health & Science University (OHSU) in

Portland, Oregon, while Maija Anderson served as interim director of library operations, she conducted an oral history program, oversaw a department of an academic library that manages collections of archives, rare books, artifacts, and digital assets, and provided services to the researchers who used them. The oral history program falls under the public history programming category, which also includes a lecture series and exhibits.[34] Transcription is extremely important to OHSU's work. "Most of our researchers access our oral histories through transcripts," she told me while she was directing the program. "We and our researchers are concerned with accuracy and authenticity, and having professional transcription is key."

Community Oral History Projects

Community oral history projects range from tiny, one-person efforts to large projects with a mixture of professional staff and volunteers. Any club, historical society, professional organization or other non-university-affiliated entity might start a community oral history project. They usually share these characteristics:

- lack of institutional support;
- organized around some sort of end product, such as a book or performance;
- deadline-driven;
- rely on volunteers;
- lack infrastructure, such as equipment, storage or office space;
- limited funds.[35]

Minnesota-based scholar Kim Heikkila, the owner and president of Spotlight Oral History, created the Eat Street Oral History Project in 2016 to document stories behind the ethnic restaurants on Minneapolis' Nicollet Avenue. Her duties included all the communications with the narrators, conducting the oral history interviews, project management, contact with the repository, public relations, marketing and research. Heikkila hired a professional transcriptionist to produce transcripts, which she believes are hugely important to researchers. "They're going to work from the transcript, particularly if they're doing any kind of written product."[36]

Historical Societies

Many historical societies around the world collect oral histories of their country, state or city, depending upon the territory they cover. Some are very broad, such as the Hong Kong Archives Society, which documents the history of an autonomous territory of more than seven million people. Others set smaller parameters. The Tinmouth Historical and Genealogical Society records long-time citizens of a Vermont town, population 600.

Jeff Corrigan was the oral historian for the State Historical Society of Missouri from 2008 until 2017. As the only staff member of the society's oral history program, he oversaw a collection of 5,000 interviews. Corrigan aimed to transcribe all the interviews he conducted, but always ran short on funding. "Transcription was definitely important, but it was the one thing that always got kicked to the back burner," he said.[37] Corrigan estimates that it would take an average of three to five years before an interview's turn for transcription came up. The society also accepted donated interviews, but didn't transcribe them.

Museums

From the Computer History Museum in Mountain View, California, which collects oral histories with computing pioneers, to catching the memories of Russian artists at the Garage Museum of Contemporary Art in Moscow, museums are seeing the value in oral history methodology.

As chief archivist and director of collections at the National Museum of the Pacific War in Fredericksburg, Texas, overseeing the museum's oral history collection is just one of Reagan Grau's duties. Their collection of nearly 5,000 interviews focuses on World War II's Pacific arena.[38] The museum transcribes all of its interviews—which may take a while, as Grau relies wholly on volunteers. "Transcription of the oral histories is vital to one aspect of the educational component of this museum's mission: providing access to the stories of the Pacific War," Grau wrote in an e-interview. "With transcriptions, researchers are able to cover more ground faster."[39] The museum posts both the audio and transcripts online.

The Canadian Museum for Human Rights in Winnipeg, Canada, relies heavily on collecting interviews, and uses outside contractors to transcribe them all. "Oral history is one of our primary research methodologies and is particularly valuable, given our subject matter of human rights," Jodi Giesbrecht, manager of research and curation, told me in an email. "It animates all of our core exhibitions and allows us to tell stories for which we might otherwise not have things like material artefacts or other assets."[40]

Independent Scholars

Independent scholars conduct oral history or other types of qualitative research, especially when writing books. Arlie Russell Hochschild, author of *Strangers in Their Own Land: Anger and Mourning on the American Right*, talked to 60 people and had 4,000 pages of interview transcripts by the time she was ready to draft her manuscript.[41]

In Australia, Carol Roberts, owner of Hawkesbury Valley Heritage Tours, uses her oral history research to enhance tours of a historic agricultural region in New South Wales, as well as in her book projects. Her research focuses on a particular local artist. "I use information from the oral histories with him to illustrate my commentary when visiting heritage sites he has depicted in his artworks," she said in an email interview.[42] Her oral history transcripts were used as the basis for the art catalogue printed in conjunction with a 30-year survey exhibition of the artist's work. Roberts transcribes all her own interviews. She diligently learned art terminology so her transcripts would be perfect.[43]

Personal and Family Historians

Personal historians interview clients and present their stories in books, audio and video formats, on websites, or simply as transcripts. The idea is to make a lasting—though not best-selling—product that can be enjoyed by family and friends. Personal historians may also work with businesses or other organizations to document their history.

Jennifer Campbell of Cobourg, Ontario, Canada, owns a personal history business called Heritage Memoirs. She records anywhere from six to 28 hours of interviews for each project, and has worked with clients ranging from a former Ice Capades skater to a World War II Russian army veteran. For Campbell, professional transcription is

> absolutely vitally important. My transcribers capture every word, every false start, every unfinished sentence. The manuscripts have to be true to the narrator's voice and I need to remember the cadence, speech patterns, even the awkward way of expressing themselves.[44]

Federal Agencies

Some American federal agencies have their own oral history projects, including the National Park Service, the Senate Historical Office, the US Census Bureau and the Federal Bureau of Investigation. According to Donald Ritchie, associate historian in the Senate Historical Office:[45]

> When the Washington-based Society for History in the Federal Government conducted a survey, it found oral history projects in all branches of the military, the intelligence agencies, many cabinet departments, Congress, the federal courts, the Smithsonian museums, and independent agencies from NASA to the National Institutes of Health.

British government oral history projects include the House of Commons staff oral history collection and the History of Parliament Oral History Project, run by the History of Parliament Trust.[46] In Australia, the National Library collects veteran oral histories.[47] Books, articles, folklife festivals, museum exhibits, radio programs and documentary films are some of the fruits of government-run oral history activities.[48]

Folklorists

Englishman William John Thoms coined the term "folklore" in 1846, replacing the term "popular antiquities" with a "good Saxon compound."[49] Folklorists often audio- or videotape people telling stories or demonstrating crafts. With folklore, the recording is clearly the primary source, the transcript, a supplement. While transcripts can do a fair job of capturing stories, poems and sayings, the audio or video recording is crucial for preserving rituals, pageants, dances, craft demonstrations and other dynamic examples of folklife. Since folklorists engage in "participant observation"—that is, doing the craft, learning the dance, cooking the food—often working a recorder is not possible. So field notes written immediately after the event are crucial for folklorists.[50]

People might picture the folklorist as traipsing through Appalachia, "catching songs" on a recorder. But folklorists find folklore everywhere. The 2017 meeting of the American Folklore Society included papers on folkways of paranormal investigators in Wyoming, stories of therapy dog handlers and fat-positive bloggers as folk groups, as well as the more predictable woodturners and basket makers.[51] Most states have their own folk heritage programs, with professional folklorists who organize festivals, exhibits and "folk artists in the schools" programs.[52]

Non-Governmental Organizations

Non-governmental organizations (NGOs) are nonprofit groups that provide a humanitarian or service function. They may be organized on a local, national or international level. Some are related to UN agencies and offices.[53]

In some places, NGOs actively collect oral testimony from the citizens they serve. They often interview refugees and other people living in dire poverty who have little opportunity to share their stories with a wider audience. Oral testimony is important to NGOs not only for preserving history and culture, but in figuring out how to best serve relevant communities. As stated in *Learning to Listen: A Manual for Oral History Projects*, prepared for NGOs working in Burma:

> the techniques of oral history can be of immediate relevance to the development of appropriate polices and in decision-making; and in the process of the recording, a lot of unexpected social, cultural and historical information can also be collected.[54]

Whether NGOs are using oral testimony to inform decisions, excerpt in local or international publications or preserve in an archive, the focus is usually on the voices of narrators. This differs from the more academic approach, where the author's analysis and interpretation often overwhelm the narrator's words. Transcripts are crucial in this type of NGO work, so that direct quotations from people served can be inserted into reports meant to change policy for the better.

Independent Oral Historians

Many trained oral historians work on their own projects, or freelance for various organizations, community or governmental projects. This can be a full-time or part-time job, or a sideline.

Australia-based oral historian Carol McKirdy heads a small company called History Herstory and authored *Practicing Oral History with Immigrant Narrators* (Routledge, 2015). She works on several projects, each with different aims, funding and expectations. "For the State Library I do interviews on specific collections such as women of influence over 90 years old and Cambodian women who lived under Pol Pot rule," she explained in an email interview.[55]

Interviews she conducts for the Royal Australian Historical Society are archived at Sutherland Shire Libraries, which eventually transcribes McKirdy's interviews. The immigrant project is chronically underfunded. "The grants I receive to do the immigrant oral histories are much appreciated but miniscule. I can't afford to get transcripts done when the project is being undertaken."[56] In the short term, McKirdy creates comprehensive timed logs or executive summaries, digital stories, podcasts and lesson materials, depending on the project. She makes digital stories to share with her narrators, in addition to giving them copies of their interviews.[57]

Corporate Historians

Many corporations value preserving their own history, whether by employing a corporate historian or contracting with somebody to build an archive and record oral history interviews with key employees. As History Associates states on its website, "an archival program can provide a favorable return on investment for your company."[58] This historical research company points out that an archive can contribute to a sound risk management program, communicate stability in times of change, help companies get the most out of their brand image, assist with marketing and PR, produce licensing revenue and strengthen consumer loyalty.[59]

For example, when Kraft Foods acquired Cadbury's, a British confectioner, it consulted its archive to smooth the transition. The company archivist pulled together an intranet exhibit of old advertising images, timelines, mini documentaries and product histories to show employees of the two companies their shared values.[60]

In 2017, the Harvard Business School India Research Center in Mumbai assembled business archivists, historians and business people to discuss the role of oral history in documenting India's growing field of business history. A project called Creating Emerging Markets tells the story of the IT industry in India.[61]

Qualitative Researchers

Qualitative researchers don't usually attempt to gather a cohesive life history of a narrator, as oral historians do. Instead, "Qualitative research is designed to reveal a target audience's range of behavior and the perceptions that drive it with reference to specific topics or issues," according to the Qualitative Research Consultants Association.[62] Researchers in sociology, anthropology, psychology and natural sciences all record one-on-one interviews and group discussions to explore research topics.

Sharon Kruse, academic director of Washington State University's College of Education, depends entirely on qualitative research in her work, which she publishes as books and journal articles. "I probe research questions related to the ways school function, both as formal and informal organizations," she said in an email interview. "Absent the ability to talk with people (e.g. interview), I wouldn't be able to obtain the narratives/stories that comprise the bulk of my cases for analysis."[63]

"Transcription is vitally important to my research," Kruse said. Not only does she want to capture exact quotations, but she finds notetaking too distracting while interacting with the teachers, principals, and superintendents she studies. Her participants appreciate receiving a transcript to review for correction and clarification.

Graduate Students

Graduate students often enthusiastically conduct interviews for their doctoral research, only to find themselves buried under hours of untranscribed audio that they're in a hurry to use. The biggest concern for grad students is usually money. Most are living on loans and low-paid, time-consuming assistantships. Some are fortunate to receive small grants for transcription. They seldom have time to type full transcripts, especially if they were overly ambitious in the collecting phase.

Alexis Waldron got a grant from her department to cover transcription for her dissertation research on the relationship between self-compassion, mindfulness and wildland fire leadership:

> By recording it and having it transcribed, as you start reading it, there's so much more in there that you see and pick up that you didn't even know. What you may have thought was a huge deal really ends up being overshadowed by other things that you just weren't privy to while you were in the middle of that interview.

The group interviews could be especially distracting. Reviewing the transcripts at a later date let her absorb the nuances of the interview sessions.[64]

Linguists

Linguists require way more information from a transcript than the average scholar in other disciplines, and their own particular transcription systems reflect this need. Within the field of linguistics, conversational analysis is a popular way to study everyday conversations, focusing on how people understand, respond to each other and take turns talking. By studying everyday conversation, sociolinguists seek to "uncover the often tacit reasoning procedures and sociolinguistic competencies underlying the production and interpretation of talk in organized sequences of interaction."[65] Conversational analysis is a challenge for transcriptionists, as they try to represent speaker overlap, emphasis, lapsed time in tenths of a second and other precise concepts. Oral historians will probably never get as detailed in their transcripts as linguists, but those who mourn the lack of orality in transcription might want to adopt some linguistic notation for their project.

Linguists commonly work on scholarly research, but they also serve some important transcript-related functions outside academia. For example, law enforcement agencies occasionally call upon linguists to transcribe and analyze recordings in court cases, with high stakes riding on accuracy. "Legal battles sometimes ensue about the often important differences found between competing transcripts prepared by the prosecution and those made by the defense," wrote Roger Shuy in *The Handbook of Linguistics.* [66]

Documentary Filmmakers

Some documentary filmmakers greatly rely on transcripts throughout their storytelling process. Louisiana filmmaker Victoria Greene watches the video while simultaneously scrolling through the transcript. Some people do a paper edit, she said, where they only look at transcripts. "But I found the way my brain works is to be able to see the words and hear it. This just reinforced it and helped me pull out the sound bites, pull out what I want to use to create the story."

The transcripts play an even greater role in editing. When working on her environmental film *Forgotten Bayou,* Greene and her film crew distilled many hours of footage into a 70-minute feature, aided by the search function in electronic versions of the transcripts. A transcript of her complete film helped her trim it to 54 minutes when shopping it to PBS. The search feature let her weed out redundancy. She sends the final transcript to the Library of Congress to copyright it, like a book or a script. "I just can't imagine not using transcripts. To me, it's best practice." [67]

Sun Yi, a documentary filmmaker in China, also relies on transcripts when making films. "Usually I will go over the transcription first (if you watch the video, it could take hundreds of hours but reading is a lot faster)," she told me in an email. Eventually she turns to the screen to pick up tones of voice and visual factors.[68]

Marketing Professionals

Marketers use qualitative research to help clients develop better strategies for improving and selling their products. Lindsey Annable, director of the UK-based Free Spirit Consulting Ltd, works on UK and international projects in all sectors. Typical deliverables include a PowerPoint deck with an executive summary of the findings. More detailed findings may include diagrams and consumer verbatims to bring the explications to life for the end client.

Transcriptions of group and one-on-one interviews are critical to good qualitative practice in terms of analysis, Annable said. As she examines the transcripts, patterns, contradictions and anomalies take shape. "Analysis is not a matter of adding together A + B but putting together a series of jigsaw pieces A + B + C + U." Transcripts jog the moderator's memory about the research group, and help quickly identify useful sound bites for presentations to clients.[69]

Others

The list goes on. Lecturers, retreat leaders, and other professional speakers often want transcripts of their speeches. They may use these for writing books, adding website content, distributing to followers, selling in the back of the room at events or creating scripts for radio or television shows. City government, business meetings, and conferences all sometimes need minutes transcribed. Journalists and authors transcribe full or partial interviews for their writing projects.

Transcription is embedded in legal proceedings. While court reporting is a separate specialty with its own skills and equipment, lawyers also need lots of ordinary transcription, including dictated notes, court proceedings and depositions. Legal firms may employ office assistants whose jobs encompass transcription and other administrative duties, or they may outsource transcription to a specialist, as needed. This type of transcription work usually involves heightened attention to confidentiality.

And, of course, medical transcription is a field unto itself. Medical transcription is hard—both psychologically, listening to the doctors' calm detached descriptions of horrific proceedings, and technically, comprehending and spelling difficult terminology. Those who aspire to greatness as medical transcriptionists need specialized study.

Bottom Line

Around the world, interest in oral history—documenting recent history through recorded personal accounts of those who lived it—continues to grow. And with this increased capture of qualitative interviews, so does the need to transcribe them. The most obvious skill a transcriptionist needs is good typing. But the role also requires patience, commitment to accuracy, careful listening, a good grasp of language, willingness to adapt as technology changes and acceptance of staying in the background.

Within oral history, transcription has its supporters and detractors. Researchers generally love working from transcripts. But many oral historians worry that scholars will overlook audio recordings, which are the primary documents. Transcripts are extremely convenient. However, they don't catch nuances of speech and are costly to produce.

As noted above, a surprising number of disciplines and professions require transcription. This book focuses primarily on oral history, with a secondary focus on other types of qualitative research. I will draw on the ways that different fields use transcripts so that they may inform each other, and to expand transcriptionists' minds about places their services are needed.

Notes

1 Oral History Association, "Oral History: Defined," available at: www.oralhistory.org/about/do-oral-history/ (accessed July 8, 2018).
2 Stephen H. Paschen, "Planning an Oral History Project," in *Catching Stories: A Practical Guide to Oral History* (Athens, OH: Swallow Press, 2009).
3 Barbara W. Sommer and Mary Kay Quinlan, *The Oral History Manual* (Lanham, MD: AltaMira Press, 2009).
4 Michael Frisch, *A Shared Authority* (Albany, NY: State University of New York Press, 1990).
5 Donna DeBlasio, "Transcribing Oral History," in Stephen H. Paschen, *Catching Stories: A Practical Guide to Oral History* (Athens, OH: Swallow Press, 2009).
6 Sherna Berger Gluck, "Refocusing on Orality/Aurality in the Digital Age," in D. Boyd and M. Larson (Eds.) *Oral History and Digital Humanities* (New York: Palgrave Macmillan, 2014), pp. 35–36.
7 Nyssa Chow, "Oral History as Poetry: Restoring a Visual Orality," available at: http://oralhistory.columbia.edu/blog-posts/People/as80byigoo84g0i5effatxx1h4zhef (accessed December 17, 2017).
8 Francis Good, email correspondence with Teresa Bergen, July 22, 2018.
9 Museum of Magnetic Sound Recording, available at: http://museumofmagneticsoundrecording.org/ManufacturersAEGMagnetophon.html (accessed February 7, 2017).
10 Linda Shopes, "Making Sense of Oral History," available at: http://ohda.matrix.msu.edu/2012/08/making-sense-of-oral-history (accessed February 10, 2019).
11 Allan Nevins, "Oral History: How and Why It Was Born," in *Oral History: An Interdisciplinary Anthology* (Lanham, MD: AltaMira Press, 2013).
12 About the Williams Center, available at: www.lib.lsu.edu/oralhistory/about (accessed February 10, 2019).
13 George Ewart Evans collection, available at: http://sounds.bl.uk/Oral-history/George-Ewart-Evans-collection (accessed July, 2017).
14 Faber & Faber website, available at: www.faber.co.uk/catalogsearch/result/index/order/date_of_publication/dir/desc/q/George+Ewart+Evans (accessed July 15, 2017).
15 Hazel Estelle De Berg, *Australian Dictionary of Biography*, available at: http://adb.anu.edu.au/biography/de-berg-hazel-estelle-12410 (accessed June 19, 2017).
16 National Archives of Singapore, available at: www.Nas.gov.sg (accessed November 11, 2018).
17 Nehru Memorial Museum & Library, available at: http://nehrumemorial.nic.in/en/oral-history.html (accessed July 22, 2017).
18 Anna Sheftel and Stacey Zembrzcki, "Who's Afraid of Oral History?: Fifty Years of Debates and Anxiety about Ethics," *The Oral History Review*, summer/Fall 2016, Volume 43, Issue 2.
19 History of Oral History, Oral History Society website, available at: www.ohs.org.uk/about/history-of-oral-history/ (accessed June 7, 2017).
20 Beth Robertson, "Long Desperate Hours at the Typewriter: Establishing the Oral History Association of Australia," *Oral History Association of Australia Journal*, No. 30, 2008. Available at: www.oralhistoryaustralia.org.au/files/about_us_-bethrobertson_longhoursatthetypewriter.pdf (accessed July 9, 2018).

21 Regional and International Organizations, Oral History Association website, available at: www.oralhistory.org/regional-and-international-organizations/ (accessed March 30, 2017).

22 History of Oral History, Oral History Society website, available at: www.ohs.org.uk/about/history-of-oral-history/ (accessed June 7, 2017).

23 Barbara W. Sommer, Nancy MacKay, and Mary Kay Quinlan, *Community Oral History Toolkit Series* (London: Routledge, 2013).

24 Mary Larson, " 'The Medium is the Message': Oral History, Media and Mediation," *The Oral History Review*, summer/Fall 2016, Volume 43, Issue 2.

25 Michael Hunt, "Why the Cassette Tape Is Still Not Dead," *Rolling Stone*, available at: www.rollingstone.com/culture/news/why-the-cassette-tape-is-still-not-dead-20160418 (accessed March 18, 2017).

26 Donald A. Ritchie, *Doing Oral History: A Practical Guide* (Oxford: Oxford University Press, 2003), p 23.

27 Di Yin Lu, "Doing Oral History in the PRC," available at: http://dissertationreviews.org/archives/950 (accessed July 10, 2017).

28 Sun Yi, email correspondence with Teresa Bergen, July 24, 2018.

29 David Beorlegui, email correspondence with Teresa Bergen, July 23, 2018.

30 Columbia University Libraries Oral History Archives, available at: http://library.columbia.edu/locations/ccoh.html (accessed December 17, 2017).

31 Baylor Institute for Oral History, available at: www.baylor.edu/oralhistory/index.php?id=931703 (accessed February 10, 2019).

32 Troy Reeves, interview with Teresa Bergen, December 11, 2017.

33 Mark Wong, email correspondence with Teresa Bergen, August 24, 2018.

34 Maija Anderson, email correspondence with Teresa Bergen, November 14, 2017.

35 Ibid.

36 Kim Heikkila, interview with Teresa Bergen, November 15, 2017.

37 Jeff Corrigan, interview with Teresa Bergen, December 18, 2017.

38 Reagan Grau, email correspondence with Teresa Bergen, November 28, 2016.

39 Reagan Grau, email correspondence with Teresa Bergen, November 8, 2017.

40 Jodi Giesbrecht, email correspondence with Teresa Bergen, July 24, 2018.

41 Arlie Russell Hochschild, *Strangers in Their Own Land: Anger and Mourning on the American Right* (New York; The New Press, 2016), pp. 247–248.

42 I realize some oral historians might object to the term "email interview." But I use it here rather than the more vague "personal correspondence" to indicate that I was asking specific questions regarding this book, with the intent that their answers could be published, rather than more casual correspondence.

43 Carol Roberts, email correspondence with Teresa Bergen, March 30, 2018.

44 Jennifer Campbell, email correspondence with Teresa Bergen, November 20, 2017.

45 Donald A. Ritchie, *Doing Oral History: A Practical Guide* (Oxford: Oxford University Press, 2003), p 42.

46 British Libraries, "Oral Histories of Politics and Government," available at: www.bl.uk/collection-guides/oral-histories-of-politics-and-government (accessed December 31, 2017).

47 National Library of Australia, "Oral History and Realia," available at: www.nla.gov.au/research-guides/first-world-war/oral-history-and-realia (accessed December 31, 2017).

48 Ritchie, *Doing Oral History: A Practical Guide*, p. 14.

49 Stephen Winick and Peter Bartis, *Folklife & Fieldwork: An Introduction to Cultural Documentation* (Washington, DC: American Folklife Center, Library of Congress, 2016), p. 1.

50 Ibid., p. 18.

51 American Folklore Association conference 2017 schedule, available at: http://c.ymcdn.com/sites/www.afsnet.org/resource/resmgr/AM17/Revised_Schedule_8-24-17.pdf (accessed December 31, 2017).

52 Winick and Bartis, *Folklife & Fieldwork*, p. 37.

53 NGO Global Network, "Definition of NGOs," available at: www.ngo.org/ngoinfo/define.html (accessed December 31, 2017).

54 Mandy Sadan, *Learning to Listen: A Manual for Oral History Projects* (Brighton: Green Centre for Non-Western Art and Culture, 2008), p. 12, available at: www.burmalibrary. org/docs21/Sadan-2008-learning_to_listen-en-tpo.pdf (accessed February 10, 2019).

55 Lindsey Annable, email correspondence with Teresa Bergen, December 8, 2017.

56 Carol McKirdy, email correspondence with Teresa Bergen, January 7, 2018.

57 Ibid.

58 History Associates website, available at: www.historyassociates.com/resource/guides/ the-business-case-for-archives-how-history-can-bolster-your-bottom-line/ (accessed December 31, 2017).

59 Ibid.

60 John T. Seaman, Junior and George David Smith, "Your Company's History as a Leadership Tool," *Harvard Business Review*, December 2012, available at: https://hbr.org/ 2012/12/your-companys-history-as-a-leadership-tool (accessed December 31, 2017).

61 Harvard Business School, "Creating Emerging Markets," available at: www.hbs.edu/crea ting-emerging-markets/resources/conferences/Pages/oral-history-business-history-a nd-business-archives-in-India.aspx (accessed July 10, 2018).

62 Qualitative Research Consultants Association, "What Is Qualitative Research?" available at: www.qrca.org/?page=whatisqualresearch (accessed December 19, 2017).

63 Sharon Kruse, email correspondence with Teresa Bergen, December 18, 2017.

64 Alexis Waldron, interview with Teresa Bergen, January 5, 2018.

65 Ian Hutchby and Robin Wooffitt, *Conversational Analysis* (Cambridge: Polity, 2008), available at: www.thoughtco.com/what-is-conversation-analysis-ca-1689923, (accessed February 10, 2019).

66 Roger Shuy, "Language and the Law," in *The Handbook of Linguistics* (Chichester: Wiley, 2017), p. 635.

67 Victoria Greene, interview with Teresa Bergen, November 18, 2017.

68 Sun Yi, email correspondence with Teresa Bergen, July 24, 2018.

69 Lindsey Annable, email correspondence with Teresa Bergen, December 8, 2017.

2

GETTING STARTED

Most people who come into contact with transcripts do so with the finished product—a transcript of a city council meeting or a legal proceeding, a radio or TV broadcast, or an oral history interview. Without much thought, they probably assume it is a verbatim document and consider it authoritative. People tend to think being in print gives something authority. In fact, there are many decisions made and skills applied behind the scenes to create the resulting transcript they read. This chapter will get you started on turning your interviews into transcripts by answering some basic questions.

Since one of the fundamental concepts of oral history is that the interview is conducted for the historical record, this book will mostly focus on creating a nearly verbatim transcript intended to accompany the recording and made available to public audiences. By nearly verbatim, I mean the whole interview minus false starts, ums and excessive verbal ticks, such as constant use of "you know" and "like." We'll also look at transcription done for more specific oral history aims, such as when the interviews are being collected for use in a book, script or exhibit.

A Note on Readership

I envision this book as having several distinct readerships, the main ones being transcriptionists themselves and oral history project managers overseeing many parts of the process, including transcription. At times I'll be addressing one of these groups and not the other. I will try to be clear as I go back and forth, explaining issues to transcriptionists and to project managers. Other reader groups include qualitative researchers, graduate students using oral history methodology or other types of qualitative research in their dissertations, individuals documenting the history of their family, church or organization, and archivists.

Maybe you are a librarian or program administrator planning a large oral history project. You don't plan to do the transcription yourself, but you need to understand the time it takes, the skills and resources (money and technology) required. Or maybe you are a lone oral historian, doing everything on your own, including interviewing and transcribing. Or maybe you are a freelance transcriptionist keen on oral history. While this book focuses on oral history, as we saw in Chapter 1, a surprising number of disciplines rely on accurate interview transcriptions. Sometimes it seems the work of a transcriptionist is never done.

When I use the term "freelance transcriptionist," I'm talking about somebody who makes all or part of her income from transcribing. Staff at established oral history programs, such as at universities or historical societies, may be paid a salary or hourly wages, plus may have a combination of benefits such as paid vacation and holidays, paid sick leave, maternity leave, health insurance, 401Ks or, for some faculty oral historians, even sabbaticals. Community oral historians may have grants or be unpaid following their strong interest. Genealogists may be interviewing relatives due to a passion for preserving family history.

One thing I've encountered many times in my 20 years of freelancing is being snubbed or looked down upon by academics for providing a commercial service. My theory is that since academics can rely on their institutions reliably depositing pay into their accounts every month, they often fancy themselves above money and forget it's a factor in their work. Freelance transcriptionists, on the other hand, are only paid for deliverables—transcripts—and then whenever the institution gets around to it rather than on a specific date. Many times I have found myself knocking at the door of an Ivory Tower,[1] asking after my fee. In a single month while following up on unpaid invoices more than 60 days out, I got the following excuses from different clients: "Sorry, I went to Europe and forgot to submit your invoice"; "Oh, our accounting person is on maternity leave"; "We're a small business and contractors get paid last." This is all too typical. So reader, if you are an academic with a reliable salary and benefits, please don't think me gauche when at times in this book I bring up the "m" word. Ten out of ten transcriptionists surveyed prefer living indoors, just like academics.

Whether you're a freelancer, volunteer, salaried professional or somebody working on a passion project, this chapter will help you make some decisions in order to get started. Then you can quickly move on to Chapter 4 to learn about the actual transcription process.

These are some of the questions explored in this chapter:

- What is the scope of my transcription project? (Number of interviews, recorded hours)
- What is the turnaround time for transcription?
- How will the transcript be used?
- What are my technology needs and resources?
- What are my budget needs and resources?

- Who will transcribe the interviews? Should I outsource or do transcription in-house?
- How do I find a reliable transcriptionist?

The Scope of the Project

Enthusiastic newbie oral historians often dive into collecting without first considering the scope of their project. But the figuring-it-out-as-you-go-along approach often results in enormous backlogs of untranscribed interviews, sometimes poorly labeled and left in a box for a future generation to deal with. Pity the transcriptionist who must open that box!

Instead, temper your enthusiasm with patience, and bravely look the project in the eye. People are often surprised by how much oral history interviewing and transcription costs in time and/or money. Senior editor and collections manager Steven Sielaff at the Baylor University Institute for Oral History (BUIOH) shares the institute's project budget and timeline. In a post for the Oxford University Press's oral history blog, he extrapolated Baylor's policies to a small project budget for a one-person shop. People unused to the rigors and details of interviewing, transcription and processing might faint when they see how much work Sielaff estimates goes into *a single* audio hour of oral history, from pre-interview to public access.

- Pre-interview research: 4–8 hours
- Interview: 2–4 hours for onsite, 8 for local travel, 16 for longer
- Audio processing/transcription: 15–20 hours
- Review: 2–3 month wait
- Post-review edits: 5 hours
- Final editing: 5 hours

Total: 30–60 hours, over 3–4 months.[2]

Sielaff noted that these times can vary widely, especially depending on how much research and travel time an interview requires. As for transcription, he wrote:

I typically tell people it will take five to ten hours to transcribe one hour of audio. The low end represents an experienced listener and fast typist, the high end a novice. I also built into this transcription category the time it will take for you to audit check and initially edit your work.

Note: Auditing means listening to the audio while reading through the transcript, adjusting it as necessary as you catch transcription errors.

So if you're planning 20 two-hour interviews, Sielaff's figures mean you should budget 1200–2400 hours to finish your project. Note, this includes all the steps to prepare transcripts for public use, not just transcription hours. Bearing these figures in mind, an oral historian planning a new project might reconsider its scope.

Instead of conducting 50 exhaustive interviews, what about paring down to 10 interviews, and aiming for 90 minutes each?

Transcriptionists are rarely responsible for interviewing narrators, or for processing or cataloging the transcripts. Table 2.1 shows the life cycle of a transcript, as it relates to the transcriptionist, and who is generally responsible. Note, in some cases the project manager might negotiate with the transcriptionist about additional tasks, such as auditing, editing or abstracting the transcript.

Timelines

Generally, the desired turnaround time for transcription is determined by the intended use of the interviews. Sometimes researchers urgently need completed transcripts within a timeframe, such as to meet a grant requirement or prepare for a public program. Documentary filmmakers and authors might also have deadlines. Other times, repositories simply want to reduce audio backlog and are happy to have transcripts trickle in as the transcriptionist completes them.

If you're a project manager, contact transcriptionists in the planning stages so they can set aside time for your project. "It's astounding that people who set up oral history projects leave the most time-consuming activity, that of the transcription, to be booked when all else is ready to go, mindlessly assuming the transcriber can almost instantly take on a large volume," said Susan Hutton, transcriptionist for the British Library.[3] Freelance transcribers regularly juggle multiple projects, but there's a limit to how much two hands can type.

Transcriptionists need to be aware of these differing expectations for turnaround. It can be catastrophic to promise fast turnaround to too many people at once. Transcriptionists and project managers must communicate in order to have clear

TABLE 2.1 Transcription life cycle

Task	Who is responsible?
Deciding whether to transcribe	Project manager
Deciding to transcribe in-house or outsource	Project manager
Finding a transcriptionist	Project manager
Negotiate terms/sign written agreement	Transcriptionist and project manager
Transfer files	Transcriptionist and project manager
Supply proper noun list	Project manager
Set up document	Transcriptionist (though project manager might provide a template)
Transcribe	Transcriptionist
Spellcheck and preliminary fact check	Transcriptionist
Audit check	Project
Editing and further fact checking	Project
Send transcript to narrator for review	Project

expectations, especially when there's a time constraint. For example, qualitative research done for marketing has some of the fastest turnaround requirements. Lindsey Annable at Free Spirit usually uses a 48-hour turnaround service for transcription, and sometimes even a 24-hour. On multi-day interviewing projects, she likes to send the audio files for transcription as soon as that day's session is finished. "This gives a drip-feed of transcriptions which enable making a start on the analysis." Even this lightning-fast timeline keeps tightening as clients want analysis and reporting faster and faster.[4] One market research client I work for instructs me to greatly shorten the interviewer's questions and comments by paraphrasing them in brackets to show that it's not a verbatim transcription. I type the participants' answers fully, unless it's irrelevant, such as [weather chit chat] and [they adjust equipment]. This allows me to turn in a transcript considerably faster.

Turnaround time for transcription may also be accelerated if narrators are old, ill, and/or have quickly deteriorating abilities. Remember, the interview is only the first step—once the transcript is complete, it should be returned to the narrator so he can review it for accuracy. In some cases, the clock is ticking against progressive dementia, sickness or death.

Minnesota-based oral historian Kim Heikkila's Eat Street project is an example of a project where the timeframe ran smoothly. She initiated the project in October 2016 with archival background research, and interviewed narrators between March and June 2017. She sent interviews to the transcriptionist as soon as the interviews were done, receiving transcripts on a rolling basis. The project was completed in time for an exhibit opening at the Hennepin History Museum in September of 2017.When I talked to Heikkila in November, she'd already delivered all the final materials to the library archive.[5] A project that runs this smoothly is every oral historian's dream.

Budget

Budget drives many decisions in an oral history or other qualitative research project, including how many interviews to collect, the desired outcomes and whether or not to transcribe. I'll quote few money figures in this book, for several reasons: Costs vary in different countries (and regions, such as around the USA); costs can change rapidly; and projects have different ratios of human resources versus expenses. For example, dedicated volunteers might run an oral history project with almost no budget, fueling it with their time and passion. At the other end of the spectrum, an oral history endeavor may operate within the framework of a large institution or philanthropic situation with a very large budget.

Funding Sources

When I talk to friends who direct large oral history centers and people who run one-person community projects, there's often a common thread: the financial fight to keep their projects alive and producing oral history. Now we'll turn our attention to how people keep the lights on and the recorders humming, from traditional funding sources like endowments to newfangled technological strategies like crowdsourcing.

Institutional Support

The university's operating budget often funds oral history programs at universities. For example, at Oregon Health & Science University, then-interim director Maija Anderson said the library's operations budget covers about six interviews a year. "I use the budget to pay for contractors, including the transcriptionist, video producers, and a project manager who coordinates everyone and tracks the production workflow."[6]

The University of Wisconsin, Madison's oral history program is part of the UW Madison Archives, and the archives are part of the larger UW Madison Libraries, Troy Reeves said:

> So it's a long way of saying that our program is funded through money that primarily the UW Madison Libraries gets from the state. We do have a little gift fund, and that allows me to hire some students, buy equipment, occasionally transcribe.[7]

Grants

For many individuals and groups conducting oral history projects, getting grants is an enormous coup. Receiving non-repayable funds from a foundation, government department or corporation feels like getting free money—unless you were the person spending hours writing the grant proposal, aware that all your hard work would be for naught if you didn't get it. Grant-getting requires skills and entails responsibility. Applicants must learn how to write successful grant applications. Upon award of funds, they must comply with the timeline and produce deliverables. For organized, dedicated people with good grant-writing skills, this can be a feasible way to fund a project.

Government entities, such as the Royal Australian Historical Society and the State Library of New South Wales, fund Carol McKirdy's oral history projects. "All the grants have a year to complete and completion depends on the community," she said. "The actual project may take five months or a year; it depends how hard it is to get everything organized. Sometimes I have a very short turnaround, maybe a month if I have to meet a deadline." Sometimes projects need to complete invoicing before a grant deadline, meaning they might have to pay for transcription before the work is completed.

Donations

Depending on the type of oral history project, the director may request donations from community members, alums, local businesses or others who they think might want to help preserve history. Occasionally a donor shows up on a project's doorstep. While Jeff Corrigan directed the oral history program at the State Historical Society of Missouri, a donor offered to match the funds Corrigan could raise, with the proceeds earmarked for transcription. Corrigan sent a letter to all the living narrators in the collection that he could find. He received donations of $25 to $750, which were all matched by this donor who wished to remain publicly anonymous.[8]

Donations can come from family, friends, businesses, and anybody with an interest in the project. While raising donations used to require more personal interaction, whether hitting up relatives at Thanksgiving or making a formal presentation to the Rotary Club, nowadays fundraising often happens online. Some groups put a "donate" button on their websites, such as the Schizophrenia Oral History Project.[9] In the USA, organizations that qualify as 501c3 charities can apply to participate in the Amazon Smile program, which funnels 0.5 percent of the price of eligible purchases to charitable organizations selected by customers.[10]

Crowdsourcing through Kickstarter has also found a democratic way to gauge interest in and raise funds for projects, though this can result in faddish pop culture triumphing over more serious scholarship As I write this, 1,871 backers have so far pledged £72,881 to a person writing a book called *500 Years Later: An Oral History of Final Fantasy VII,* which promises to offer "a thrilling deep dive into the creation of the revered PlayStation RPG. Comprising over 30 interwoven voices, this beautifully produced book will offer unprecedented insight into the craft and ambition behind the game."[11] Meanwhile, the author of *Mormons in Northern New Jersey: An Oral History* has raised only a single dollar.[12]

Private Clients

Personal and corporate historians conduct oral histories on a fee basis. For example, Kitty Axelson-Barry owns the Amherst, Massachusetts-based, Modern Memoirs. She and her staff specialize in assisted memoirs and family histories, which they self-publish for families. Services include interviewing, transcribing, editing, designing and printing books. According to the Modern Memoirs website, the company has published more than 160 memoirs since its founding in 1994. Clients hail from the US, Israel, Colombia, England, France and Spain.[13] At the time of this writing clients could expect to pay about $8,000 for 15–20 hours' worth of transcribed interviews, including the cost of the interviewer traveling to the narrator. A commissioned memoir costs upwards of $40,000.[14]

Self-Funding

Some projects are self-funded by individuals, often those who work full or part time, and are passionate about documenting an aspect of history. They might be turning this documentation into a creative product, such as a book or film. Louisiana filmmaker Victoria Greene said she self-funded about 80 percent of her film *Forgotten Bayou,* a movie that chronicles the environmental disaster of the

Bayou Corne sinkhole. This very expensive proposition included hiring an editor, post-production people, shooters and a transcriptionist. She describes her experience as typical. "Unless you're really like Ken Burns or very well known, mostly you do put your own money in or your own time. You don't get paid for it."[15]

The Phnom Penh-based Cambodian Women's Oral History Project, led by Dr. Theresa de Langis, is a self-funded crusade to reveal an especially ugly hidden corner of history. The Khmer Rouge crammed an unbelievable number of atrocities into less than four years, many of which have been chronicled elsewhere. But de Langis' project goes deep into gender. As the project website explains:

> In having their voices heard, their faces shown, the women whose testimonials are featured here break age-old taboos against survivors speaking out about violence against women. Although victims of horrendous crimes, the narrators are active agents of change, refusing to be fully defined by the violence afflicted against them and determined to share their stories to end violence against women in any and every context.[16]

Such an urgent, heartfelt mission may inspire self-funded projects.

Volunteer Hours

Recruiting volunteers is a popular way to partially power community history projects. Organizers may still need to find a way to fund equipment, space or travel, but volunteer interviewers and sometimes transcribers may be enticed to take part in a worthy project. The Stanford Historical Society at Stanford University seeks volunteers to serve as interviewers, editors, writers, indexers, curators and videographers.[17] The Veterans History Project at the Library of Congress runs one of the largest oral history programs to depend on volunteers to interview veterans within their communities. The American Association of Retired Persons is the Veterans History Project founding corporate sponsor. They are a major funder, and spread the word to their 37 million members, some of whom will want to volunteer.[18]

Fundraisers

Oral historians can get creative about funding their transcription budget. Instead of crossing their fingers waiting to hear the results of a grant application—or, better yet, in addition to—some plan their own fundraising events. For several years, Jeff Corrigan raised transcription money by tacking a wine raffle and silent auction onto the State Historical Society of Missouri's annual dinner meeting. Corrigan collected wine donations from trustees and staff, aiming for two to three cases. The raffle typically raised around $500. Coupled with the silent auction, he raised about $2,000 per year for transcription.[19]

Corrigan knew of a small historical society in Missouri that funded their transcription with an annual spaghetti dinner. Depending on the community, chili, corned beef and cabbage or catfish could also lure potential donors to a fundraising night. "Something along those lines where it's an easy, one-pot meal that you can overcharge a little bit for a good cause," Corrigan recommended. "People are willing to come out because A, they support it, B, they get a meal out of it, and C, they get to be with their community members, interact with each other and have a good time." Such community events create a far more personal tie to the oral history project than sending a check in the mail.

Partnerships

Many large oral history centers partner with outside entities to grow their collections. The T. Harry Williams Center for Oral History at Louisiana State University works closely with many community history projects, class projects and individuals at other institutions. Director Jennifer Cramer said the Williams Center often provides training and loans recording equipment to these projects, who then house their collections in the center. "If they do actually have cash to spend, we advise them to hire a contract transcriptionist. Or if they have access to a student assistant, we will train that student assistant," she said.

> Every time anybody has a little bit of funding, I always suggest that they use it for the hardest part. Nobody wants to do the transcription. I can't tell you how many times I've seen people's beautiful, wonderful projects languish because they procrastinated the transcription part.

To show their appreciation for good donated collections, and out of respect for community historians who spend their free time preserving history, Cramer said that for every 10 interview hours a partner donates to the Williams Center, the center will transcribe one hour of the project's choice:

> So they pick the one that they want to see transcribed immediately and we'll do that. Then we have an idea of how the interviews are going. And once they see the transcript, then sometimes it will help that person to say, okay, let me find the funding and finish this out.[20]

Transcription: In-house vs. Outsourcing

One of the biggest transcription decisions for an oral history project is whether transcription will be done in-house or outsourced. The interviewer is often the ideal person to transcribe an interview, since he or she is already familiar with the narrator's cadence, accent, stories and content. Often an interviewer's memories of the session can help fill in parts of the audio that are difficult to hear. But interviewers may be unable or unwilling to transcribe their interviews. To do transcription in-house, you or somebody on your staff will need sufficient:

- time;
- skill;
- technical aptitude;
- interest in transcribing.

The Veterans History Project estimates that it takes 6–12 hours to transcribe a single hour of audio.[21] Where will that time come from? How can work responsibilities be shuffled around so that someone on staff has that amount of time to transcribe each interview? Is this something you're willing to take on in your free time?

The main skills necessary are close listening, accurate typing and the ability to use punctuation to translate voice to text. This is best done by a native speaker of the language of the recording.

While transcription isn't highly technical, a certain amount of comfort with computers, software and file formats is necessary. You'll need to learn to use transcription software. You may have to troubleshoot audio file formats. In some cases, being able to perform special audio processes, such as boosting volume or reducing background noise, will make a big difference in the end result. If this paragraph increases your blood pressure, delegating transcription to a staff member or outsourcing entirely is a good plan.

If you're fortunate enough to have interns, consider teaching them to transcribe. Linda Valois' interns transcribed interviews while she was managing the museum collection at the Santa Monica Mountains Recreation Area. "It was a way for interns to learn what constituted a good interview (or bad interview) before they went out and conducted an oral interview."[22]

Table 2.2 summarizes the pros and cons of transcribing in-house and outsourcing:

TABLE 2.2 Transcription: in-house vs outsourcing

	Pros	Cons
In-house	• No extra monetary costs • More familiar with project and terminology • Is presumably interested in the project	• May dislike transcription or lack appropriate skills • May need equipment and software
Outsource	• Transcription done quickly and professionally • Transcriptionist supplies her own equipment and workspace, so no overhead costs	• Monetary investment • Lack of knowledge about community or language of project • May not be interested in subject

Choosing a Transcriptionist

If you have decided not to do transcription on your own, it is time so look for a professional to get the job done. How do you choose? Most of my clients have found me through word of mouth, or by meeting me at a conference. I maintain visibility in oral history circles by attending and presenting papers at the annual Oral History Association conferences, writing book and media reviews in the *Oral History Review,* and serving on committees and/or as an officer in the Oral History Association and the Northwest Oral History Association. Lois Glewwe, who is also an author, has met transcription clients at a local history group. In the USA, some transcriptionists take out advertisements in the annual program of the Oral History Association conference, a crucial form of support for the organization. The Audio Transcription Center pays for a booth at the annual conference.

Most transcriptionists are either independent or work for a large company. The Audio Transcription Center (ATC), located in Boston, is the great-granddaddy of all transcription operations. Owner Sandy Poritzky founded ATC in 1966.[23] Its transcriptionists—some working on-site, some typing remotely—promise a fast turnaround in more than a half dozen languages. GoTranscript, based in Scotland, is a gargantuan enterprise which employs nearly 20,000 professional transcriptionists, proofreaders, and customer support specialists.[24]

Each setup has its advantages. I am a freelance transcriptionist. Many of my clients are return customers because they like to know exactly who will be transcribing their work. Large transcribing companies disperse work between a large staff, but they are better at guaranteeing quick completion of big jobs. Much as I hate to turn down work, I occasionally refer a client to one of these large concerns. After all, my two hands can't compete with GoTranscript's 40,000.

The most common routes to locating and evaluating a transcriptionist are referrals and online searches. If you work at an established oral history program, transcriptionists may occasionally contact you, promoting their services. Newer or more obscure projects would be wise to contact an established program and ask for referrals. Try contacting your nearest university oral history program or large historical society. If you are searching online for a transcriptionist, be extra wary. If you contract with offshore transcription companies that employ non-native speakers of your language, you may have to spend more time fixing your transcripts later. A well-written response from a transcriptionist is a good sign. If an email is riddled with typos, the transcript is unlikely to be clean. Consider her academic background, native language, language skills and competencies relative to the work you need done.

"Oral history can be a little messy," said Reeves, offering a point of view from the director's seat:

> For our program, we're always interested in somebody who has a track record of transcribing oral history interviews. And then once we hire somebody, we're looking for what it costs, what they charge us, how quickly they can

turn a transcript around, and then the quality of it. Because we'll go back and do an audit/edit of the transcript to compare the audio to what the transcriptionist gave us, and see if we are getting our money's worth from that transcriptionist.[25]

Transcriptionist Susan Hutton warns that you get what you pay for. "A basic transcript will need to be worked on by the recipients; a professional, comprehensive one will require minimal post-delivery work," she said. "In recent years online agencies have taken much transcribing work, but it would appear that people are realising that it comes at a cost." She attributes these poor outcomes at least partially to agencies paying miserable rates.

Also, I have received transcripts to correct which have been mind-bogglingly bad, some being quicker to do again from scratch than to correct. As a professional, I take a personal interest in all my work, however small or large, and communicate with the client throughout—of course, impossible when clients farm out to an agency.[26]

The question of how you're charged is also tricky. "I think you have to be really careful if people are like, 'Oh, it's a buck a page,'" said Jeff Corrigan. "Great. What does your page look like? Does it have three-inch margins? Do you have like three inches of spacing? Do you single space, do you double space?" If you choose a transcriptionist who charges by the audio minute, you'll have a good idea of what you're getting into. Be sure to ask about situations that will lead to higher charges, such as interviews with more than two speakers, poor audio, thick accents or rush jobs. Corrigan also suggests hiring a prospective transcriptionist to transcribe a single interview before signing any contracts. That way you can evaluate their skill level, turnaround time and how easy they are to work with.[27]

Barb Jardee, owner of Jardee Transcription, charges by the page. She ensures her pricing is fair by initially typing all clients' documents in the same format. Jardee bases her billable page on double spacing, 27 lines per page, no indents, no footers/headers/page numbers, left justified, Courier New 12 point typestyle, 10 characters per inch. She calculates the number of estimated billable pages by dividing the number of recorded minutes by two. "So a 60-minute recording, divided by two, equals approximately 30 billable pages. If the narrator is a fast talker, I usually add 20% to my estimates for cost and time to process."[28] Once she determines the correct price, she'll format to the client's preferences. If you contract with a per-page transcriptionist, be sure to ask for clear parameters.

Be aware that you might encounter a generation gap between older narrators and young typists, some of whom have never heard the names and phrases the narrator is using and therefore cannot decipher them from the tape. I have been on both sides of this problem. When editing transcripts prepared by students who were 20 years younger than I am, I found they didn't recognize politicians and celebrities that I consider household names. But when transcribing an older collection of lectures, I failed to recognize the majority of names of European intellectuals from the first half of the twentieth century. Many of them, I'm sure, were household names in Europe circa 1930. So in that case I had both a generational and a culture gap (plus an accent and old audio) that reduced my ability to produce a stellar transcript.

Whether you're the transcriptionist or the project manager, you also want to make sure you're contracting with somebody *simpatico*. The early stages of communication can be revealing for both sides. Does the transcriptionist take feedback cheerfully, or get defensive? Does the project manager communicate clearly? Does the other person promptly respond to emails?

As project manager, you want a transcriptionist who can efficiently deal with your project, who asks for clarification when necessary but doesn't bother you with niggling little questions. You are paying a professional to make your life easier.

Meanwhile, the transcriptionist is vetting the project manager. Does she clearly express her preferences and expectations? Does she seem reliable enough to follow through with this project and eventually pay?

Student Transcriptionists

University oral history programs often hire students to do transcription. At LSU's Williams Center, director Jennifer Cramer uses both professional contract transcriptionists and student workers, depending on the project. "If the funding is available and we need a transcription done quickly and efficiently, we turn to our contractors," she said.

In addition to the professional's higher level of experience, they're usually more focused. Student workers, Cramer said, often have their responsibilities split over numerous tasks. "Maybe they're filing. Maybe they're helping curate an exhibit. Maybe they're helping us move to the basement once again. Who knows? But their full-time attention isn't always geared toward it," she said. "And so they're stopping and starting, and stopping and starting. It isn't as efficient as a professional who does this for a living."[29]

It may take the students longer, but they cost less than professional transcriptionists and generally catch on quickly, Cramer said. Staff review the student's first transcription attempts, giving them feedback to help them improve. The center has developed a detailed transcription manual chronicling its transcription style, from formatting to time stamping to dealing with false starts. After the students' initial training, referring to the manual answers many of their transcription questions.

In India, oral historians often turn to students due to a shortage of professional transcriptionists. "Thanks to medical transcriptions (mainly for the US insurance companies) that are now done in India at a high price, the cost of transcriptions for oral history interviews have gone up making it unaffordable for many projects to hire professional transcriptionists," said Indira Chowdhury, founder-director of the Centre for Public History at the Srishti Institute of Art, Design and Technology in

Bangalore. "Such projects end up using students as transcribers or interviewers do it themselves." Even when projects can afford the services of medical transcriptionists, they need training in oral history standards, she said.[30]

Working with Volunteer Transcriptionists

I am a rare person who enjoys transcription. As long as the audio is clear, I usually find it interesting, relaxing, and even meditative. But if I wasn't getting paid, would I still do it? Probably only for my own research, as a writer transcribing my own interviews. Assuming I didn't need the money, I'd probably spend my spare time writing fiction, painting, hiking, kayaking, doing yoga, and learning to play bossa nova music on my bass. If I did volunteer work, I'd be more likely to teach adult literacy or work with refugees than transcribe interviews.

Yet some project managers expect they'll find plenty of volunteer transcriptionists. Jeff Corrigan often heard this when trying to get transcription funds:

> People need to understand that no, every retired court reporter that you know does not want to transcribe your stuff for free. How many times have I heard that? I just want to ask those people, do you plan to do the same job when you retire, and other people want you to do it for free?[31]

During Corrigan's time running the oral history program at the State Historical Society of Missouri, his volunteers were more willing to audit transcripts—that is, listen to the audio while correcting the rough draft of a transcript—rather than transcribe. His most dedicated volunteer did some transcription, as well as other tasks around the office. But even then, she chose interviews that interested her, such as civil rights, environmental interviews, and rural topics. "When you're giving up your time, you get to have some say in it," Corrigan said.

In my experience working with projects around the USA, it's much easier to find volunteer interviewers than volunteer transcriptionists. The interviewing process is seen as relatively glamorous—you get to meet an interesting person and coax out their best stories. Transcription? Grunt work, to most. Several projects hired me after their volunteer transcriptionists went AWOL.

But some projects manage to engage and retain volunteers. The History Center at the Linn County Historical Society in Iowa recruits volunteer transcriptionists through its website and through local volunteer organizations. According to Jami Roskamp, the center vets prospective volunteers by checking the facts on their volunteer application form and doing an online search of social media platforms, looking for consistency. Then they send out transcription guidelines and instructions. "It is all rather informal and they are encouraged to ask questions as they have them," she said. "Since nearly all of our transcription volunteers do their work from home I usually don't interact with them much." The center asks that transcription volunteers either commit to at least four hours per week, or volunteer on an interview-by-interview basis. They can work onsite or at home. When I talked to Roskamp, she said she had four or five volunteer transcriptionists. The center hoped to retain them by inviting them to special volunteer events and activities, and giving them a sense of belonging on the volunteer team.[32]

At the Williams Center, Cramer has seen some of their project partners succeed with volunteers, but she advises budgeting for paid transcription if possible:

> Volunteers are volunteering their very precious time. And transcription is the hardest part. A lot of people try and they want to do it. They have jobs, they have families, they have lives, and they've already volunteered their time to do the background research and conduct the interview and manage a project. So it's hard to also talk them into okay, now for every hour of interview, can you sit down for ten hours and transcribe your own voice?[33]

Using volunteers to audit computer-generated transcripts is on the rise. See Chapter 3, Transcription vs the Alternatives, for a look at how this is working in New South Wales, Australia.

Reagan Grau at the National Museum of the Pacific War cherishes his volunteers, but admits the challenges of managing them:

> I think our timeline is all shot to pieces. Relying on volunteer labor makes for some unreliability when it comes to timely completion of transcription. Not that I am unappreciative of what I do receive from volunteers, because I am, but sometimes it takes a while to get a complete transcript. Volunteers work on their own schedule and at their own pace. The professional transcribers are very punctual and timely.

Some of the museum's interviews are transcribed quickly, while other audio languishes for a decade. "In our collection of approximately 5,000 interviews, there is no hard and fast rule about timely transcription. Over the years, we have taken what we could get when we could get it."[34]

Deciding What to Transcribe

By this point in the chapter, you might realize that money, time, and staffing constraints preclude transcribing your entire collection. So what do you do? Prioritize.

Top priorities include:

- interviews of important research value;
- interviews with important donors to the collection;
- interviews that the interviewer or project feels came out especially well;
- interviews with the most elderly, since time could be limited to get your narrator to review the transcript.

The points above might not all apply to the same interview. Some interviews fail to live up to best practices, but are popular with researchers because of the content. For example, the Williams Center at LSU houses a collection of interviews chronicling the history of McKinley High School. Established in 1926 as the first high school for African American students in Baton Rouge, the school has a vital legacy to the city, with many prominent Louisiana citizens among its graduates. The project started in 1995 with high school students interviewing community members. Interviews focus on African American businesses during the period of segregation, the history and role of African American churches, the Baton Rouge bus boycott, and African American social organizations.[35]

The McKinley High interviews don't necessarily reflect best practices, Cramer said.

> I see this a lot with student interviews, where the narrator bails out the unprepared student because they have a story to tell, and they have been waiting a lifetime to tell this story. And so it doesn't matter whether the student is not asking follow up questions, or talking too much, or asking yes or no questions, or cutting the interview short.

This happens a lot in the McKinley interviews. Despite the inexperience and awkwardness of the student interviewers, this series has yielded vital content. "It's a hugely popular collection among researchers," Cramer said, explaining that topics like the 1953 Baton Rouge bus boycott—which predated the more famous Montgomery bus boycott by two years—weren't widely known before this project. "Later on, different researchers came and did more polished documentary-style interviews," Cramer said. "But a lot of these stories were first told to these students by people who have long since passed."[36]

Sometimes oral histories are conducted to please a donor as much as for the sake of scholarship. When partnering with another organization, leaders there might identify people of particular importance. "So they may tell us that there are some people's interviews that because of who they are, that should definitely have a transcript," said Reeves. "And that's fine. I mean, that's part of what a project is, is negotiating all the levels of it."

Reeves has to make a lot of decisions about interview priorities, since so much of his collection will not be transcribed. For example, Reeves was planning an oral history project on the history of the book arts program at the University of Wisconsin, Madison, when I spoke with him in December of 2017. His budget would allow him to only transcribe some of the interviews. "We won't probably even think about transcription until we get fairly deep into the project, meaning getting most if not all the audio," he told me. "I want to know what I think will be the best interviews to transcribe in case we don't have enough money to transcribe it all."[37]

When evaluating on interview content, Reeves asks himself, "Are the answers to the questions illustrative and in depth?" Rather than a tight paragraph to each open-ended question, he looks for narrators who really reflect. "Part of it actually depends on the interviewer, too. Like, is the interviewer willing to ask good follow-up questions?"[38] Challenging the narrator to think more deeply leads to richer anecdotes and worthier transcripts.

Sometimes narrators want their interviews transcribed in a hurry, often for their own reasons that have nothing to do with the institution's goals. For example, they want to bind the interview as a Christmas gift for children and grandchildren. Corrigan occasionally had narrators ask if there was a way to speed up the transcription process by jumping to the top of the list. "I would give them the option if they wanted to pay for that, I would outsource it and they could have it as soon as I could get it done. And several people wanted that option."[39]

One of the biggest reasons to opt out of transcription is when the audio is subpar. The project manager may realize this, or it might come to the attention of the transcriptionist. I occasionally encounter audio that a project optimistically thinks I can transcribe but has a high percentage of undecipherable words. In that case, the best practice for the transcriptionist is to produce about two minutes' worth of the best transcript she can manage from the recording, then send it to the client. The client can then decide if it's worth proceeding with—and probably paying extra—for this transcript.

Preparing for the Transcriptionist

Let's say you've sorted out who will do your transcription, whether in-house or outsourced, and which interviews are priorities. You're all set, right? Well, for optimal results you should prepare a little bit more. Here's what you should send:

- the contract;
- a sample transcript;
- a style guide;
- a list of proper nouns;
- any other paperwork mandated by your institution, such as confidentiality statement, purchase order or invoice format.

Contracts and Agreements

You may work for a big institution that requires a 10-page contract for everything. Or you might be a tiny community oral history project, making it up as you go along. If you work at that big institution, it will probably dictate what paperwork you need to send to a transcriptionist.[40] Most likely, your institution will have some sort of independent contractor or outside vendor form that human resources or payroll can help you set up. If you are that tiny project, you and the transcriptionist can decide whether or not to have a formal contract. It's important to have something in writing, just to clarify expectations on both sides.

At minimum, include the following in your contract:

- the expected number of audio hours;
- the transcriptionist's rates – including things like difficult audio, more than two speakers, or rush transcription, if applicable;
- estimated turnaround time (The turnaround time should be based on when the transcriptionist receives the files, not when the agreement is made.)
- any special directions.

See a sample contract in Appendix 4.

If you're the transcriptionist, you might want to add a payment timeline to the contract, such as requiring invoices to be paid within 30 or 60 days of receipt. Project managers, make sure that you know exactly how your contractor will be paid. Susan Hutton, transcriptionist for the British Library, mentioned to me a frequent "lack of concern regarding the setting up of proper and efficient payment of invoices prior to engaging freelancers."[41] If the person who commissions the work doesn't plan ahead for payment, they might face bureaucratic obstacles that take months to clear up. Meanwhile, the transcriptionist's bills are due, and she may have to jump ship in favor of prompter payers.

Sample Transcript

Every oral history collection should strive for consistency in the look and feel of the transcript. It serves as a "branding" for the collection, it is easier for the reader, and it gives a professional look to the document.

If you already have some transcripts, send the transcriptionist a sample transcript so she can match the format. People get so used to their own format—whether or not there's a cover page, introducing each speaker by full name or initials, to bold or not to bold—that they often forget to include details, such as spacing or non-standard margins, in the style guide. But as somebody who has worked on more than 100 different projects, I can tell you that there is no standard transcript. A sample eases the process. Even if you cover formatting in your style guide, a sample transcript is easier for a transcriptionist to quickly visually comprehend, and can serve as a template with which to start each new transcript. See more on format options in Chapter 4.

If the project is new and no transcripts exist, project managers can leave the preliminary format up to the transcriptionist's best judgment. Together you can tweak it until you're satisfied.

Style Guides

Some larger institutions produce their own transcribing style guides. These may include how to deal with nonstandard grammar, use of ellipses, transcribing non-verbal vocalizations, and other decisions a transcriptionist makes on a minute-to-minute basis. For example, here's a section from the excellent style guide assembled by the T. Harry Williams Center for Oral History.

BOX 2.1 STANDARD SPELLING

Use standard spelling. Do not try to reproduce accents or dialects. If you are unsure of a word, try looking it up in the dictionary or searching on Google.

- You may use yeah, ain't and y'all.
- If someone agrees by saying um-hm or uh-huh, type "yes" or "[agrees]."
- If someone disagrees by saying uh-uh or nah-uh, type "no" or "[disagrees]."
- Gonna should be typed as "going to."
- Gotta should be typed as "got to."
- 'Em should be typed as "them."
- Nothin' should be typed as "nothing."
- Cause should be typed as "because."
- Et cetera instead of "etc."
- Alright instead of "all right."
- Okay instead of "OK."
- Miss, Ms. or Mrs. ("Ms." and "Mrs." can sound alike, so "Miss" is a good default).
- Mr. and not Mister.
- Dr. and not Doctor. *Source: LSU Transcription Guide.*

Think how much time this saves auditors and editors at a later date. It is always best practice to create a style guide for a project. See the Resources section for examples.

Proper Noun List

The proper noun list is an essential component that can be used as a spelling guide, index, and a discovery tool. Almost every project has specialized vocabulary, ranging from family and geographical names to occupational lingo. For example, I've worked on medical history projects where I needed to correctly spell medical tests and procedures, a project on nuns that required terminology about religious education, ceremonies, and parts of the habit, and a couple of projects with equestrian terms. Prepared project managers will send a list of proper nouns along with the interview files. I usually transcribe on a desktop computer with a large monitor. In that case, if there's a lot of use of unfamiliar vocabulary I can have the documents side-by-side for quick referral.

Project managers should require the interviewer to submit a proper noun list along with the recording. The interviewer should make notes during the session, being sure to verify spelling with the narrator either during or after the interview. The narrator may not know how to spell all the terminology or proper nouns. In this case, the interviewer and/or project manager may need to do internet or other research to verify spellings. It's unlikely they'll catch everything; the transcriptionist will probably add to the list as she transcribes.

I've often encountered project managers who don't want to prepare a proper noun list because they are busy, and are thinking of more immediate things than the time when the transcripts come back and will need corrections. If they address the situation at all, they say, "Leave blanks and we'll fill those words in later." This is a colossal waste of time for the whole project, setting yourself up for hours of fixing spellings later instead of getting them right in the first place.

When preparing a proper noun list, keep in mind who will be transcribing the interviews. At Baylor University, which employs student transcriptionists, Sielaff tells interviewers to imagine a 19- or 20-year-old when creating a proper noun list. "Think of the things you said, or the names, or turn of phrases or whatever that you use, that a 19- or 20-year-old might not know, and write those down," he said. This could include words and expressions younger people might not be familiar with, rather than just proper nouns. The interviewer can prepare a word list for a single interview, or for a project where street names, terminology, and/or people's names reoccur.

The Proactive Transcriptionist

What if the oral history project is new and has not yet developed a format or style guide? Transcriptionist Barb Jardee sends a preference list to clients to help them build their style guide—and to save everybody lots of time and frustration. Her three-page document allows clients to state myriad preferences, from margins to font to "okay" versus "O.K." She has allowed her form to be reprinted in this book in Appendix 3 because, as she said, "I'd be happy if the whole transcribing world used my preference list!"[42]

Recording

No matter how good the proper noun list and style guide, it all comes down to the recording. In some cases, I'm transcribing audio that was recorded long ago. Noise reduction programs and pumping up the volume generally only help a little. Basically, you have what you have.

But if you are recording audio for a new project, please do it right! Transcriptionist Susan Hutton said:

> I'm forever bemused at the number of professional oral history interviewers who apparently dive into recording an interview without doing a sound check, let alone monitor levels and quality during the interview. Even interviews conducted over more than one session, the previous sound quality doesn't appear to have been reviewed. This despite many having attended a course or workshop on oral history interviewing.[43]

Remember, it is all about the narrator. Test the recorder with the narrator sitting an appropriate distance from the microphone. If the narrator drops to a mumble, leans way back or moves to a different place in the room, be aware that this will affect future listeners' ability to hear your research. Same for a dog barking, a cat purring beside the microphone, a clock ticking, air conditioner kicking on, or an interviewer's constant interjections of "yes, mm hmm, got it." I've transcribed so many interviews where the interviewer is crystal clear while the narrator sounds muddy and faraway. If you can only clearly capture one side of the interview, err on the side of the narrator.

If you are recording an interview over the phone, there are apps for that. Placing a recorder next to the phone and setting your phone on speaker is not a best practice.

One of the things that most annoys me is when interviewers aren't sure about how good the recording is, or they know the environment is too noisy, and they laughingly make remarks to the narrator about how they feel sorry for whoever is going to transcribe this. Talk about shooting yourself in the foot! Sure, the transcriber will suffer in the agonizing moments of wading through subpar audio. But ultimately, it's the project and future researchers who suffer. Transcriptionists don't have supersonic hearing. If the recording is inaudible, I'm going to put [unclear] or [inaudible] and move on. And I'm going to bill extra for having to spend three times as long to produce this poor transcript. Interviewers, you don't want to waste everybody's time and money—the narrator's, the transcriptionist's, the project's, and the future researchers'. Figure out how to work your machine, and find a quiet place to record.

Bottom Line

People often underestimate the cost and time that go into an oral history project, and transcription is a significant percentage of that cost. It's important to be realistic at the outset about how many interview hours you can produce and transcribe.

Budget, funding sources, and timeline are important factors in a project's decisions about transcription. You'll likely need to prioritize which interviews get transcribed first, or at all. Deciding whether to transcribe interviews and who will do it is one of a project's biggest decisions.

Useful Documents

- Sample transcript, see Appendix 1.
- Proper noun list, see Appendix 2.
- Transcription preference list, see Appendix 3.
- Sample contract, see Appendix 4.

Notes

1 As defined by the Merriam-Webster dictionary, "a state of privileged seclusion or separation from the facts and practicalities of the real world."

2 Steven Sielaff, "In the Oral History Toolbox," University of Oxford Press Blog, September 16, 2016. Available at: https://blog.oup.com/2016/09/oral-history-tools/ (accessed December 10, 2017).

3 Susan Hutton, email correspondence with Teresa Bergen, December 9, 2018.

4 Lindsey Annable, email correspondence with Teresa Bergen, December 8, 2017.

5 Kim Heikkila, interview with Teresa Bergen, November 15, 2017.

6 Maija Anderson, email correspondence with Teresa Bergen, November 7, 2017.

7 Troy Reeves, interview with Teresa Bergen, December 11, 2017.

8 Jeff Corrigan, interview with Teresa Bergen, December 18, 2017.

9 Schizophrenia Oral History Project website, available at: www.schizophreniaoralhistories.com/donate (accessed December 10, 2017).

10 Amazon Smile website, available at: https://org.amazon.com/ (accessed December 10, 2017).

11 Kickstarter website, available at: www.kickstarter.com/projects/darrenwall/500-years-later-an-oral-history-of-final-fantasy-v, (accessed December 10, 2017).

12 Kickstarter website, available at: www.kickstarter.com/projects/1842010623/mormons-in-northern-new-jersey-an-oral-history, (accessed December 10, 2017).

13 Modern Memoirs website, available at: www.modernmemoirs.com/modern-memoirs-inc/ (accessed December 10, 2017).

14 Modern Memoirs website, available at: www.modernmemoirs.com/process/ (accessed December 10, 2017).

15 Victoria Greene, interview with Teresa Bergen, November 18, 2017.

16 Cambodian Women's Oral History Project website, available at: http://cambodianwomensoralhistory.com/about/ (accessed December 10, 2017).

17 Stanford Historical Society website, available at: https://historicalsociety.stanford.edu/volunteer/oral-history-volunteer-opportunities (accessed February 11, 2019).

18 Veterans History Project, available at: www.loc.gov/vets/about.html (accessed February 11, 2019).

19 Jeff Corrigan, interview with Teresa Bergen, December 18, 2017.

20 Jennifer Cramer, phone interview with Teresa Bergen, January 23, 2018.

21 Veterans History Project, "Indexing and Transcribing Your Interviews," available at: www.loc.gov/vets/transcribe.html (accessed January 14, 2018).

22 Linda Valois, email correspondence with Teresa Bergen, June 4, 2018.

23 Audio Transcription Center website, available at: https://audiotranscriptioncenter.com/our-staff/ (accessed January 14, 2018).

24 GoTranscript website, available at: https://gotranscript.com/ (accessed January 14, 2018).

25 Troy Reeves, interview with Teresa Bergen, December 11, 2017.

26 Susan Hutton, email correspondence with Teresa Bergen, December 9, 2018.

27 Jeff Corrigan, interview with Teresa Bergen, December 18, 2017.

28 Barb Jardee, email correspondence with Teresa Bergen, May 4, 2018.

29 Jennifer Cramer, interview with Teresa Bergen, January 23, 2018.

30 Indira Chowdhury, email correspondence with Teresa Bergen, August 25, 2018.

31 Jeff Corrigan, interview with Teresa Bergen, December 18, 2017.

32 Jami Roskamp, email correspondence with Teresa Bergen, January 15, 2018.

33 Jennifer Cramer, interview with Teresa Bergen, January 23, 2018.

34 Reagan Grau, email correspondence with Teresa Bergen, November 8, 2017.

35 McKinley High School Oral History Project, LSU Libraries, available at: www.lib.lsu.edu/oralhistory/collections/mckinley (accessed January 27, 2018).

36 Jennifer Cramer, interview with Teresa Bergen, January 23, 2018.

37 Troy Reeves, interview with Teresa Bergen, December 11, 2017.

38 Ibid.

39 Jeff Corrigan, interview with Teresa Bergen, December 18, 2017.

40 Sometimes it's a little crazy. I once had to sign a pile of papers promising I would not molest any children, even though I was working at a home office in a different state with only a cat (unmolested, I assure you) around.

41 Susan Hutton, email correspondence with Teresa Bergen, December 9, 2018.
42 Barb Jardee, email correspondence with Teresa Bergen, May 9, 2018.
43 Susan Hutton, email correspondence with Teresa Bergen, December 9, 2018.

3

TRANSCRIPTION VS THE ALTERNATIVES

Oral historians have long debated whether or not to transcribe interviews, and this conversation has intensified now that new technology offers more alternatives. There are compelling reasons both for and against (Table 3.1).

Reasons Not to Transcribe

As someone who has earned part of her living doing transcription for more than 20 years, I might be biased in favor of transcripts. But there are perfectly good reasons that people overseeing oral history collections don't transcribe interviews, including:

- lack of funds
- lack of time
- concern for the loss of "orality"
- poor content of interviews.

Lack of Funds

The cost of transcribing a collection adds up fast. Project directors often have to prioritize interviews, deciding to transcribe only part of a collection, or none at all. Many projects languish, untranscribed and inaccessible, for years. Funds for timed indexes—a list of topics and time codes, as described in depth later in this chapter—stretch farther than for transcription, which is more detailed and time-consuming.

TABLE 3.1 Should you transcribe your interviews?

Pros	*Cons*
Many researchers prefer working with a transcript than with audio	Transcripts are costly and time-consuming to produce.
A transcript provides correct spellings.	Even the best transcript fails to capture every nuance of speech and tone.
It's easier to search an electronic version of a document than to search audio.	The existence of a transcript often discourages researchers from listening to the primary source, the audio.
The transcriber clarifies the hard parts of a transcript so that the researcher doesn't have to.	Technology continues to introduce new alternatives to transcripts.
Producing a transcript allows the narrator to review and verify how researchers will quote the interview.	
A paper version is still the best preservation format.	

Lack of Time

Depending on the project, timelines can be tighter or looser. While some oral history archives accept nothing less than a full transcript, others who use qualitative research must find ways to quicken their access to the information.

Concern for Loss of "Orality"

As I mentioned in Chapter 1, a certain amount of backlash against transcripts exists in the oral history field, since anecdotal evidence shows that many researchers prefer the transcript to the recorded interview. The word "orality" often pops up in discussions of transcript versus audio. The *Oxford English Dictionary* defines orality as "the quality of being verbally communicated."[1] Critics of transcription point out that changing voice to text mediates and flattens those voices, wringing much of the meaning, life, rhythm, and expression out of the spoken words.

Poor Interview Content

If the audio *quality* is bad, researchers will find a transcript prepared by a patient, dedicated professional extremely helpful. But what if the *content* is poor? For example, I've worked on some projects where high school students were the interviewers. While some grasped the idea of probing follow-up, others seemed to think the point was to get through a list of questions as quickly as possible. This led to transcripts of mixed value.

Some narrators are unable or unwilling to share much due to dementia, speech impediments, mental illness, a preference for privacy, or other reasons of their own.

These disappointing interviews sometimes don't warrant the cost of transcription. For example, retired physician Neal Ross Holtan interviewed former staff and mental patients for an oral history project about Anoka State Hospital in Minnesota. Sadly, one of the patient interviews was so repetitive, rapid and stream of consciousness that the project ultimately decided not to transcribe it.[2]

Should I Transcribe My Interviews?

Box 3.1 will give you some directions on how to decide.

BOX 3.1 SHOULD I TRANSCRIBE MY INTERVIEWS?

These questions will help you decide if your oral history project needs transcripts.

1. What is the intended use of the interview?
2. What are the expectations of the archive or other place where I'm depositing this work?
3. What are my resources—financial and human?
4. What is my timeline?
5. Is the content of this interview worth the cost of transcribing?
6. Is the whole interview useful, or just selected parts?
7. How many interviews are in the collection?
8. How will researchers access these interviews?

Interpreting your answers:

1. Certain types of projects, such as documentary films, warrant full transcription so you can edit your video. If you know you'll need the full text right away, transcribe. If you're capturing something solely for future generations to access in archives, transcription is kind, but optional.
2. Unless you have a special partnership with the archive, it's highly unlikely they'll transcribe your interviews for you. If you want them transcribed, you'll need to get it done.
3. If the interviews went well and you have funds for transcription, or reliable and willing volunteers, go for it. Otherwise, consider indexing.
4. If you are working against a deadline or the public needs access to these interviews in a hurry, index now and transcribe later, if desired. Or employ students or a transcription service that can quickly turn your audio or video into transcripts.
5. If the content doesn't merit transcription, index instead.
6. This is a highly subjective question, and mostly applies to people working on projects with a certain end product, such as a book or museum exhibit.

> In these cases, a researcher might choose to index the whole interview and selectively transcribe the parts that are relevant to their project.
> 7. The more interviews you do, the higher the transcription cost. Depending on your budget, you might index the collection or transcribe selectively.
> 8. Many researchers prefer transcripts. Consider your audience of scholars, and your budget.

Alternatives to Transcription

Of course, if projects don't transcribe interviews, they need to come up with a different way for interested parties to access the information. A collection with no discovery tools is useless. So project teams need to decide whether interviews will be transcribed or, if not, what alternative aids will be created so that researchers can find the collection.

A timed index is one popular solution. There are different ways of making indexes, but they all indicate where particular topics come up within the audio. For example, if 3 minutes and 27 seconds into an interview the narrator begins describing her childhood in Paris, "3:27 childhood in Paris" could be a line in the index.

Some alternatives (or supplements) to traditional transcription include:

- timed indexing using word processing programs
- timed indexing with spreadsheets
- voice recognition software
- digital indexing
- OHMS.

Timed Index with Word Processing

This tried and true method is easily creatable on your computer and requires no special training. Back in the days of cassette tapes, we indexed using tape counter numbers. In the 1990s, I had a job supported by a six-month grant to create indexes from 500 cassette tapes of interviews and performances from Louisiana folklife festivals. Once I started digitizing cassettes, I was shocked to learn how inexact cassette tapes were. Instead of a 90-minute cassette measuring 45 minutes on each side, I'd wind up with nearly 47 minutes. With digital timestamps, timing seems much more reliable.

By making a simple index with word processing software, you can add a time stamp whenever a new topic starts. In this example from the University of Wisconsin, Madison, the index of an interview conducted with Nancy M. Abraham begins with a list of titles she held at UW, year and length of the interview, names of the interviewer and indexer, and an upfront list of major topic areas covered (Box 3.2). Then we get into the breakdown of topics by time code. This is a detailed style of index, and written in complete sentences. While quicker than transcription, the UW index still required careful listening and several hours to prepare.

BOX 3.2 EXCERPT OF TIMED INDEX FROM UNIVERSITY OF WISCONSIN, MADISON ORAL HISTORY PROJECT ARCHIVES

ORAL HISTORY PROJECT

Interview #436

ABRAHAM, NANCY M.

ABRAHAM, Nancy M. (1934–)

Undergraduate and Graduate Student; Staff; Assistant Director of Summer Sessions; Associate Director of Special Students; Associate Director of Inter-College Programs; Associate Dean of Summer Sessions and Inter-College Programs at UW: 1954–1955; 1959–1989
Interviewed: 1993
Interviewer: Barry Teicher
Indexed (time code) by: Haochen Wang
Length: 3 hours, 14 minutes

> Early childhood and education; Undergraduate work; Office of high school relations; Graduate work; Summer sessions; Director Clay Schoenfeld; Dean's Council; Office of special students; Budget; Protest on campus; Facilities; Bicentennial festival; Enrichment and enhancement programs; Dean Harland Samson's emphasis on enrollment management, budget reduction, upgrading facilities, streamlining and enhancing creativity; Committee work; Summer sessions service organizations; Mental illness organizations; Other interests and activities.

First Interview Session (October 14, 1993): Tapes 1–2

Tape 1/Side 1

> 00:00:17 NA came from a blue-collar family in Sheboygan, Wisconsin. She loved school while she was growing up.

00:01:47 She mentions two teachers who influenced her. NA's wonderful first grade teacher made an impression on her at an early age. In high school, she enjoyed all courses she took in the college track. Her history teacher/debate and forensics coach also had quite an impact on her. He was very demanding and taught students to question without fear. He recruited her for the debate and forensics team, participation which she regards as one of the single most important learning experiences in her life. This involvement helped her to overcome her shyness and required she do research on debate topics, an activity she enjoyed. McCarthyism was one of the topics she remembers.

00:06:10 Promising students were encouraged into the college track by principals and teachers.

None of NA's relatives had gone to college, so there was no expectation that she would.

Her father did not see any reason for her to go because the assumption was that she would just get married. She proceeded to check into scholarship opportunities on her own.

A simpler index model would summarize information and might employ sentence fragments. For example, instead of saying, "Her history teacher/debate and forensic coach also had quite an impact on her. He was very demanding and taught students to question without fear ..." That whole five minutes might be summed up with, "Relationships with and lessons learned from teachers."

In an article on transcription, Francis Good asks, why transcribe at all? He mentions "enthusiastic 'no transcription' advocates" who relish forcing researchers to listen to the audio by only providing a scant index of interview contents. "Any oral historians with a feeling for orality and experience of the way researchers will rarely access a sound recording where a transcript is available must sympathize with this view." However, he reminds us that indexing involves a strong element of mediation and many subjective decisions, and makes an excellent point:

> There's also considerable disquiet that the absence of a transcript cleared by the interviewee puts the onus on users to ensure professional and ethical approach to quotations they idiosyncratically transcribe for themselves. Many collecting agencies believe they have a responsibility to clear interpretations of language used with narrators.[3]

Indexing is, of course, highly subjective—much more so than transcription, since so much is left out. Indexers inevitably vary in the sections they deem worth indexing and in the language they use as index terms. The level of detail will depend on project aims and interest, budget, expertise of indexers and guidance from the project manager. Training indexers upfront, and carefully reviewing their first few indexes for quality, cohesiveness and adherence to project style, can save many hours of redoing work later. And, to solve the problem Mr. Good mentions above, consider clearing indexes with narrators, just like you would transcripts.

Timed Index with a Spreadsheet

Spreadsheet programs are another useful tool for indexing. The University of Wisconsin, Madison, switched over to spreadsheets from the Microsoft Word example already shown. "We've moved to Excel, because it's easier to cut and paste it into OHMS or to, if needed, export the rows and columns out to some other software or tool, like an Access or FileMaker Pro database," Reeves explained.[4] (See section on OHMS later in this chapter.)

Scholar and writer Mary Contini Gordon has developed a detailed and carefully planned method using Excel for indexing massive amounts of narrative data which is adaptable to most projects (Figure 3.1). This is part of what Gordon has trade-marked as *Her-His*tory Method™ which she uses in interview-based research reports and in her published books. This method is very powerful and convenient, as most people have Excel on their computers and it's easy to share spreadsheets via email or shared access sites like Google Docs.

As shown in Figure 3.1, Gordon charts this metadata in separate searchable columns. Different researchers might chart different metadata, but Gordon said most people will need:

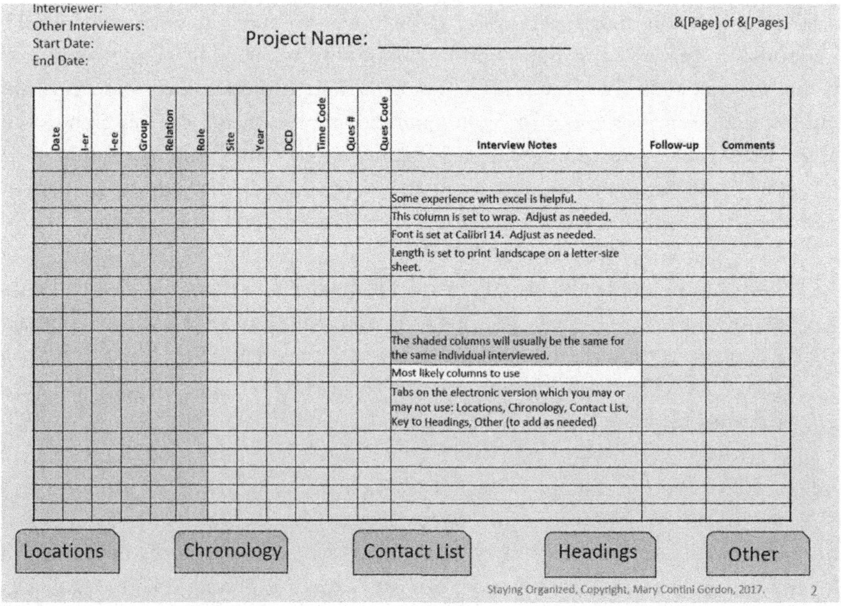

FIGURE 3.1 Mary Contini Gordon's spreadsheet log

- Date of interview
- Name of interviewer
- Name of narrator
- Group
- Time code
- Question number
- Question code
- Interview notes
- Follow-up

She deems "interview notes" as the major column, where the researcher types in his or her notes. To keep everything in one place, Gordon adds tabs at the bottom of the spreadsheet to track chronology, contact info and locations.

Gordon sees the two greatest strengths of her method as being accessible and sortable. Instead of keeping each person's index separate, as happens with Word documents, Gordon logs all her interviews for a project into the same Excel spreadsheet. She's added up to 70 interviews in a single index. Then she can easily use the "find" function to search all her interviews in seconds for a certain location, topic or keyword.

Just as oral history projects usually send a draft transcript to the narrator to check accuracy, Gordon sends a spreadsheet—but only the section that logs that individual's interview. If there's a part she doesn't understand, she might make that text red and ask the narrator to further explain.

Gordon said the ideal situation would be to have both a full transcript and her index. "But if I had to choose, frankly I would choose the Excel spreadsheet."

Gordon offers these tips about her method:

- Careful notetaking during the interview will save you time when reviewing the recording, and is an important back-up for technology that fails.
- Promptly download recordings before anything happens to them.
- Enter time codes immediately while your memory of the interview is still fresh.
- Create and stick to definitions. Clearly define categories to avoid confusion when sorting.
- Track changes, such as when adding new data or when the narrator sends back an approved index.
- Add columns as needed when you realize a new one would be helpful.
- Be flexible as project objectives evolve, changing column headings or definitions accordingly.[5]

Voice Recognition Software

Voice recognition software that really works could revolutionize transcription and sway the long-standing debate back in favor of transcribing, as it would solve the problem of transcription's high cost. But at the time of writing, it's not there yet. When I talked to Baylor's Steven Sielaff about voice recognition software in summer 2018, he said he hears of a new app every month. At the time of our talk, he was conducting tests using a mid-level typist versus Pop Up Archive, one of the speech-to-text online services. Automated services are fast—you can often get your transcript in less than an hour—but the error rate is high.

Sielaff said:

> And then it becomes the issue of how much time do I spend A, transcribing from scratch with a standard student typist, versus B, running a piece of audio through an automated transcription service and then having someone edit that into a form that's usable, basically ready to move on to the editing phase that we have at our institute.

So far, it's a draw. "From what I've seen, what I would probably say is it takes just as long to edit an automated transcript as it does to transcribe it from scratch," Sielaff said. So which approach is better depends on the situation. If you're working on a large project and have reliable transcriptionists, he thinks transcribing from scratch is better because you can train them in project terms and knowledge as you go along. This is especially true if the audio quality is less than stellar, or if there are accents and/or multiple speakers. However, voice-to-text might be a good solution for less adept typists. "If someone is more comfortable being an editor than a transcriptionist, it might work for them," Sielaff said.[6]

Before this new crop of online voice-to-text services, Sony's Dragon Naturally Speaking was long the leader in voice recognition software. Its speech to text function works well for some people. The catch? It responds best when trained to understand a single voice. This means if you're a lecturer, writer, or anyone else who wants to organize thoughts verbally, it might be worthwhile to spend some time training the software to your voice. Then Dragon can probably produce a useful text for you. But in the messy world of oral history—with regional and foreign accents, unanticipated noises, people talking over each other, varying distances from the microphone, and the joy of recently discovered boxes of mystery tapes that have spent the last three decades without the benefit of climate control—well, you can see what I'm getting at.

In 2017, IBM proudly announced that its newest speech recognition system had only a 5.5 percent word error rate, down from the 2016 system's 6.9 percent error rate.[7] This new rate is roughly akin to human hearing. But how does it compare to a transcriptionist's hearing? Unfortunately, I lack supersonic hearing or other audio superpowers. But I do have the diligence to go back and listen to that one tricky word over and over. Because if a client gave me an interview with decent audio and I missed every twentieth word in the transcript, I wouldn't have that client for long. In other words, IBM's 5.5 percent error rate isn't acceptable.

Some transcriptionists use the new crop of audio-to-text online services to produce the first draft of a transcript, then go back and audit the text, fixing mistakes. I can be something of a purist, so this idea made me uneasy, as though it were cheating. But in the interest of scientific research for this book, I decided to try out a service called Trint. In an article entitled "Transcribing Audio Sucks—So Make the Machines Do It," *Wired* lauded Trint. "An unprecedented voice-transcription technology can tell you not only what's being said, but who is saying it."[8] This new technology could supposedly discern multiple voices with ease.

I have to admit that reading about Trint seduced me, just a little. Unlike the writers at *Wired,* I love transcribing. Usually. But what if I could offload some of my more trying audio? Specifically, a collection recorded in the 1970s on cassette, later digitized, featuring a speaker with a very heavy German accent.

Okay, this wasn't really a fair test, especially since Trint warned me it didn't want to deal with these recordings, either. According to the Trint site,

> Our machine-learning robots are pretty neat, Trinting your audio or video files into text – at lightning speeds. But they're not miracle workers (just magicians). Nine times out of ten when we see people confused or disappointed by the accuracy of their transcription, it's because of one of two things: 1) recording quality; or 2) heavy accents.[9]

My candidate had both these strikes against it.

I registered for an account, which included 30 minutes free. Since my file was 48 minutes long, I paid $15 to cover an hour of transcription. I uploaded the MP3 to the Trint website and within ten minutes I had a transcript.

The transcript was worse than useless, but the entertainment value was high. I laughed so hard my dog got nervous. Here's a sample of the actual transcription, as close as I could get it. The speaker is George L. Mosse (1918–1999), eminent historian of fascism and Nazi Germany, and the first scholar-in-residence at Washington's Holocaust Museum. This is the first minute and 35 seconds of a 1979 class lecture at the University of Wisconsin, Madison, by Mosse.

> Last time I tried to tell you how the war was built into people's lives, how they coped with the unparalleled confrontation of mass death and life in the trenches by lifting it either into the sacred or into the trivial. And when I talked about lifting it into the sacred, building this kind of bridge, I tried to tell you that this was connected to two things: to the stereotype of the hero, of the young hero, which continues in a third way the rediscovery of the body, the idea of Arcadia, of innocence, the idea of flowers and then the design of military cemeteries. And I ended last time by saying something about the greatest experience for all of them, the experience of camaraderie, wartime camaraderie, in the trenches. And that this idea of camaraderie became an idea of equality. That the officers, the second lieutenants, who were also the [administrators?] of the war, of the writers, all of this sort of thing, how these second lieutenants believe, which may or may not have been true, that the relationship between them and their

men was indeed a democratic relationship in the front line, in the trenches. There is actually another truth to that.

Here's what Trint managed to capture of the same 1 minute, 35-second passage:

[00:00:04] All people like cope with the pain of day and night the sacred oranges. That was the stereotype. OH OH OH OH GOD. OH YEAH. OH. OH.
[00:01:00] Really. I hear all.
[00:01:09] The majors all the same. Oh really. Which may be true that there may well be related to the point line. HEY. OH HEY. OH HEY HEY HEY HEY HEY HEY HEY HEY. In this wall on this. War.

That's it. Trint recognized "war," "stereotype," and "sacred," or three words out of a 1:35 segment. A little further on, Trint has Mosse using the phrases "you go girl" and "hey bro," and mentioning Home Depot, all terms that Mosse never used in his discourse, according to Skye Doney, director of the George L. Mosse Program in History.[10]

Obviously, the cards were stacked against Trint with the Mosse recording, which takes me multiple listens to decipher what he said. To make up for over-taxing Trint on our first date, I gave it a second chance with the easiest audio I could find, a clearly recorded interview with a nun reflecting on her life.

At first glance, I was impressed with how well Trint got the rough transcript. Most of the information was down, and it even correctly identified some non-obvious proper nouns for capitalization, such as the name of a religious order.

But as I worked through the transcript, I realized how rough it was. Trint doesn't have the same ear for punctuation that I do, so I had to track every sentence very carefully for commas and periods. Trint seems to think there's a new speaker every time someone pauses, so I had to do a lot of paragraph reformatting. Before uploading the audio to Trint, I'd only listened enough to note its clarity. I didn't realize there'd be some Hawaiian names, which completely threw the automated service. Bottom line: Even though the raw Trint transcript initially looked impressive, it took me about twice as long to fix it up than it would have taken me to type it. Plus, I had to pay 15 dollars.

My experience may not reflect the general consensus. I'm a professional transcriptionist who types fast and has my own way of doing things. For example, I'm very accustomed to ExpressScribe software and much prefer controlling it with the function keys, rather than the excessive mousing the Trint editor required. I found it a little faster to export the Trint as a Word document and audit it with ExpressScribe than use the Trint editing function.

However, if I were a slow typist and didn't already have a system in place, Trint might be useful. If I was running a program at a large institution with lots of student help, it might be cheaper to get a Trint subscription for $120 a month (at press time) and pay student workers minimum wage to fix the machine-made transcripts. This would only work with the clearest recordings and the most diligent, detail-oriented students willing to chase down every missing comma and rogue paragraph break.

Some programmers are working hard to adapt speech-to-text technology to their specific oral history collection needs. At the 2018 International Oral History Association meeting in Finland, oral historian Almut Leh presented a paper about work she and her colleagues are doing in Germany. They have been developing the Fraunhofer IAIS Audio Mining system, which is designed to

> create a time-aligned transcription of the spoken words, as it is normally made by professional human transcribers. To achieve an optimal result this does not only include automatic speech recognition but an entire workflow including segmentation of the audio signal, speech detection, speaker analysis and keyword extraction using several state-of-the-art pattern recognition algorithms.

This system detects gender and can identify which speaker is speaking. Engineers are training the system using a subset of the archives "Deutsches Gedächtnis" ("German Memory"), which consists of 2,500 oral history interviews conducted from 1975 to the present. So far, only half of these interviews have been transcribed. The chosen test set is representative of the collection, with all interviews easily understandable to the human ear.

While this project is specific to the German language, oral historians around the world will relate.

> Other big challenges posed by oral history interviews are colloquial language used in spontaneous speech, hesitations, age- and health-related changes in the way of speaking and domain-specific words used in the interviews that usually do not occur in everyday speech (e.g. Kriegerwitwensöhne, German for sons of a war widow).

So far, the results are promising, with a descending percentage of error rates and continuing addition of domain-specific language.[11]

All over the world, effective voice-to-text methods are the holy grail for oral historians. "We are desperately in need of effective tools," Sun Yi, a documentary filmmaker in China, told me in an email. They do have some voice-recognizing tools, she said, "but they are not widely adopted in China and it may not apply to some dialects."[12] It's a bit perplexing that the voice-to-text quandary has been so difficult to solve. As my husband puts it, "They have self-driving cars, and you're still in business?!"

Transcriptionist Susan Nicholls worries about being put out of work by voice recognition software:

> I'm quite surprised that I'm still in work now! However, there is a company that I've worked for, for several years, who stopped using me just over a year

ago, and as a cost-cutting exercise started using a computer program for their transcripts instead. But I'm pleased to say, they've come back to me again, having found that the quality of the transcripts wasn't good enough and they preferred the human version.[13]

Transcriptionist Barb Jardee figures that transcription work will continue to evolve in tandem with technology:

> As voice recognition gets better and better, computers will take over the task of typing the rough draft transcripts. Humans who used to perform this task will become verifiers of the computer's work, correcting misinterpretations, standardizing punctuation, and inserting paragraph breaks, etc. "Woman without her man is lost" takes on a whole new meaning when punctuated, "Woman: without her, man is lost." There will also be times when the computer may "recognize speech," but the human verifier realizes what was really being said was "wreck a nice beach." So will there be employment for people like me in the future? Yes, but the nature of that work will be slightly different. We will adapt.[14]

Case Study: Crowdsourcing and Voice-to-Text in New South Wales

The State Library of New South Wales launched a crowdsourced transcription program called Amplify in October 2016. It lets anybody online read—and edit—computer-generated transcripts while listening to the audio. Since users don't have to log in to participate, statistics are hazy. But library staff know that as of July 2018 11,000 sessions from 6,000 users in 55 different countries were noted, marking 160,000 individual edits across their collections. Of those users, only 37 created their own account. So far this has resulted in 80 completed transcripts. "There's probably another 100 or so that are 80% complete or higher," Jenna Bain, digital projects leader, told me in an email. "There can be a long tail in getting items completed."

The State Library of NSW worked with existing platforms and used open-source code that had been developed by another institution. The New York Public Library's open-source Transcript Editor was especially helpful:

> We took this codebase and modified it to our own requirements with some custom development as the original version didn't quite have all the features we wanted but provided a fantastic baseline. Working with a developer, we were able to get our version of the application and its customisation up and running in about five weeks. We have also made our version open-source which means that others can take a copy of our code and spin up their own version much more quickly—it could be done in a day, assuming that an organisation had access to a skilled web developer (or the money to outsource).

This is a revolutionary approach, and right in line with conversations I've had with oral historians who have told me that it's easier to get volunteer auditors than volunteer transcriptionists, and then only if it's a subject that interests them.

Amplify displays icons of each available interview. Click an icon, and you have the option to listen or join in as an editor. One of the things that's made the program successful so far is how it seduces visitors into participating. "We had found in previous crowdsourcing experiences that requiring users to create an account before getting started was a barrier to participation," Bain said.

> We also promote Amplify as a listening platform as well as a tool for transcription—which supports a more serendipitous editing experience we have found. Someone might at first be interested in just listening to an audio file, but if they see an obvious error in the text it takes no more than a few key strokes to make a correction. We benefit more by not making people log in first.

Before you know it, you're a volunteer.

Amplify works on a sophisticated consensus algorithm which means that users of the platform effectively review each other's work, Bain said.

> If your consensus threshold is programmed to three, for example, it means that each line of a transcript is in draft and must be transcribed/corrected by three people before being considered complete. If those three people have transcribed the line identically, the line is considered to have met consensus and locks for further editing.

If the three people disagree, the line goes into a verification stage where a fourth editor can then indicate which of the previous edits they feel is the most correct. Occasionally a State Library staff member steps in to moderate. Since some people only edit a handful of lines at a time, it can take many more than three people to complete a transcript.

"This consensus algorithm is an excellent way to mitigate risk and has been really transformative for us actually, especially in terms of winning staff and stakeholders over who may have ordinarily had an aversion to using computer-generated transcripts," Bain said. Amplify has made the State Library of NSW the first cultural institution in Australia to use artificial intelligence/machine learning across its collections in this way.

According to Bain:

> A.I. in libraries is an especially burgeoning area—two years ago when we launched it was virtually unheard of, especially for audio materials, so we had a huge amount of interest from other cultural institutions about our use of speech-to-text. What has been fantastic has been the way in which Amplify

has opened up discussion about the possibility of using A.I. in a library context—10 or even 5 years ago even this would have been a taboo subject.

So, what's in it for volunteers? A good story, and the chance to help. In addition to more general calls for volunteers, the library targets their communication to communities they've identified as stakeholders in particular collections. Bain's conference papers on Amplify have also helped to spread the word. "We do have a few super users who are passionate oral historians or just historians in general, but for the most part they come because they have an interest in a specific collection," she said.

As I write this, the library is developing version 2 of Amplify, due in large part to feedback from other institutions. Bain said that she'd expected other institutions would adapt the open source code developed by the NYPL for their own collections, but soon realized many lacked the technical resources. The new version of Amplify will help other institutions crowdsource transcription of their oral history collections. Bain also foresees bringing collections of different institutions together online for the first time and linking these collections together via common themes for users to browse. Sounds like volunteers will be able to follow their favorite subjects across—and perhaps edit for—multiple institutions.[15]

Oral historian Mark Wong said that the National Archives of Singapore has also been crowdsourcing transcription through its Citizen Archivist portal:

> This portal allows members of the public to participate in tasks such as writing captions for uncaptioned photographs, transcribing manuscripts and transcribing oral history interviews. So far, we've found that members of the public find transcribing oral history interviews most challenging. It may be due to the challenges and demands of real-time listening. One good aspect about these efforts is in terms of educating the public in what we do, and for them to have a try at it themselves to better appreciate the challenges of our work.[16]

Randforce

Oral historian Michael Frisch formed Randforce Associates in the State University of New York at Buffalo's Technology Incubator in 2002. It aims to advance oral history scholarship and public practice through technology, making best use of digitization. The website clearly states their mission: to "put the oral back in oral history."[17]

Randforce basically provides customized, high-powered audio and video indexing to oral history and other qualitative research projects, with or without transcripts. As Frisch explained in an abstract for a keynote speech:

> Audio and video documentation is conventionally encountered in one of two states—relatively "raw," in archived collections, and relatively "cooked," in

constructed, selective, and linear documentary forms. In this presentation, I discuss and demonstrate how new digital tools open an important non-linear, multi-pathed ground between these poles. By permitting direct indexing, cross-referencing, and searchable access to audio and video documentation—to collections of recorded voice or music and, in video, to bodies, gestures, performance, and non-verbal demonstrations—these tools stand in sharp contrast to conventional modes grounded in the limited (and limiting) world of text transcription and broad-brush content summaries.[18]

The Randforce system works with digital tools, including InterClipper Audio, which offers real-time media bookmarking for qualitative researchers. This means scholars can bookmark highlights while watching a video interview, then later return to edit, review and/or export clips to use in presentations.[19]

Randforce offers services ranging from overall project design and development to media-based annotations of recordings, and a lot in between. Users appreciate that indexes are tied to the audio, so that they can click on a term and be taken immediately to the corresponding place in the audio or video. This also makes it easy to search across a collection of interviews.

Large Randforce projects include partnering with the Illinois State Museum to index an extensive oral history of Illinois agriculture, and with Arkansas Educational Television to index 200 hours of video for a World War II documentary. Randforce also works with community projects, small museums and collections, including the Brooklyn History Society and the Multicultural History Society of Ontario. They pride themselves on quickly making small collections accessible to the public.

OHMS

The Oral History Metadata Synchronizer (OHMS) is an open source software application developed by Doug Boyd and his team at the Louie B. Nunn Center for Oral History at the University of Kentucky. His aim was to improve access to the center's extensive oral history interview collections through automated indexing.

When Boyd came to the Nunn Center in 2008, scholars used about 300 interviews per year "despite terrible access," he said.[20] He felt frustrated that researchers weren't using the oral history materials more. "Untextualized audio and video is the biggest challenge since the beginning of oral history. We still need those transcripts. The problem is, we still can't afford those transcripts on a huge scale."

Early versions of the OHMS indexing system were only written for in-house implementation. But in 2011, the Nunn Center hired Artifex Technology Consulting, Inc. to rewrite the OHMS code, improve indexing capabilities, integrate video compatibility and optimize it for open-source distribution.[21] That year, the Institute of Museum and Library Services (IMLS) awarded the University of Kentucky Libraries a National Leadership Grant to further develop OHMS.[22] The system went public in 2014. As of late 2018, over 500 individual and private OHMS accounts are in use in 35 countries, according to Boyd.[23] Meanwhile, back at the Nunn Center, the collection is fully digitized with 3,000 indexes and very few transcripts. Thanks to OHMS, scholars are now accessing Nunn Center interviews 10,000–12,000 times per month.[24]

OHMS is free and open source, but how does an individual oral history project get started? First, a project team member applies online for a free account by providing their name, email, institution, location, whether the account is personal or institutional, the proposed OHMS repository and how the project will be using OHMS. Once approved they download the OHMS viewer and start studying the ways to use the tool.

The two main parts of OHMS are the application—the back-end where the oral history project team load recordings and metadata—and the viewer interface, where a user listens to and/or watches the chosen interview.[25]

For example, a Nunn Center interview with François Erlyne lists:

> 2:35 –The experience of the earthquake
> 7:58 –Reactions in the aftermath of the earthquake
> 9:53 –Balance of mixed emotions
> 11:48 –Funeral ceremonies

Click on any of these segments and you see a partial transcript, segment synopsis, keywords, subjects, and GPS and map coordinates. The Erlyne interview, conducted in Haitian Creole, offers the added option of clicking to an English translation.[26] If a transcript is available for the interview, researchers can also switch back and forth between the full transcript and the index, depending on their needs. Many institutions are now indexing first, then transcribing when and if the funds become available.[27]

Boyd points out that indexes are more subjective than transcripts, since so much is left out. OHMS developers are now exploring models where multiple indexes could represent different perspectives, such as that of a student, archivist and interviewer.

The indexing, adding of metadata and prepping of the transcript, if one exists, sounds like a lot of work. At an OHMS workshop I attended in Minneapolis, an audience member asked Boyd skeptically. "Isn't it easier to just transcribe than do all this?"

"It costs one-tenth as much to pay students to do these indexes," Boyd replied. The previous year, $16,000 in student hours got 900 interviews online, he said, estimating that it would have taken $160,000 to get full transcripts.[28]

Another benefit of the index model, Boyd said, is that's it's easier to get an index than a transcript approved by the narrator. Instead of being confronted with messy "uhs" and false starts, the narrator only need approve a list of topics. "It removes that burden of perfection," Boyd said. "I love sending them an index. It's a different vibe. Ninety-nine percent of the time they're like, 'This is awesome. Thank you.'" With transcripts, he said, that only happens 10 percent of the time. Transcripts made to go with OHMS are the ugliest of all, since proper synching of audio and text require every "like," "you know," "um," and false start to be left in. Narrators are often appalled when they see themselves looking so inarticulate on paper.

While attending the workshop, it struck me that OHMS is perfect for a larger program with lots of student and volunteer help, or for a smaller one with very techy folk. But lacking inexpensive labor and/or a tech-savvy staff, preparing OHMS indexes would still be extremely time-consuming and costly—perhaps rivalling transcription.

At the University of Wisconsin, Troy Reeves' student workers haven't had any trouble learning the OHMS basics. He points them toward YouTube tutorials, has them read an introductory article, and they're off. "Hardly any of them ever sort of come back to me with, 'I don't get this,'" he said.

> So, at the student level, I think it's pretty intuitive. Now for those of us who weren't born in the digital age, aren't digital natives, I don't know for sure. I mean, I use it a little bit, but really the students use it ten times more than I do.[29]

Bottom Line

Not every collection has to take the traditional transcription route. Lack of funds, lack of time, or concerns about transcripts overshadowing audio are a few good reasons collections might choose another way for researchers to access their interviews.

Various types of indexing can substitute for transcripts, from relatively low-tech timed indexes made with word processing programs or spreadsheets to the complicated and versatile Oral History Metadata Synthesizer (OHMS), which synchs transcripts or indexes with audio.

As voice recognition and voice-to-text technology improve, the need for human transcribers may eventually disappear. But the need for human auditors will likely remain. While a human-prepared transcript can't fully capture the nuances of the audio, a computer will do a much poorer job. Human auditors will still need to verify the computer's work, standardize punctuation, insert paragraph breaks, and correct misinterpretations.

Useful Documents

- Index from University of Wisconsin, Madison – word processing document, see Appendix 5.
- Index from University of Wisconsin, Madison – spreadsheet, see Appendix 6.

Notes

1 *Oxford Dictionary* website, available at: https://en.oxforddictionaries.com/definition/ora lity (accessed December 17, 2017).

2 Oral History Association meeting presentation, "Public History Sites and Community Oral History Projects," Minneapolis, MN, October 5, 2017.

3 Francis Good, "Voice, Ear and Text. Words, Meaning and Transcription," in R. Perks and A. Thomson (eds), *The Oral History Reader*, 3rd edn (London: Routledge, 2016), p. 462.

4 Troy Reeves, email correspondence with Teresa Bergen, December 13, 2017.

5 Mary Contini Gordon, email correspondence with Teresa Bergen, April 26, 2018.

6 Steven Sielaff, interview with Teresa Bergen, June 29, 2018.

7 George Saon, "Reaching New Records in Speech Recognition," IBM website, March 7, 2017, available at: www.ibm.com/blogs/watson/2017/03/reaching-new-records-in-sp eech-recognition/ (accessed January 1, 2018).

8 Jesse Jarnow, "Transcribing Audio Sucks—So Make the Machines Do It," *Wired*, April 26, 2017, available at: www.wired.com/2017/04/trint-multi-voice-transcription/ (accessed December 24, 2017).

9 Trint website, available at: https://support.trint.com/hc/en-us/articles/115004257869-Rot ten-Transcription-We-re-only-as-good-as-what-you-give-us-just-saying- (accessed December 24, 2017).

10 Skye Doney, email correspondence with Teresa Bergen, December 27, 2017.

11 Michael Gref, Joachim Köhler and Almut Leh, "Improved Transcription and Indexing of Oral History Interviews for Digital Humanities Research," in *Proceedings of the Eleventh International Conference on Language Resources and Evaluation* (LREC 2018), available at: www.lrec-conf.org/proceedings/lrec2018/summaries/137.html (accessed February 11, 2019).

12 Sun Yi, email correspondence with Teresa Bergen, July 24, 2018.

13 Susan Nicholls, email correspondence with Teresa Bergen, December 9, 2018.

14 Barb Jardee, email correspondence with Teresa Bergen, April 4, 2018.

15 Jenna Bain, email correspondence with Teresa Bergen, July 26, 2018.

16 Mark Wong, email correspondence with Teresa Bergen, August 24, 2018.

17 Randforce website, available at: www.randforce.com/ (accessed December 24, 2017).

18 New York Folklore website, available at: www.nyfolklore.org/progs/conf-symp/a rchws-060906.html (accessed December 24, 2017).

19 Interclipper website, available at: www.interclipper.com/ (accessed December 24, 2017).

20 OHMS Workshop, Minneapolis, October 8, 2017.

21 OHMS website, available at: www.oralhistoryonline.org/ohms-history/ (accessed December 24, 2017).

22 University of Kentucky website, available at: http://uknow.uky.edu/research/uk-libra ries-receives-grant-web-search-technology (accessed December 24, 2017).

23 Doug Boyd, email correspondence with Teresa Bergen, November 26, 2018.

24 OHMS workshop, Oral History Association conference, Minneapolis, October 2017.

25 Information about the latest version and getting started with OHMS is available at: www.oralhistoryonline.org/ (accessed November 26, 2018).

26 Louie B. Nunn Center for Oral History website, available at: https://kentuckyoralhis tory.org/oh/render.php?cachefile=2011oh060_hmp008_ohm.xml&translate=1&time= 34&panel=1 (accessed December 24, 2017).

27 OHMS workshop, Minneapolis, October 2017.

28 Ibid.

29 Troy Reeves, interview with Teresa Bergen, December 13, 2017.

4

TECHNOLOGY AND EQUIPMENT

As in every field, technology makes transcription both better and more complicated. I entered the transcription field at the end of the cassette era. Cassettes were much more standardized than digital files. The choices were basically 30-, 60-, 90- or 120-minute tapes, or the inferior microcassettes. The digital universe presents a much wider choice of video and audio file types. And that's just one example of a major technological change in transcription. Almost all oral history interviews today are recorded on digital media and transcriptionists can expect to transcribe from a digital file.

While a few issues raised in this chapter involve the person overseeing the project, we'll mostly discuss the equipment and the technology that the person doing the transcription will need. To try to keep things straight, I'll sometimes directly address certain sentences to project managers or to transcriptionists, if they only apply to one reader group.

So, if you're a freelance transcriptionist, a one-person oral history project, somebody capturing family histories, a graduate student, a qualitative researcher without an assistant, or anybody else about to tackle transcription, read on.

We'll cover:

- Delivering and receiving files
- File formats
- Transcription tracking
- Transcription software
- Equipment
- Transcribing from cassette
- Digitization
- Managing audio files
- Naming conventions
- Text expansion

Delivering and Receiving Files

Once the project director reaches an agreement with the transcriptionist (see Chapter 2), they decide how to deliver the audio or video files in a way that they both can access them. Before the digital age, project leaders sent cassette tapes and, later, CDs through the mail. Even now, some people prefer to mail a flash drive rather than to propel their audio into cloud-based file-sharing options.

Mailing a flash drive is still a legitimate delivery method. This can be a good choice for projects where the people aren't so tech-savvy, don't want to use cloud-based file-sharing and/or feel like the files are taking way too long to upload. Some organizations don't allow employees to use commercial file sharing services due to security concerns, preferring to trust the postal service. If your transcription client wants to send you a flash drive, request a self-addressed stamped envelope with sufficient return postage. Project managers working within big organizations or universities usually have easy access to outgoing mail. They might not think about the freelancer spending an unpaid hour driving to the post office and waiting in line.

Some universities and federal agencies have internal ftp sites that they can grant contractors access to so they can download files. Transcriptionists, note that sometimes this access is only available for a limited time, such as a week. Be sure to download these files promptly, and to leave these audio or video files in your downloads folder after you load them into your transcription software. It's easy to accidentally delete an audio file, and embarrassing to ask a client to re-send it after the link expires. For the same reason, I keep clients' flash drives until transcription is complete.

Most file-sharing services offer free accounts with limited amounts of storage. Transcriptionists, if you find yourself using one or two of these services so much that you're maxing out your free account, consider upgrading to a paid plan. This will make it easier for clients to work with you, as you won't have to request that your client upload just a few files at a time, wait for you to download them, then upload more. If you're working with video files, which are very large, you'll quickly run out of free account space.

Project managers, please think of the bigger picture when labeling a shared folder. Include both the name of the institution and the name of the transcriptionist. For example, Transcription_Bergen_LSU. Remember that your contract transcriptionist probably has multiple clients. When clients all give shared files generic names like "Transcription," "Audio Files" or "Transcription for X," things quickly become confusing at the transcriptionist's end.

Transcriptionists, note the location of shared files in your transcription tracking system (see below). When you have different clients who use three or more different file-sharing systems, and one of them sends a note telling you they added audio or video files to your folder, it's easy to forget the whereabouts of said folder.

File Formats

In a digital environment, information is organized into file formats that tell the computer about the kind of information included, such as the kind of data—sound, visual, text—or the resources needed to process it—kind of operation system, display requirements, and so on. We humans recognize file formats by the suffix appended to the filename: .docx, .wav, and .mp4 are examples of file formats for text, sound, and video respectively. The codec is the way audio is stored and compressed and determines the file size. Some file types always use the same codec. Other files may support several types of codecs. Within one file type, there can also be different bit rates, which are the number of bits per second transmitted on a digital network. The higher the bit rate, the better the quality and the bigger the file size. All this gets very confusing very fast. If you're the transcriptionist, the main thing you'll need to know is what file formats your transcription software supports.

In addition to agreeing on a delivery system, the project leader and transcriptionist must also decide which file formats they can use. Table 4.1 presents some common file formats.

So what are the best file formats? WAV is a standard audio file format for storing uncompressed sound files, usually in Windows PCs. The high quality of WAV files means they are good for archival storage of oral history interviews and work reliably with transcription software. But they take up a lot of space and are slow to

TABLE 4.1 Common file formats

File format	What is it?	Notes
WAV	Uncompressed audio file, can require 10 MB of storage per minute of audio	Open format
MP3	Compressed audio file	Open format
OGG	Usually uses the audio codec Vorbis. Similar to mp3 in quality, but more obscure	Open format
DCT	A file type designed for dictation with header information that can be encrypted, which complies with medical privacy laws	Open format
AIFF	Apple's standard audio format, comparable to a WAV	Open format
WMA	Microsoft's Windows Media Audio, designed with digital rights management for copy protection	Proprietary
DVF	A compressed audio format often used by Sony recorders	Proprietary
DSS	Olympus audio format	Proprietary
MP4	Multimedia format that most commonly stores video and audio, but can also store subtitles and still images	Industry standard, works with most operating systems

upload on the project manager's end and download on the transcriptionist's computer. The compressed MP3 files are best for transcription, as they take up a tenth of the computer space and sound just fine.

WAVs and MP3s are two examples of open format files for storing digital data, which are maintained by a standards organization and available for use by anyone. The transcription software I use, Express Scribe, currently supports 10 different types of open file formats. You can tell one from another by their file extension, such as Bergen.mp3 or Bergen.wav. Other examples of open formats include OGG, DCT, and AIFF. Many brands also have their own proprietary formats, as shown in Table 4.1. So, if you use a Sony recorder, you might automatically record in an MSV or DVF file format. Yes, this rampant proliferation of file formats is enough to make me miss cassette tapes at times. While Express Scribe claims to be able to work with all of these formats, sometimes I've had to work hard to figure out why a file wouldn't open, or how to convert it from one file type to another so it would be compatible with my transcription software.

My clients are often confused by these file problems. Usually they say, "The file opened just fine on my computer." But the transcriptionist needs to be able to open the file *within the transcription software program,* not open it with just any program.

Transcription Software

People often confuse transcription software with voice recognition software. With transcription software, you still do all the typing yourself, but its features make your life easier. Transcription software is crucial for efficient transcription, as it lets you play and stop audio with either a foot pedal or with the function keys. If you had to mouse your way between screens to the player every time you needed to hit stop, it would take you ten times as long to get anywhere. Nowadays, as most interviews are digital, transcription software has pretty much replaced the old transcription machines. This software is not just for professionals. Even if you're a grad student or an individual working on a small family project of half a dozen interviews to transcribe, I recommend taking an hour or so to learn to use one of these programs. They will more than pay back your learning investment by saving you many hours while transcribing.

Several transcription software packages are on the market. I'm devoted to Express Scribe, made by the Australian company NCH, which I've been using for about 15 years (Figure 4.1). The basic version, which supports common audio formats like MP3 and WAV files, is available for free download from the NCH site. The professional version, which works with more formats, including many proprietary file types, costs $70 at the time of writing, but seems to usually be on sale at half price. Baylor University's Institute for Oral History uses Express Scribe, and has an enterprise account with about 20 log-ins.[1] If you're working on a small community or family project and dealing with common file types, the free software is probably all you'll need.

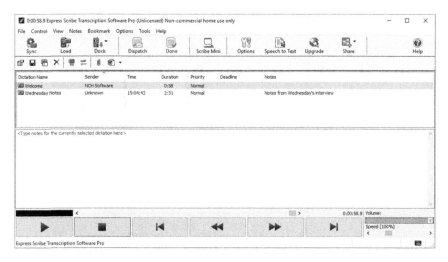

FIGURE 4.1 Express Scribe features

A few of my favorite Express Scribe features:

- Works with function keys instead of requiring a foot pedal.
- Automatic backstep means that it automatically backs up a little whenever the transcriptionist stops then starts again.
- Customizable playback options, such as for playing at a slower speed. I can choose that slower speed to be 50, 80, 90, or whatever percent.
- By enabling systemwide hot keys (Figure 4.2), users can type in a regular word processing program while using the function keys to stop, start, speed up, slow down, etc.
- Three special audio processes—background noise reduction, volume boost and high pass filter—improve common sound problems.

Start Stop is another brand of transcription software that's been around for a long time—since 1997. The Start-Stop UNIVERSAL transcription program plays just about any file type and comes with a foot pedal, headset, and lifetime technical support.

A newer transcription option is a web app called simply Transcribe. Instead of buying the license outright, users pay a yearly fee, currently $20, to use the software. With Transcribe, you type in its program, then export the text as a .doc file to your computer when you're through. Transcribe seems to be slightly more limited in file types than Express Scribe, and suggests using a file converter tool to convert all file formats to MP3s before transcribing. On the plus side, you can open YouTube videos in Transcribe, which could come in handy.

Barb Jardee uses GearPlayer. It's more expensive than Express Scribe, but has nice features like built-in line counting and pitch-corrected speed control, which allows you to slow down the audio without distorting the voice. Indira Chowdhury of the Centre for Public History in Bangalore said when they train oral

FIGURE 4.2 Express Scribe hot keys

historians, they recommend Express Scribe, but many prefer using the open source VLC media player in conjunction with Word.[2]

I'm tempted to make a comparison chart of the leading transcription software, but by the time you're reading this book one or all of them will probably have a new version. Instead, I suggest you review their websites and see which one best fits your project's needs. For example, check to make sure it supports the type of audio or video files you'll be transcribing. Compare prices. Try out the free version or free trial of the software that looks most promising. If it feels comfortable to use and does the job, stick with it. I've been using Express Scribe with the function keys for so long that my fingers automatically hit F4 to stop and F10 to start my audio, making for more seamless transcription.

Headphones

Aside from a computer and software, headphones are the most essential part of a transcription setup. I've tried many kinds, from the cheapest to sets that cost about $100. And you can go even higher than that. But if I'm home in my mostly quiet office and the audio is clear and sufficiently loud, it doesn't make that much difference. Good headphones matter more if you're working with difficult audio or if your environment is louder than optimal.

Besides audio quality, there are a couple of other things to consider when choosing headphones. The main types of headphones are:

- Over-ear – These are the biggest headphones, resembling earmuffs. Also called "around-ear" or "full-size," they feature cushioned ear cups to enclose the ears, isolating you from outside sound.

- On-ear – These similar but slightly smaller headphones have cushions that sit on your outer ears, rather than enclosing them. You'll hear more outside sounds while wearing on-ear than over-ear models.
- Earbuds – These lightweight sets are small and easy to transport in purse or pocket. You insert them just inside your ears, where they sit on the outer concha ridge. You'll still hear some sound around you.
- In-ear – These headphones insert into your ear canal. This sounds creepy but is good for transcription, as it seals you off from most outer noise.

I've experimented with all of these types. For a while I used high-end over-ear headphones. They worked well for audio, but even though they're not very heavy they made my neck ache after an hour. I switched to an in-ear set with a USB plug and have found them a success. One irksome thing—for some reason, the slithery cord on my headphones is 10 feet long which is forever sliding off the desk and winding up under the wheels of my office chair. This is not recommended for the longevity of any cord—I've destroyed two sets so far. So, if you don't need all that cord length, get a shorter pair. Then again, many prove to be too short. Necessary cord length will depend on your setup. Or go wireless, if you don't mind frequent charging.

Foot Pedals

Foot pedals are a classic piece of transcription gear and were essential with the old cassette transcribers. But now some software programs give the option of controlling playback with either the pedal or the function keys.

The world seems split between early adopters and those who like to hold onto their comfortable ways. I'm often in the latter category. So, when I first started receiving digital files, I was hesitant. I decided to postpone investing in a compatible foot pedal until I found out if this digital thing was going to catch on. By now I'll admit it decidedly has. But in the meantime, I got so used to controlling playback with the function keys that I never did get that new pedal.

Jeff Corrigan falls in the pro-foot pedal camp, proclaiming, "The foot pedal's the best thing in the world." When I pointed out that using the function keys frees you up so you can change your position more frequently, not always having to keep one foot on the floor, he said, "But you're at home and I was in an office. It wasn't like I could just kick back on the couch and transcribe."[3] Which is an excellent point. If you're a novice starting out, it's easier to use a foot pedal to stop and restart your recording. This way, you don't have to move your hands out of typing position every time you need to peck a function key to stop or start. But if you're more experienced and want to transcribe on your laptop in various locales, the function keys are more practical than a foot pedal.

The most common types of foot pedals have a USB connection. You plug the connection into your computer's USB port and give the computer a minute to recognize this new bit of hardware. Then you open your transcription software and select the foot pedal so they're connected. Pedals usually have three basic components:

- Play—This is the largest center portion of the pedal.
- Fast forward—a smaller rectangular area on the left.
- Rewind—rectangular bar on the right.

A rarer type of pedal these days, a serial pin transcription foot pedal plugs into a serial port on the back of your computer. This can be useful for older computers that quickly run out of available USB ports. Otherwise, they're not so convenient.[4]

Office Chair

A superior office chair is an oft-overlooked piece of equipment. Don't try to make do with a kitchen chair or a cast-off office chair. Go to an office furniture store and find one that's comfortable and adjustable, preferably in an appealing color. In the long run, spending money for a good chair can save you many appointments with doctors, chiropractors, masseuses or acupuncturists.

Transcribing from Cassette

Digital files have replaced cassettes—almost. Occasionally cassettes rise out of somebody's vaults to haunt me, usually in the form of long-forgotten collections newly discovered. What if you, the transcriptionist, find yourself faced with interviews on tape? Tell the project manager you only accept digital files.

The only exception I make to this is for one long-time client who is flummoxed by digital recorders. She's been loyal to me for nearly 20 years. For her, I descend into my basement and drag up my cassette transcription machine—a cumbersome, bulky thing from days of yore, like a pterodactyl compared to a svelte modern digital bird. Cassettes are fragile, so I insist she send me a copy, not her original. But unless you happen to have a cassette transcription machine and an extremely loyal client, just say no. Box 4.1 explains how to digitize cassettes.

BOX 4.1 DIGITIZING CASSETTES

So, your client has discovered a treasure of old cassette tapes. Or maybe this is a family project, and you've found recordings from your parent or grandparent. How can you bring this audio into the modern era?

Digitizing cassettes yourself is fairly easy if you have the right equipment. You'll need some type of cassette deck, an RCA cord and free software called Audacity (or something similar). Here are the basic steps to complete this operation. Keep in mind, equipment varies.

1. Connect the RCA end of the cord to the output jacks (might also be labeled as earphone) in the back of your cassette deck and the stereo mini-jack end to the line-in jack on the back of your computer. This jack is usually color-coded blue. Don't plug it into the mic jack on your computer.

2. Open Audacity on your computer. You'll have to figure out the settings for your computer, such as the right input.

3. Hit record on Audacity, then hit play on the tape recorder. You'll see the digital soundwaves onscreen when your interviewer and narrator start talking.

4. Adjust the volume on your tape recorder so that the soundwaves are medium-sized. Too big, you'll clip the audio. Too small, it will be barely audible.

5. Hit stop when the recording ends. Go to the File dropdown menu and export the file as an audio WAV or MP3 file. Name it and save it in your desired folder. From there, load it into your transcription software and get to work.

If you get stuck, YouTube has many useful how-to videos on converting tapes to digital files.

After my last cassette deck broke, I bought a little cassette-converting device for $30. Like the setup described above, it works with Audacity. But instead of dealing with audio cables, it plugs directly into the USB port on the computer. It worked fine for four or five cassettes, then the buttons jammed so badly I had to throw it away. It was a rickety and cheap piece of equipment from the start, but a more robust version of the same type of thing would be a good investment if one needed to transcribe a collection of tapes.

Either the project manager or transcriptionist can also outsource digitization to a specialist. Some large services allow you to mail in your cassette tapes, VHS tapes or reel-to-reels, then receive digitized versions on CDs, DVDs, thumb drives or via digital download. Larger cities may have somebody local who provides this service. I'm fortunate to have AVP Media, a home-based digitization business, a couple of miles from my house. I've partnered with John Croy to turn a nightmare box of 1970s cassette tape interviews into digitized tracks I could somewhat decipher. Advantages of hiring out digitization include that pros have much better equipment and more advanced skills. Croy has 30+ years doing sound, lighting, video and other techy things. If you are digitizing old, damaged and iffy cassettes, outsourcing digitization might make the difference between an audible and inaudible track, and thus a useful or useless end product for research.

Managing Audio Files

When I interview people, I'm careful to give the MP3 or WAV file a name that includes the narrator's name and the date of interview. For example, Belden_Trixie 1–31–18 would be a typical file name I'd use. But when you're receiving audio to transcribe, you never know what might show up. To save yourself endless frustration, be slow and methodical when first encountering these files.

Project managers, please label files in a sensible way that includes the narrator's name, the segment number (if the interview has multiple digital tracks) and the date. This is best practice. If you're a one-person operation, follow this same protocol. You will save yourself lots of headaches later.

Fellow freelance transcriptionists, we must deal with reality. People don't always follow best practices. When the project manager is labeling files, they're thinking from a project-centric perspective. For example, one of my client's research all focuses on one person. Most of the audio files are simply that person talking, so the project manager labels the files only by date, not including the narrator's name at all. Makes perfect sense to him. But when I receive these files and load them into Express Scribe, where they're rubbing shoulders with a dozen other projects, suddenly I have a bunch of mysterious date-only files. If your memory falls short of perfection, the best policy is to rename each file in your transcription software as it comes in. Be sure to number them if you have multiple interviews with the same person. For example, Belden_Trixie 1 1–31–18, Belden_Trixie 2 1–31–18, etc. If the file name is long, you might not see all of it in the window of your transcription software, which is why I recommend putting the segment numbers right after the name. Note: If you're confused about digital files, keep in mind that there's no need to "return" your copy, as clients might have expected in the old cassette days. So whatever you do that file—such as renaming it or enhancing the volume—is your business and won't affect the original.

Project managers might name files with the narrator's last name first, or first name first. They could start each file with the project name, or a date, or words like "interview" or "oral history," or, in the case of social science researches, a code. Worse, a pseudonym. You might find yourself filling up the "notes" column of your transcription tracking spreadsheet.

Transcriptionists, be especially on guard for the people who don't name their audio files at all. I've had a couple of clients whose audio came to me in many five-minute tracks, all with names like MZ00001, MZ00002, etc. Worse, each narrator's set of audio files would start the default naming convention over at MZ00001. So if I tried to download all these project files at once, I'd get multiple files with the same name but different people talking. In this case, I had to load one narrator at a time, renaming each five-minute track before starting over with the next narrator. This is time-consuming work and it's easy to lose count and misorder the 20 or 30 audio files from one narrator. This is obviously terrible practice on the part of project managers. If you're working with someone on an ongoing basis, ask them to please label audio with name, segment number and date before sending it to you. That said, as contractors we are always trying to please clients, so be sure to suggest this in a kind and helpful way.

I was perplexed why somebody would record in five-minute increments. But I heard one possible explanation from Steven Sielaff at Baylor. He said they record in 15-minute segments. That way, if the recorder malfunctions, they don't lose the entire interview.[5] Why 15? "Mainly because of the setting options of the Marantz 661 recorder. Other recorders might not have the same options," Sielaff told me.[6]

Makes sense. But as the transcriber, see if the project manager can merge all those small files together into one or two longer files before sending them your way. The more individual files you deal with, the more chance to mislabel, get out of order or accidentally delete. And the more unpaid time you're spending managing them.

Naming Conventions

Transcriptionists, now that you have all your equipment and software ready to go, it's time to create the document that will turn into a transcript. We'll get to the nitty gritty of that in Chapter 5. Here we'll look at the bare bones of how to set up your files.

Oral history programs quickly recognize the need for consistent file organization. Even if you're working on a small, one-time project, this is a good habit to adopt. You never know if your project will expand. At Baylor, Sielaff has created a normalized method for all different types of documents involved in each interview. They use the first five letters of the last name, then the first initial of the first name, the first initial of middle name, and the interview date in YYYYMMDD format. For example, if Baylor interviewed me on February 1, 2018, they'd label the transcribed interview Bergetl20180201_transcript. When somebody indexed the interview, that document would be entitled Bergetl20180201_index.[7]

At LSU, the Williams Center adheres to consistency so much that they still assign each interview a "tape number" to match the system that was in place during the years of interviewing on cassette. They name documents by name and tape number. For a single narrator, they follow the convention Lastname_Firstname_T####. For two narrators, the file is named Lastname_Firstname_and_Lastname_Firstname_T####. More than two? Lastname_Firstname_et_al_T####. There's a limit to how long a file name should be. Transcripts that cover multiple interviews on different dates are described by multiple tape numbers. For example, Bergen_Teresa_T112_1113_1114 would indicate an interview that unfolded over three sessions. When LSU indexes an interview, they name the document Lastname_Firstname_T####_index.

Again, the point here is consistency. If you are the project manager at an institution or a one-person operation, set up a naming convention. If you're the transcriptionist, ask if there's a naming convention. If not, pick one that makes sense to you and follow it.

Text Expansion

If you have ever programmed a macro on your computer—a saved sequence of keyboard strokes or commands that are stored, then recalled with a single keyboard stroke or command—you've used text expansion. The idea is to program shorthand into your computer to save time in typing. Nowadays you can download text expansion apps that will work system-wide, whether you're typing in MS Word or Pages, writing emails, or using any other program. Programs like PhraseExpress and

Breevy let you abbreviate frequently used or complicated words, automate repetitive tasks, customize boilerplate templates and will autocomplete text as you type. Most text expander apps offer 30-day free trials, then charge a fee if you decide to become a long-term user.

You can also program shortcuts into MS Word AutoCorrect. When my friend and fellow transcriptionist Mary Hunger showed me how to do this about 10 years ago, she revolutionized my keyboard. The AutoCorrect function is what automatically fixes spellings as you type. A long list of common typos is pre-programmed into Word. For example, if you type "thign," AutoCorrect will change it to "thing" unless you turn off the feature.

But AutoCorrect can do much more than fix spellings. You can program in your own shorthand system so that you only have to press a few keys and whole words or phrases will appear.

For detailed instructions for creating keyboard shortcuts in Microsoft Word, do an online search on "customize keyboard shortcuts." Trust me, it's easier than copying the unwieldy URL. You'll notice the instructions look long and painful. But once it's set up, it's brilliant. I assigned the combination CTRL+Q to bring up the window that lets me add a new entry to my AutoCorrect.

Here are some of the common words I have programmed in with shortcuts:

- st = something
- eb = everybody
- cg = college
- itt = institute
- orgz = organization
- fe = for example
- aed = at the end of the day
- idw = I don't know
- eg = everything

You can add proper nouns, phrases and project-specific lingo as needed, then delete them from AutoCorrect when you're finished with that project. One of my non-oral history clients specializes in improving companies' automated phone systems. When I transcribe their marketing research, it's easier to type in "aps" instead of "automated phone system," and "apss" instead of "automated phone systems" every time somebody says it. I've probably programmed more than 200 shortcuts into my AutoCorrect. Of course, if I have to type on somebody else's keyboard, I must remember my shorthand won't work. And I'll probably never pass a typing test again, since I automatically use my shorthand.

Bottom Line

As anyone who has ever used a computer knows, when things are going right, technology speeds up the job and eliminates countless tedious hours. For example, remember White Out? No need for that anymore. But when technology is bad, it's horrid. If you work at an oral history center at a large university, lucky you. There are probably IT guys and gals on staff. Make the most of them. If you're running a tiny project or are a freelance transcriptionist, you'll need to be your own tech problem solver. You must have patience with inanimate objects. Hurling thumb drives won't make those files playable.

Consistency, organization and communication with other team members will make your project run more smoothly, including the technological aspects. Agree on naming conventions and a file delivery system.

For young readers, technology is likely to be second nature. But all people of working age need to keep up with technology in their field if they want to stay employable, whether they consider themselves techy or not. This is especially true for individuals running their own oral history projects, and freelance transcriptionists. Even if no one would ever hire you for your computer aptitude, congratulations: You're now your own head of IT.

Notes

1 Steven Sielaff, interview with Teresa Bergen, June 29, 2018.
2 Indira Chowdhury, email correspondence with Teresa Bergen, August 25, 2018.
3 Jeff Corrigan, interview with Teresa Bergen, December 18, 2017.
4 Association for Healthcare Documentation – Western Region, "How to Choose a Transcription Foot Pedal," available at: www.ahdi-west.org/how-to-choose-a-transcrip tion-foot-pedal/ (accessed January 29, 2018).
5 Steven Sielaff, Oral History Association conference, Minneapolis, October 2017.
6 Steven Sielaff, email correspondence with Teresa Bergen, July 20, 2018.
7 Sielaff, OHA conference, 2017.

5

TRANSCRIPTION STEP BY STEP

Everything is a go. You've identified your top transcription priorities and decided who will do the transcribing. You've secured funds or volunteers and have agreed upon a timeline and budget for the job. The transcription software is on the computer, the headphones are plugged into your headphone jack or USB port. You're ready to turn that audio into text.

Now we will get down to the nitty gritty of transcribing. This chapter should be of great use to anyone learning to transcribe, and even experienced transcriptionists might learn something new—I know I did while researching this book. We'll explore questions so specific you may not have thought of them before. Here's just a sampling of what we'll ponder:

- Should I mention the narrator is coughing?
- What do ellipses convey versus choosing an em dash?
- Should the narrator's name be in bold or all caps?
- How do I keep track of project-specific lingo?

Let's start transcribing.

Your Transcript Template

Consistency is an attractive attribute for a collection of transcripts. If the project doesn't already have a style in place, the project manager should decide on one. However, in my experience the busy project manager often tells me to start transcribing and they will sort it out later. In these cases, I choose a simple style which the project often winds up retaining.

The first decision is what information to include at the top of the page. Some projects I've worked on even like a separate title page, so the completed interview resembles a book manuscript. Things to include at the top of your page could include:

- Project name
- Narrator's name
- Interviewer's name
- Other people present
- Interview number
- Date of interview
- Location of interview
- Name of transcriptionist
- Name of editor
- Date of transcription

The essential elements are the narrator's name, the interviewer's name, the names of other people present, the date of the interview and the name of the transcriptionist. Here's an example:

Narrator:
Interviewer:
Date:
Transcribed by:

The main body of the transcript shows the back and forth dialog between narrator and interviewer. Simple enough. But even that part requires decisions. Do you use last names? Initials? To bold or not to bold? Last names in all caps? How many spaces after the colon? While project managers have their preferences, the following is a simple, clean style. Type the first and last name when the person first speaks, then last names, no bold, regular case, two spaces after the colon, as follows:

Trixie Belden:
Nancy Drew:
Belden:
Drew:

Again, the important thing is consistency. A collection looks so much better when it matches, and is more comfortable for a researcher to sink into.

Once the style is decided, you can set up your document. Assuming this is the agreed upon format, before I start transcribing I prepare the document like so:

Narrator: Nancy Drew
Interviewer: Trixie Belden
Date: February 2, 2018

Transcribed by: Teresa Bergen
Trixie Belden:
Nancy Drew:
Belden:
Drew:
Belden:
Drew:

Keep pasting the names for pages, estimating how long the transcript will be.

48:32 [or however long the audio track runs]
[End Interview.]

Having the document prepped like this lets you fly through it—or at least trudge more efficiently, without having to stop and type names over and over.

Some oral historians don't use the names, or even initials, throughout the transcript. "If there are only two speakers on the recording, there is no need to identify the interviewer and interviewee by name throughout the transcript," wrote Beth M. Robertson, whose *Oral History Handbook* is widely used as the standard practices book in Australia. "Instead, differentiate between the speakers by typing the interviewer's words in bold print and the interviewee's in normal print. Indent the interviewee's words four or five spaces from the left margin. The result is an attractive, uncluttered presentation." Robertson recommends using initials if the audio includes more than two speakers.[1]

Keeping Track of Project Notes

If you're a freelance transcriptionist working on multiple projects, you'll be expected to keep discrete sets of guidelines straight. One uses initials, another spells out the narrators' and interviewers' names. One needs time stamps every 30 seconds, another requires double spacing, another wants everything verbatim and yet another uses pseudonyms for the narrators. Instead of receiving a tidy style book, project notes are likely to arrive in a series of emails. I like to put all of this info about special requests and requirements in a document I entitle "Notes" and stick in the folder where I'm storing that set of transcripts. Then when I'm switching between projects and starting a new transcript, I review the project notes to make sure I'm formatting the transcript according to that client's wishes.

Verbatim vs. Lightly Editing as You Go

Should you type every *um, you know, and so forth*, and *like*, no matter how painful? This is a decision for the project manager. Settling this matter before starting transcription will save a lot of time for both parties. Large programs, such as university oral history centers, will already have a style. The style guide for the T.

Harry Williams Center for Oral History advises transcribers to handle crutch words this way.

Stutters and Crutch Words
You do not need to include every single sound that an interviewee utters. For example, do not transcribe "ah" "er" "um" or other similar sounds:

SMITH: Well, ah, I graduated from high school in, uh, 1934. And I graduated from college in 1938, er, I mean 1939.

Can be transcribed as:

SMITH: Well, I graduated from high school in 1934. And I graduated from college in 1938, I mean, 1939.

If a speaker stutters, it is not necessary to transcribe every repetition of every sound:

PORKY: Th-th-th-th-th-th that's all folks!

Can be written as:

PORKY: That's all folks!

Sometimes a speaker will repeatedly use a word or phrase such as "you know," "you see," "like," or "okay" while he or she is speaking. These repetitions are known as crutch words.

- Include all crutch words in the first three pages of the transcript.
- Beyond page three, if the phrases are so constantly used that they negatively affect the flow of the dialogue, you may drop any crutch words that do not contribute to the understanding or meaning of a sentence.[2]

As oral historian Willa Baum said, "In speaking, crutch words may slip by almost unnoticed, but written down they will leap out from the page as a proclamation that the narrator could not get her thoughts together instantaneously."[3]

I worked for one project where all the narrators were college students. These bright, educated young people were extremely serious about the subject matter, but their incessant use of "like" – sometimes five or six in a single sentence— undermined their authority. After I turned in the first couple of transcripts, the program director asked me to please leave out the likes, which were driving her nuts during editing.

If you're on the project management side and just starting to get your interviews transcribed, consider how you plan to use your interviews. For example, programs that plan to index and make their interviews available through OHMS (see

Chapter 3) will need every "uh" and "you know" so that the transcript will synch with the audio when a researcher plays it back together. If you're depositing transcripts into an archive for later use, light editing will make them less painful to future researchers, and to the narrator.

Documentary filmmakers need every crutch word and false start, as that's what the film audience will see. When you leave those out, said filmmaker Victoria Greene:

> Then you don't really get a true depiction of the interview. Because not everybody talks without the ands, the buts, the uhs. And when you see it, all of that may make for a poor sound bite, or something you just have to edit.[4]

Market researcher Lindsey Annable explained that, in the UK, she encounters companies offering different levels of transcription. These range from full transcription to

> slightly shorter ones where "irrelevant" chat is removed or a notes and quotes style product whereby verbatims that might be of interest are highlighted. With these types of graduated products, we are more reliant on the skill of the transcriber to recognise what "matters."

Identifying what's important requires transcriptionists to have additional skills. "I always as a matter of course share the aims of any project with a transcriber to make sure they understand what we are trying to achieve. I believe this contributes to better quality outputs."[5]

As somebody who transcribes professionally, I appreciate being recognized as an intelligent collaborator on a project. I've often thought that project managers could get a lot more use out of transcriptionists. For example, by asking them to mark especially good quotes for an exhibit, or, as Annable mentions above, useful verbatim excerpts for a presentation to a client.

Style Guides

As mentioned above, a style guide covers the degree of editing, what to do with false starts, and many other aspects of spelling and punctuation. What if a project doesn't have a style guide? Devise your own or pick one to follow, and stick to it. Again, consistency.

Baylor University Institute for Oral History has compiled one of the most popular style guides in the field and updates it approximately every two years. It covers many decisions that come up while transcribing, including words which should and shouldn't be capitalized, what not to abbreviate, use of commas, crutch and compound words, how to handle incomplete sentences, writing numbers, dates, and times of day. It names the latest version of the *Merriam-Webster's Collegiate Dictionary* as the last word in spelling and follows the *Chicago Manual of Style*. The style guide is packed with useful information. For example, Baylor's list of common pitfalls and distinctions can save transcriptionists from many embarrassing mistakes. You can access Baylor's guide online.[6] It makes an excellent default style guide if your project doesn't have one.

A project manager might decide to follow a standard style guide popular in his or her country. For example, in the United Kingdom, the *New Oxford Style Manual* is widely used. It's the successor to *Hart's Rules for Compositors and Readers*, originally published more than a century ago. Other British style guides include several produced by media organizations—the BBC, the newspapers, such as the *Guardian, Times* and *Telegraph*— and the *Modern Humanities Research Association Style Guide*, used for writing theses. Australia has *Style Manual: For Authors, Editors and Printers,* published by Snooks & Co. Canadian academics depend on *The Canadian Style: A Guide to Writing and Editing*. In the US, *The Chicago Manual of Style*, first published in 1891, is one of the top style guides. The Associated Press puts out a style guide that's popular with journalists, while social scientists often use the American Psychological Association style guide and other academics and students may turn to the Modern Language Association style guide. The best style guide to adopt is one that is most specific to your country's language and your field's conventions.

Punctuation and Rendering of Speech

Willa Baum wrote, "Transcribing is a work of art, a little akin to translating from one language to another, but with less latitude allowable."[7] Punctuation is responsible for much of this translating work. While the transcriptionist can eliminate false starts and crutch words—if that's the project's policy—she can't "improve" word order, word choice or grammar. If the narrator describes everything from pasta to his partner as "great," the transcriptionist can't slip in a "wonderful" or "fabulous" just for variety's sake. If the narrator uses strange grammatical constructs like "might could" and "might should," the transcriptionist might can't alter these.

One note about false starts: While often ripe for elimination, sometimes you need to include them if key pieces of information aren't repeated in the new start.

People often speak in endless run-on sentences, which look like stream-of-consciousness and mentally undisciplined in print. Unless your project manager is a stickler about verbatim transcription, you can stick in periods and begin new sentences where appropriate. Future researchers will appreciate it, as will the narrator.

Remember that commas are especially prone to changing the meaning of a sentence. Double check that your commas make sense and are faithful to what the narrator is conveying. Note the difference between "Let's eat, Grandma!" and "Let's eat Grandma!"

Using quotation marks to punctuate dialogue within oral history is one of the trickier everyday tasks a transcriptionist faces. Narrators often recreate dialog in their interviews, such as:

I yelled at him, "Get your head down! The enemy's coming!"
He said, "What? Where?" God, he should have done what I said. Not asked questions.

But often, it's hard to tell where the dialog ends and where the narrator has drifted back into monologue. Many a time I've pondered lines of text, wondering where that point was and feeling sort of silly since I'm 99 percent sure the recreated dialog from a 30-year-old scene is unreliable anyway.

Baylor offers this excellent note about dialogue:

When a person repeatedly breaks up recreated dialogue, whether internal or external, with phrases such as I said, she said, I told him, I thought, etc., it is permissible to leave some of them out. Compare these two versions of the same passage:
I said, "No." I said, "I'm done." I said, "I'm just waiting to retire."
I said, "No, I'm done. I'm just waiting to retire."[8]

Interior monologue can also trip up transcriptionists, who wonder whether sentences starting with "I said to myself" or "I thought to myself" deserve quotation marks. No, they don't. Unless your project style guide tells you differently, treat interior monologue as ordinary text without quotation marks. Some projects may decide otherwise. For example, the Historic Columbia River Oral History Project advises its transcriptionists:

Never use quotes for interior monologue, which is by definition thought, not said. Instead, indicate the thought with *italics* if it's a short passage. Example: I thought, *What kind of a question was that?* [9]

Depicting a broken-off sentence is also tricky, with oral historians having differing views on dashes and ellipses. The clearest way to depict a broken-off sentence is with an em-dash, like so—Beth Robertson, author of the popular Australian *Oral History Handbook,* wrote, "Three dashes are used to indicate unfinished sentences that are a normal part of conversational speech." She gives the example, "I don't know, we didn't - - -. Well, you didn't know any better, and you didn't look for anything better, if you can understand what I mean, and - - -. (telephone rings, break in recording)."[10]

Not being accustomed to this three-dash construction, I would not know what it meant if I were reading such a transcript. But I do agree with Robertson's stance on ellipses:

Do not use dots "..." to indicate pauses or an unfinished sentence. In the academic world, three dots (known as an ellipsis) mean that something has been left out and a different use will only serve to confuse some readers.[11]

I edited for one project that used ellipses to convey broken off sentences, and it was difficult for me to adhere to the guidelines for this reason.

Listen Closely for the Everyday Words

One of the easiest mistakes to make—and one that I am constantly correcting in my own work—is mis-typing everyday, interchangeable words. Did the narrator say "that" or "which?" "Everybody" or "everyone?" "Somebody" or "someone?" My mind likes to fill these in for me, so I frequently have to back up and make sure I'm being true to the narrator's speech pattern. Some people might say, what does it really matter if the person said "everybody" or "everyone?" But for a transcriptionist, getting this sort of thing right is crucial. If I don't discipline myself to go back and make sure these little things are right, who knows what liberties I'll be taking next?

I also type "yeah," "yup," "mm hmm," "uh huh," "yes," or however the narrator responds in the affirmative, unless I'm transcribing for a project whose guidelines have me convert these all to "yes." The exception is when somebody says the opposite of "mm hmm," which I've never figured out how to render. Then I type "no."

Paragraphing

Paragraphing makes transcripts much easier to read, since huge text blocks are daunting. Most projects like the transcriptionist to break the transcript into paragraphs. However, at some larger programs, paragraphing falls to the editor. If in doubt, communicate. If you're the transcriptionist, ask the project manager. If you're the project manager, convey relevant details to the transcriptionist. If you have multiple questions or points to make, include a few in the same email, as most everybody complains of too-full inboxes.

Overly Vocal Interviewers

One of the biggest nuisances is the interviewer who gives constant verbal approval. Not only is it annoying to try to figure out how many times I should include a "yes," "got it," or "mm hmm," but worse, these interviewers undermine their own research. Interviewers have a knack for sitting closer to the mic than their narrator—probably so they can keep an eye on the recorder—and too often the "yes" or "mm hmm" renders some of the narrator's words inaudible. This is one of my pet peeves, since all the missing words make my transcript look like Swiss cheese. Unless instructed otherwise, I leave out many of the interviewers' superfluous interjections. I'll allow one in every once in a while to demonstrate the flavor of the communication, similar to the strategy of including enough "you knows" and "likes" to indicate a narrator's speech pattern without making them look inarticulate.

Few interviewers appreciate a direct critique from the transcriptionist. But if it's an ongoing problem, I sometimes indicate this verbal tic in the transcript, hoping the interviewer will notice and improve. Like so:

INTERVIEWER: Yeah, I see.
NARRATOR: [unclear, both speaking at once]

What I really mean is:

NARRATOR: [unclear, drowned out by interviewer AGAIN]

Marking Things Other than Speech

Many non-speech sounds happen during an interview. Some deserve to be noted, others don't. Relevant non-verbal sounds can be indicated by parentheses or brackets. I routinely include:

- (laughs) – for the person talking
- (laughter) – if more than one person laughs
- (applause)
- (snaps fingers)
- (crying)
- (imitating sound of rooster) – or car starting, whistle blowing, whatever sound the narrator is using to illustrate a story

A few narrators laugh like a verbal tic, after almost anything they say, funny or not. In this case, I leave much of their laughter out, as it's confusing on paper.

Other sounds are worth including if they affect the interview. If somebody's incessant coughing prompts offers of water and pauses in the tape, I'll note they're coughing, or if the interviewer's coughing obscures the narrator's words. Same for when a barking dog renders the humans' words inaudible, or if the woofs elicit words directly to the dog. If a narrator suddenly says, "Shut up!" or "Get off the couch!" in the middle of an interview, I'll explain he was addressing the dog, not the interviewer.

I usually use parentheses to indicate a sound, such as laughing or coughing, and brackets for more of a stage direction or explanation, such as [reading from newspaper] [talking to dog] or [interruption for telephone call]. Many stage directions are only possible if the interviewer transcribes the interview, or if it was captured on video. Otherwise, the transcriber won't know the narrator was [pointing at window] or [dropping head into hands].

Long ago, in an attempt to be faithful to capturing sound, I'd transcribe phone calls received during the interview or people entering the room and saying random things. But I've since realized this is obnoxious and an invasion of privacy. Noting [interruption, phone conversation] in brackets is a better policy.

If someone else enters the room during an interview, it may or may not be appropriate to transcribe. Listen first and see. Maybe they come in and say something like, "Oh, hi, what you doing? Oh, an interview? How interesting. Okay. Later." Then you can sum it up by saying [interruption by person entering the room].

But maybe they come in and the narrator says, "Oh, this is my friend who marched with me in the civil rights march you're asking about," and invites the friend to stay and comment. In that case, if you're lucky the interviewer will get the friend's name and you can add him or her into the transcript.

I avoid getting too descriptive. If a researcher is interested enough that she wants to know if the narrator giggled, chortled, squealed or guffawed, she should listen to the audio. As Baum wisely put it, "Some indications of emotion are best limited to the tape where they can be evaluated in their full sound context."[12]

Projects recording on video might want the transcriptionist to include visual data. "The aims of the project should dictate whether visual information is necessary for data interpretation, for example, room layout, body orientation, facial expression, gesture and the use of equipment in consultation," wrote Julia Bailey, a London-based physician and qualitative healthcare researcher. "However, visual data are more difficult to process since they take a huge length of time to transcribe, and there are fewer conventions for how to represent visual elements on a transcript."[13]

Time Coding

Many researchers find time codes in transcripts useful. The most basic reason to note the time is so researchers who want to listen to a certain passage in the interview can find it easily. Again, different projects have different standards. The Williams Center at LSU includes a time code on each page of the finished transcript. Some clients might want a time code every five minutes, or when there's a change of topic. When I work with documentary filmmakers, who are extremely interactive with their transcripts, they might want every 30 seconds marked. Social scientists sometimes request a time stamp at the beginning of each new question.

It's also worth noting timecodes at points in the transcript where you can't make out what somebody is saying because the voice is inaudible, there's a word you can't even guess at, or the narrator is drowned out by the interviewer, a dog barking, a truck passing or other audio distraction. A timecode here lets an auditor—or, better yet, the interviewer, who might remember what was said—skip right to the trouble spot and perhaps fill in a few more words.

My preference is approximately one time code per page, inserted between speakers. Or, if the speaker is going on for multiple pages, between paragraphs. So it looks like this:

BELDEN: How did you know something fishy was going on at Lilac Inn?
30:22

DREW: Well, when somebody stole my aunt's jewels while she was lunching there, I suspected the staff were involved.

Or you can insert the timestamp into the line of dialogue. In this case, bolding the text will keep it from getting lost.

DREW: **[30:35]** And I was right. The maid was part of that jewel heist gang.

To mark an inaudible or unclear passage, or when you're guessing with a phonetic spelling:

DREW: Her brother and his gang almost drowned me on a [unclear] **[30:48]** but in the end I caught them.

When You Can't Understand

Speaking of inaudible and unclear, sometimes you can't understand the audio, no matter how hard you try. When I first started transcribing a million years ago, my mentor told me to listen three times and then move on. This is good advice, though I don't always adhere to it. Sometimes I listen ten or more times trying to get some stubborn word or words to reveal themselves. Once I must have listened to an elderly retired petroleum plant worker from Louisiana say "catalytic cracking" about 50 times before I finally got it. Then I did a victory dance. I decoded this mystery with an online search (see section below), because while catalytic cracking is a common term in the world of oil refineries, it isn't in my world.

There are many reasons you might not be able to understand a word or a passage, including:

- The narrator is too far from the microphone.
- The narrator's voice drops at the end of sentences, is feeble, raspy, or otherwise does not project well.
- The narrator has a strong accent.
- The interviewer keeps saying "yeah, mm hmm."
- Another person interrupts.
- A dog barks.
- A cat meows.
- A cuckoo clock chimes.
- The interview includes many foreign words unfamiliar to the transcriber.
- The interview involves jargon or geographical place names the transcriber doesn't know.
- Coughing, laughing or other human sounds obscure the narration.

When the problem is volume, I mark the word or passage [inaudible]. When there's another reason I can't get it, I put [unclear]. If I want to hazard a phonetic guess, I use brackets and a question mark to indicate I'm guessing. [Phu Song Gia?] Valley.

"It's easy, especially when you're new to this, to get too carried away with trying to find that one word," said transcriptionist Sue Shackles. "Quite often you'll find that the word will become clear to you later in the transcript when either someone else says the word more clearly or you are able to figure it out because of the context."[14]

Different projects have their own protocol. A project manager might want the text in question highlighted in yellow or typed in bold font. As usual, consistency is key. The auditor and editor should be able to easily find the questionable passages and perhaps be able to fill in a few mystery words.

Video is extremely handy when trying to decipher difficult-to-hear words. If you're working with video files, a bit of lip reading can boost your comprehension and possibly fill in some blanks.

Making Your Own Proper Noun List for a Project

As explained in Chapter 2, the proper noun list is an essential component that can be used as a spelling guide, and an index and a discovery tool. The project manager should supply the transcriptionist with a list of specialized vocabulary used in the project, ranging from family and geographical names to occupational lingo. Proper nouns are important search terms and, for researchers, one of the most valuable parts of a text version of the interview. It is essential that proper nouns be recorded, and the spelling and accuracy verified.

Ideally the interviewer compiles the proper noun list, with input from narrators. The project manager is another likely candidate for this task. But sometimes the project manager fails to provide a list. Then the transcriber can compile her own list from the recordings.

Transcriptionists, if you're working on a series of interviews, request a proper noun list. If the project manager is not forthcoming, start your own when you fact check your first completed transcript. Then you can refer to this list when you're transcribing the next recording so you don't waste time with duplicate internet searches for the same term. If you're given a proper noun list, use it as a starting point. You'll probably need to add more words as you go along. Even the most diligent interviewer or project manager can't remember all the names and places that pop up in a series of interviews.

So what goes in your proper noun list? That depends on the project. My proper noun list for a project on the Nez Perce Indians included names of prominent leaders, white settlers in the area, Nez Perce terms that were frequently used, and place names. For a project on the history of medicine in Oregon, my list included names of physicians, medical procedures, drugs and places. I created these lists organically. Every time I'd fact check an individual transcript and discover the correct spelling of a name usually through online research. I'd add it to my list.

One more note on the proper noun list: Even when the interviewer gets the spellings directly from the narrator, further verification is recommended. Narrators often think they know the spellings, or don't want to admit their uncertainty, so they spell names and places with great confidence. I've found many errors in proper noun lists. If you're the project manager, you might have to take narrators' word for family names, but double-check place names, book titles, historical figures, etc. The transcriptionist can follow up with these names with a small amount of research but the final verification is the responsibility of the project.

Post-Transcription Steps

Congratulations, you've finished the first draft of the transcript. Don't turn your computer off yet. There are still a few more steps to make it the most polished first draft possible.

Spellchecking

Once I finish typing an interview, it's time to review it. My next step is spell and grammar check. While I ignore most of the grammar check—I'm not fixing the narrator's grammar—it does catch some typos, such as using the wrong homonym or typing "the" instead of "them," and it identifies sentences in which I neglected to capitalize the first letter.

I use MS Word, which underlines spelling errors in red and grammatical errors in blue. This makes it easy to fix things while I transcribe. But I always miss a few, so spellchecking afterwards is essential. The red-underlined words are often proper nouns, so spellchecking morphs into fact checking.

After the automated spell checking, I go back and check anything I've marked with [?]. I search for "?]" in the transcript and address issues one by one. Often my guesses pass spellcheck because they're real spellings, but they might not be the correct spelling in this case. For example, was the narrator talking about David Gray or David Grey?

When I started transcribing in the 1990s, spellchecking proper nouns felt like going the extra mile. The internet was not what it is today—dial-up took forever to load. I had to use hard copy resources to track down correct spellings. I remember ordering Baton Rouge phone books to be sent to my home in Portland so I could correctly spell family names, street names and businesses. I even called a reference librarian in Baton Rouge once or twice. I bought paper maps for other projects, so I could get the names of towns, rivers and mountains right. I checked out library books that included subject matter terms used in interviews.

Fact Checking and Name Verification

Nowadays, failure to fact check marks a transcriptionist as lazy. Internet searches can quickly solve many spelling dilemmas. Maps, obituaries, business listings, phone directories and lists of company personnel all contain the answers. I've found correct book titles on Amazon, and Wikipedia is a fairly complete and accurate source for verifying spellings, dates and correct version of proper names. Notably, it helped me verify many names of twentieth-century European philosophers, writers and artists for one project. If you find multiple spellings online, defer to the most official sites. For example, the National Park Service site is likelier to spell the name of a national park correctly than a travel review site or a blog.

The timing of the fact checking step is up to the transcriptionist. I like to wait until the end and look up all my spellings at once, rather than constantly stopping and starting my transcription. The exception is when a narrator keeps talking about a place or person and I get the feeling they might continue to do so. Then I start to think of how many times I'll have to go back and fix that spelling. So I might choose to take a break and track down the right way to spell Ab Kettleby, Kootenai or whatever the proper noun in question.

Project managers may cut the transcriptionist some slack if she's in another part of the country. "Missouri is very good at having city names and places that are spelled like other places but are pronounced totally different," Jeff Corrigan told me, citing the town of Milan being pronounced My-lin, and Aux Vasse sometimes called Oxvessy. "But if you can find the answer in less than a 10-second search on Google, I think you just look it up," Corrigan said. "But to some people, that's not how they transcribe. They look up nothing. Then you have a lot more work to do on your end [the project manager's] to clean up the transcript."[15]

The editor is usually responsible for supplying missing information in brackets, but occasionally a project manager might request this of the transcriptionist. This could include names of states or provinces when it isn't obvious, such as Lac du Bonnet [Manitoba], or a full name when the narrator uses only the first, last or a nickname, as in Priyanka [Chopra]. Spelling out an acronym the first time it's used also warrants brackets, such as ANC [African National Congress]. I also tend to fact check book titles, especially when narrators stumble over them as if they can't quite remember. If the narrator mangles a title while mentioning a book, I try to supply the correct title in parentheses. Amazon and WorldCat are very useful for proper titles and spellings of authors' names.

Lois Glewwe, an author and transcriptionist in Saint Paul, uses her knowledge of Minnesota history and geography to go above and beyond. "Some projects I spend more time than I should because I really get into the research of the names, the dates, the places, or trying to find local addresses," she said. "I try to think like the reader or the listener. I tend to spend a lot of time filling in some of those annotated explanations." For example, when I talked to her she was embarking on a project about Vietnam War protests in Saint Paul and Minneapolis.

> If the person being interviewed said, "We picketed at the federal building," well, then, I would take the time to find out which federal building. Because we have one in Saint Paul, we have one in Minneapolis. And figure out where it was in 1970, because it's no longer at the same location. And I think that's just helpful to people to be able to visualize, oh, that's where the demonstration was.

She'd include the address in brackets for benefit of future researchers.[16] This example also shows where working with a local transcriptionist can be very useful.

As someone with a more macro view, Sarah Milligan, head of the Oklahoma Oral History Research Program, has a huge number of interviews to process. Unlike me—who sometimes obsesses over a term I can almost make out while listening to an interview, or the proper spelling of a river I'm sure I can find on online maps if I look a little harder—she is realistic about the return on time investment. She counsels transcriptionists not to replay the audio over and over and over. "If you can't figure it out in two tries, move on, because we're sending it back to them [the narrator] anyway."[17] Nor does she want staff to spend endless time on fact checking:

> It's an interesting dilemma because the longer that you spend on it, the more backlog you get. And if you have a pressure on that backlog already, it's just that question of what's the return on the investment that you're putting in for that. How much do people really care if we get three words wrong?[18]

Backing Up, Storing and Managing Files

A good backup system is essential, lest you lose your precious transcripts. After having multiple crashing and dying computers, I err on the paranoid side and use multiple backups. These include physical solutions, such as saving some files on both my laptop and desktop computers or on external devices such as flash drives, and cloud-based storage. Each has its pros and cons.

Cloud-Based Storage

If I'm working on my desktop computer, I have it set to automatically back up on two different cloud-based storage systems. When I'm using my laptop, if it's connected to Wi-Fi I also use cloud-based storage. Costs add up if you pay for multiple backup systems. But if I were to lose a single two-hour transcript from my computer, having a backup would more than make up for the cost of storage.

Flash Drives

When I'm working on my laptop and lack connectivity, I save important documents to a flash drive (also called a thumb drive). Remember to store your laptop and flash drive separately. If somebody stole your bag and both your laptop and flash drive were inside, that backup would be useless.

Transcriptionist Barb Jardee dedicates a separate thumb drive to each client that produces a lot of work. "I have another USB storage device that stores several clients that individually do not produce enough work to warrant a dedicated backup device," she said.[19] She keeps all documents on backup for at least a year, or longer if she has the capacity.

LOCKSS

Many curators and researchers live by the acronym LOCKSS: lots of copies keep stuff safe.[20]

For contract transcriptionists, backing up is more than simple diligence; we only get paid for deliverables. That is, transcripts. This is very different from an employee with a traditional nine-to-five job. If something goes wrong with an employee's computer, he or she will be frustrated and stressed to have to recreate a day's or week's worth of work. But that employee still gets paid. If I lose a transcript, I have to start all over again and I won't get paid for lost time. I routinely work on transcripts that run four or five audio hours. This means many paid hours lost if that transcript disappears. That's why it's especially important for contractors to have good backup systems.

This scenario is similarly heart-rending for unpaid people working on family or community histories. If you're doing something because of your passion rather than pay, you'll be nearly as sad as the contract transcriptionist when your computer crashes and you have to start all over.

Managing Files

I never intentionally delete transcripts or audio files until I get paid. This way, if the project manager loses a transcript and disputes that I ever sent it, I simply send it again. After getting paid, I usually keep the documents and delete the audio. The exception is when I work for social scientists with confidentiality agreements that require me to delete transcripts and audio from my computer.

Some contracts will instruct you to delete transcripts as soon as you send them to the researcher. Don't do it! Again, wait until you're paid. Keep your sent email, too, until you've been paid. If a transcript disappears, it's your word against the researcher's that you delivered it. Being able to refer to, "Per my email of November 13, 2018…" is very handy in establishing the veracity of your claim.

Oral historians are generally fine with me keeping copies of the transcript. While I don't volunteer myself as an archive, there have been at least five times when I've been able to save the day for somebody who lost a transcript—even a few years later. This is a good feeling, so I like to keep transcripts on my computer, space permitting, as long as there's no confidentiality issue.

Barb Jardee has had the same experience:

> I've had several clients contact me with their hair on fire, hoping I've got their documents on backup. They don't know how they did it, but they managed to delete their originals and all their backups. They're always relieved when I'm able to say, "I've got 'em!" I don't charge for this service. The good will it generates is worth far more.[21]

Of course, if you're the person responsible for preserving the transcripts, you have an additional set of responsibilities, including making sure that the interviews are stored on accessible media. Who is able to access laser discs, mini cassettes and floppy discs now?

Keeping Track of Transcription

Devising some way of tracking transcription will save lots of trouble later. Otherwise, it's easy to forget how long audio tracks have been waiting, whether or not you invoiced, whether you got paid, or how many interviews are awaiting transcription from each project.

As a freelance transcriptionist, I typically have several projects in at once and am rotating through them, trying to keep my clients happy. If I stopped and did one whole project from start to finish, I'd be neglecting the other projects. And if I only accepted one project at a time, everybody else would go find a different transcriptionist.

My most important tool for keeping track of multiple clients is my massive spreadsheet, which I call Transcription Log. I've been using this same Excel workbook for ten years and am now on line 2810. Here's what my nine-column format looks like (Figure 5.1):

My spreadsheet is simple, tracking my small part of the operation. Oral history projects and centers will have more complicated spreadsheets tracking many more details of the workflow.

Institution	Narrator	Time in minutes	Date received	Date Transcript sent	Invoice Date	Invoice Amount	Date Payment received	Notes
Monsters University	Terri Perry	123	7/1/2019	7/9/2019	7/27/2019			time stamp every 5 minutes
Tech U	Coleman "Booger" Sykes	47	7/4/2019	7/10/2019	7/10/2019			Tech U files on Google Drive
Faber University	John Blutarsky	256	7/8/2019	7/15/2019	7/15/2019			high priority
Mars University	Professor Farnsworth	87	7/12/2019	7/16/2019	7/29/2019			Mars University files in Dropbox
Wossamotta U	Bullwinkle	61	7/13/2019	7/18/2019	7/18/2019			Bullwinkle's cousin also present
Monsters University	Randy Boggs	241	7/20/2019	7/27/2019	7/27/2019			
Mars University	Gunther	66	7/20/2019	7/29/2019	7/29/2019			

FIGURE 5.1 Using a spreadsheet to track transcription

Transcriptionist Barb Jardee makes a weekly to-do list that she calls her action plan:

> I revise the list as I go through the week, keeping the old document, and saving the new version under the current date. I list each client or project by name, the date the recording was received, the due date, the length of each recording, my estimates for billable pages and time needed, and any other pertinent notes.

Jardee sets up a directory on the computer for each client where she stores their preference list, their recordings, and their transcripts, and an analysis document where she jots down notes about them. She also keeps a list of invoices, with unpaid invoices in bold. Once she receives payment, she deletes the bold and notes the date the payment was received. She stays on top of when to send thank you notes asking for more work, and when a payment reminder is in order. Jardee also relies on sticky notes, which cover the edges of her computer screen and the front of her CPU.

When Jardee has multiple projects in, she uses a ranking system to determine which project to work on next:

> I ask myself the following questions and assign a numerical order to the response to each question, then add up the scores, and that tells me which project deserves my attention next. When conditions change (i.e., a client calls with a rush job; a new project arrives, I get sick and can't work for a day or so) then I have to go through the ranking process again, considering the new factors.

Here are Jardee's considerations:

- arrival date, earliest to most recent;
- deadline (theirs or perceived by me, mostly one month from arrival);
- my time commitment needed for one chunk (smallest to greatest);
- my time commitment needed (smallest to greatest), whole project;
- last worked on (longest ago in time to most recent);
- total points accrued for each project.

> Then I consider the gut factor: How fast does the client pay? Do they treat me like more than a dirt clod? Do they owe me money? Have I completed some work for the client and I'm waiting to bill until the project is finished? I don't assign numerical rankings to these gut factor responses—it's more of a feeling.[22]

Transcriptionists can devise whatever system suits them. The important thing is to have one and faithfully follow it, so that you can instantly see where you are in any project.

Jardee raises an important point about payment. It astonishes me when a client presses me for speedier transcription when I've been waiting for their invoice to be paid for two months. Often these are researchers at big universities who either have a mega-bureaucracy to deal with, or who left my invoice in their inbox months ago and forgot to send it up the chain for payment. Contract transcriptionists, part of being a freelancer is asserting yourself when clients fail to pay. Project managers, please turn in those invoices and make sure your transcriptionist is on the road to payday.

Bottom Line

Transcription is a process of constantly making small decisions. If the project already has guidelines, this decreases the number of decisions the transcriptionist makes herself. Good communication between the project director and transcriptionist makes the whole process smoother, more efficient and enjoyable. But sometimes the transcriptionist is more experienced in oral history than the project manager. A professional transcriptionist should be able to supply a format and adhere to a reasonable set of style guidelines if the project does not yet have one. In that case, the project manager and transcriptionist can work together to develop the format.

Consistency is key. A collection of transcripts is most attractive and reliable when it agrees in style and formatting. Consistent file naming makes transcripts easier to find and organize. Diligent spellchecking and light fact checking render transcripts much more useful to future researchers. Even if you're a family or community historian, you never know where your transcripts will wind up and what future scholars will be thanking you for preserving history. So produce the best transcripts possible.

Notes

1 Beth M. Robertson, *Oral History Handbook* (Adelaide: Oral History Association of Australia (South Australian Branch), 2006), p. 79.
2 T. Harry Williams Center for Oral History Transcription Guide.
3 Willa K. Baum, *Transcribing and Editing Oral History* (Nashville, TN: American Association for State and Local History, 1977), p. 29.
4 Victoria Greene, interview with Teresa Bergen, November 18, 2017.
5 Lindsey Annable, email correspondence with Teresa Bergen, December 8, 2017.
6 The full Baylor style guide is available at: www.baylor.edu/oralhistory/doc.php/14142. pdf
7 Baum, *Transcribing and Editing Oral History*, p. 26.
8 BUIOH Style Guide, p. 17.
9 Historic Columbia River Oral History Project, "Guide to Transcribing and Summarizing Oral Histories," 2010, p. 8.
10 Robertson, *Oral History Handbook*, p. 80.
11 Ibid., p. 80.
12 Baum, *Transcribing and Editing Oral History*, p. 34.

13 Julia Bailey, "First Steps in Qualitative Data Analysis: Transcribing," *Family Practice*, 25(2) (1 April 2008): 127–31.
14 Sue Shackles, blog, "Tips and Advice," available at: http://waywithwordsblog.com/2011/11/24/a-career-in-transcribing/ (accessed February 10, 2018).
15 Jeff Corrigan, interview with Teresa Bergen, December 18, 2017.
16 Lois Glewwe, interview with Teresa Bergen, January 15, 2018.
17 Sarah Milligan, interview with Teresa Bergen, May 11, 2018.
18 Ibid.
19 Barb Jardee, email correspondence with Teresa Bergen, May 4, 2018.
20 Steven Sielaff, Oral History Association conference, October 2017, Minneapolis.
21 Barb Jardee, email correspondence with Teresa Bergen, May 4, 2018.
22 Ibid.

6

HARD DECISIONS

Many interviews are conducted under less than perfect conditions, but the content is important enough that they be "rescued" and the interview made available however possible. Most of the time that means a rendering of a bad recording into a fair-to-middling transcript. In some cases, the transcript is the only version of value. Who ends up rescuing them? You guessed it; most of the time it's the transcriptionist. Here are some problems I've come upon and how to deal with them.

This chapter delves into common transcription problem areas, including:

- unidentified speakers
- group interviews
- inadequate or missing sound files
- sound files that don't play
- improperly edited sound files
- mislabeled files
- foreign language passages
- interviews conducted in a narrator's non-native language
- the question of dialect
- difficult terminology
- extremely difficult speech
- nuances of false starts
- narration of photo albums
- profanity
- discovering conversation that is dangerous, illegal, or inappropriate

Unidentified Speakers

The transcriptionist must deal with unidentified speakers when media gets separated from labels, such as when boxes of mystery tapes are discovered years after the interviews. Or, the first of several sound files—the one that introduces the speakers—may be missing. Or maybe someone besides the narrator and interviewer is present through all or part of the interviewer but is never identified. In some interviews, a friend or relative may not plan to talk, but once the stories get going, he or she can't resist adding details, prompting or correcting the narrator. To make these third wheels even worse, usually they're sitting far from the microphone, since they hadn't planned to contribute. Once they start talking, they still hang back because they know it isn't really their interview and they should probably stop. Unidentified speakers far from microphones are the nemeses of transcriptionists.

So, what do you do? First, ask the project manager to get in touch with the interviewer and see who else was present. If the interview happened recently, this can easily solve the problem. But if it's an older collection, the interviewer might have moved away, died, or might also be unidentified on the audio.

When no identification help is forthcoming, I default to calling the main speakers "interviewer" and "narrator." Additional unidentified participants get the catchy names "unidentified male" and "unidentified female." Sometimes I detect a relationship through the interview content, allowing an individual to be upgraded to "narrator's husband" or "interviewer 2."

Group Interviews

While group interviews are the bane of my professional existence, they sometimes serve an important purpose. Like many projects, the Reed College Oral History Project began by interviewing the oldest surviving alums first. "But a lot of the alumni, we found out, they were at the point in their lives where they didn't have great recall about the details," said John Sheehy, who worked on the project.

Therefore, they tried a new strategy: group interviews at the reunion weekends every June. "I'd have, like, 30, 40 people in a room, and we'd spend 2½ hours," he said. If you've ever transcribed, your blood pressure is probably spiking as you read this, and hyperventilation may have set in.

> We would get a sense of who had great recall and also not just detail recall, but who was a good storyteller, who could frame it together and have themes and a narrative running through it. So that was how we transitioned out of just going after the oldest alumni. We had fifteen, sixteen thousand alumni we had to identify storytellers among. And that was one of the ways that we sourced them.[1]

Top storytellers were invited to do one-on-one interviews.

These Reed reunion interviews were popular with participants, who found it a moving, cathartic experience to share coming-of-age stories with their peers. So cathartic, in fact, that they often forgot to follow the ground rules, such as talking one at a time and stating their name each time they spoke. Again, no picnic for the transcriptionist and really no way for the transcriptionist to solve it. Their best bet was having the facilitator go back over the recording and try to sort it out.

Recording interviews on video can help solve this question of who in the group is talking—but only if the equipment is set up very well. In a big group, ideally, somebody would actively work the camera, training it on the narrator. It can be difficult for a static camera to capture all the participants, depending on the configuration of a room. I recently worked with some dreadful video where people were sitting around a table and the camera was mostly focused on the interviewer. I never saw some of the participants at all. Nor did they go around and identify themselves at any point, so I couldn't begin to attribute verbiage to a particular name. So if you're responsible for recording the group session, don't expect video to automatically solve the problem of IDing participants. Instead, put some thought into setting up your gear and be sure to clearly introduce everybody.

Inadequate or Missing Sound Files

Sometimes I don't want to get up in the morning because I know what awaits me: interviews with dreadful sound quality. As transcriptionist Sue Shackles describes such audio:

> There are always going to be clients who think the optimal way to record a one-on-one interview is to stick the recorder under their own nose and have the interviewee sitting across the other side of the room, causing the transcriber to have to turn up the volume so that the interviewee is audible. And then, of course, the transcriber will get their ears blasted every few minutes by the interviewer's unnecessary "mm-hmm"s and "uh-huh"s. These are usually going to be the clients who want full verbatim transcription. Bonus points if the office where they're conducting the interview is being remodeled at the time, as the sawing and hammering just adds a certain *je ne sais quoi* to the whole thing. Those of us who power our way through those kind of audio files and manage to come up with a coherent transcript are not just typists. We're miracle workers![2]

Here are a few reasons the audio may be terrible:

- Poor placement of the recorder.
- Recorder set to "voice-activated" during recording.
- Narrator who has trouble speaking due to advanced age and/or ill health.
- Speakers with speech impediments.
- Cassette tapes recorded decades ago and recently digitized.
- Recording made in a restaurant, highway underpass, construction site, heavy metal concert or other noisy place, or with a TV or radio on near the microphone.

- Unregulated group interview with simultaneous talking.
- Interviewer who talks over the narrator.

The recording session is over. The damage is done. What can the transcriptionist do now? I can make slight improvements to the audio with a "special audio processes" feature on Express Scribe. This is extremely easy to do, so is my first line of defense. For very soft-spoken narrators, I highlight the audio file, then hit "extra volume boost" in Express Scribe. It takes a couple of minutes to make the track a little louder. The enhancement I use most is "background noise reduction." If many people are talking in the background, this feature turns their voices into a swirly, psychedelic sound—annoying and disorienting, but less distracting since their words aren't fighting with the narrator's. Express Scribe's other special audio process is a high pass filter, designed to remove rumbles the microphone picks up. As stated in Chapter 2, transcriptionists don't need to worry about enhancing their copy of the audio for better comprehension. This has no bearing on the project's sound files since it's only for use on the transcriptionist's computer. If you're a one-person project, make a copy of the sound file before attempting to enhance it, in case you fail to improve on the original.

If the project you're working on is based at a university, you might have access to an IT department, or somebody on the oral history staff might be especially good with audio. The project manager can preview the sound files and get the IT person to improve poor quality tracks. Or, if this slips past the project manager, the transcriptionist can identify the dreadful sound files and ask for cleaned-up versions.

There have been times when the audio is so bad, I miss whole phrases or even sentences at a time. One way to manage this is to transcribe a three- or five-minute chunk of the recording and send it to the project manager, explaining it's the best you can do with the audio and asking for guidance. Usually once they realize what kind of subpar product they'll be spending they're funds on, they'll tell the transcriptionist to cease and desist. Freelancers, this can be hard if you were counting on the work, but letting the project know upfront is better than surprising them with—and charging for—useless transcripts. Turning in poor transcripts is no way to build a reputation in the field.

Sometimes the interview content is important enough that the project manager considers any transcript better than none at all and asks me to soldier on. This isn't great news, as even my higher rate for poor audio can't fully compensate me for the excessive time it takes, not to mention pain and suffering. If it's really awful, I work on a transcript for 10 or 15 minutes at a time then give my ears a break by switching to an easier task. This makes the process endurable. Straining to hear a soft voice through cacophony hurts the ears and is mentally tiring and stressful.

Sound Files That Don't Play

On several projects I've hit an audio snag before I even start transcribing. Something is wrong with the audio file. It might be a type of file format that's incompatible with my transcription software. Sometimes somebody weirdly renamed it so that the file extension (the part after the period) makes no sense. This is one of the most frustrating parts of being a transcriptionist, and many times I've lamented not having a normal job with an IT department down the hall. I envy those people who can call the IT guy and go to the break room or chat at the water cooler while somebody else fixes the problem—while being on the clock the whole time.

But as freelancers, one-person projects, family historians or grad students facing a mystery file all alone, when tech problems rear their ugly heads, we must do everything in our power to find out what's wrong and fix them.

Here's my best advice for dealing with non-playing files:

- If you run into trouble, search online for solutions. If you're having a problem, 1,000 other people have probably had the same problem and at least a few have discussed it somewhere on the web.
- When searching online for solutions, you'll come across free software designed to convert one type of file to another. Be careful about downloading free file converters, as they may be loaded with malware.
- If you have any techy friends, consult them.
- Try to contact the support staff for your transcription software.
- Freelancers, if you've put in an hour or two of problem-solving and are getting nowhere, ask your client. If they're part of a large institution, especially a university, they're likely to have an IT department that can help. If they're a small humanities nonprofit or a single researcher working on a project, they might be as clueless as you are. It's important to try to solve your own problems. But ultimately, they're employing you for your transcription skills, not your tech savvy, so tell them ASAP if you really can't figure it out.

Improperly Edited Sound Files

Project managers, one more note about delivering files: Only send what you want transcribed. Sometimes project managers send transcriptionists files with directions to only transcribe part of it. As Barb Jardee explains:

> They want me to skip around in a recording, jumping to the time elapsed codes they provide—often many within one recording. Sometimes their digital readings do not coincide with mine, and I have to hunt for the place to start in order for the passage to make sense. This jumping and hunting takes time, and as I've mentioned before, if my fingers aren't moving on the keyboard, I'm not making money. Also, I often overrun the place they want me to stop, so then I have to erase, and I don't get paid for the words I've transcribed that weren't wanted by the client. That makes me watch the time-elapsed chronometer like a hawk, which means I'm not giving my full

attention to the recording. I wish they'd do their own editing of the recording before they send it to me, and then I wouldn't have to worry about where to start and stop.[3]

Why wouldn't the project director edit their file before sending it? Because it takes time to edit, and time to learn how to edit. That's work they sometimes want to pass on to the transcriptionist. This is unfair, and not all transcriptionists will be as accommodating as Jardee. Project managers, expect the transcriptionist's bill to reflect the length of the file they're handling, whether or not you want every passage transcribed.

Mislabeled Files

A transcriptionist may also receive a collection of audio that's mislabeled, unlabeled, incomplete or out of order. For example, a track labeled "file one" might start in the middle of the interview, but then when you get to file three, the interviewer introduces herself and the narrator. If possible, I put these in the correct order and alert the project manager that the audio was mislabeled. Since researchers are more apt to seek the transcript anyway, why confuse them by being true to mislabeled audio? The project manager can relabel the audio tracks before letting the public access them.

You might suspect a file is missing, either because there's a big gap in the interview—one track ends in the narrator's childhood and at the start of the next she's practicing law—or because you get files labeled 1, 2, 3, 5 and 7. Ask the project manager. Maybe 4 and 6 weren't transferred properly, or the recorder malfunctioned, or the interviewer mislabeled them.

Foreign Language Interviews and Passages

Best practices for oral history recommend that the interview be conducted in the language the narrator feels most comfortable communicating in. When the languages of the narrator and the interviewer are different, usually a translator is a third participant in the recording. Occasionally a project will face the question of whether it should bypass the native language and have an interview simultaneously transcribed and translated into another. The UK-based Green Centre for Non-Western Art & Culture takes a strong stance that an interview should first be transcribed in the original language no matter what, with the only exception being when the language has no written form. Sometimes people are unwilling to do this, because funds are tight and the speakers of the language in question are few. But it's important to the integrity of the interview to start with the original language and then translate it into other languages as necessary to reach the intended audience.[4]

Oral history projects often include interviews that are partially or entirely in a foreign language. If the narrator uses only a few short phrases, indicate it in brackets. [speaking German] But when larger sections are in a different language, the project needs to find a competent bilingual transcriptionist.

Depending on where the interview takes place and which language the narrator is speaking, it can be difficult for the project manager to find a person qualified to take this on. Ideally, the language issue should have been part of the project planning. Without a competent bilingual transcriptionist, the recording could be doomed to a lonely life in an obscure, unvisited corner of an archive.

When Kim Heikkila conducted the Eat Street project in Minneapolis, chronicling the multicultural Nicollet Avenue, several of her interviews were partially or fully in Vietnamese. "One of those interviews, the amount of Vietnamese that was spoken was very minimal, so I really worked with the narrator and her daughter on the transcripts, for those very small sections of the transcript," she said. In the other Vietnamese language interview, the narrator spoke about half in Vietnamese and half in English. So Heikkila hired Phuoc Tran, a bilingual author, oral historian and transcriber, who lives in Minnesota.[5]

Bilingual transcriptionists can be found via online transcription services. Of course, these transcriptionists might be anywhere in the world. The farther you go from home, the more time you'll probably spend fixing geographical proper nouns and differences in the way language is used in the different countries.

Nongovernmental organizations (NGOs) gathering oral histories for policy change face translation challenges that academic researchers might not. "Most development projects recording oral testimony are sooner or later faced with the issue of translation," according to the Panos Network, an international network of NGOs that have used qualitative interviewing to foster public debate, pluralism and democracy:

> The answer to some key questions—who is to benefit from the project? How is the material to be used? What other audiences do we wish to reach?—will dictate which languages are required and what the translation and transcription procedures should be. A project that aims to influence policy matters may need testimonies recorded in a local language to be translated into both the national, official language (for example, Arabic) and the national, international language (for example, English or French).

According to a Panos Network publication:

> Since both transcription and translation are time-consuming processes, the question of how many layers of language are needed becomes very important. In the Sahel Oral History Project [in Ethiopia], most tapes were transcribed directly into English or French by the interviewers, on the grounds that there was no immediate use for a written version in the local language, which was anyway preserved on tape. But in the same project, transcriptions have been made subsequently in Soninke (Senegal) and Hausa (Niger), as part of literacy programmes.[6]

Two translators can come up with very different renderings of the same passage. If at all in doubt about the accuracy or adequacy of a translation, the translator should indicate those passages in brackets.

University-based oral history projects may be able to form partnerships with foreign language classes. At Louisiana State University, Oral History Center Director Jennifer Cramer works with a French professor on a class project to transcribe and translate interviews done in Cajun French. A German professor has also helped her with transcribing and translating German-language interviews. Depending on the languages in the collection and resources available on campus, language departments can be an affordable way for a center to get interviews transcribed and translated, and a valuable learning exercise for students.

Sometimes interviewers ask a bilingual family member for help during the interview. Transcriptionist Phuoc Tran has been in frustrating situations where the interpreter didn't completely or accurately translate what the narrator said, leaving her feeling that the narrator's statement was inadequately heard and expressed.[7]

Dialect, slang and pronunciation style also pose problems for translators. "I come from the South of Việt Nam and once in a while I have a hard time to listen to interviewee's accent variations," Tran told me in an email. Also,

> Vietnamese interviewees have the tendency to drop the last consonant of the words when speaking English due to the Vietnamese language doesn't spell the last consonant of the word. So the transcriptionist takes extra efforts and time to transcribe it accordingly.

Another problem that transcriptionists face when working with different languages is accessing the right script. Unicode is an encoding method that lets people type many languages—including Latin, Greek, Cyrillic, Armenian, Hebrew, Arabic, Syriac, Thaana, Devanagari, Vietnamese, Bengali, Gurmukhi, Oriya, Tamil, Telugu, Kannada, Malayalam, Sinhala, Thai, Lao, Tibetan, Myanmar, Georgian, Hangul, Ethiopic, Cherokee, Canadian Aboriginal Syllabics, Khmer, and Mongolian—using a standard keyboard.[8] This might involve a little work to set up, such as installing the proper keyboard driver software. Once the driver is on the computer's task bar, you can easily switch between languages.

Oral historians in many countries have the built-in challenge of having multiple official languages. Zimbabwe, India and South Africa all have more than ten.[9] At the National Archives of Singapore, oral historian Mark Wong said:

> Where possible, we translate non-English interviews to English to increase access to the interview contents. However, our resources are largely optimised for transcription (rather than translation) as the majority of interviews are conducted in English, and the cost of translation is higher than transcription.[10]

In India, oral historians also feel the financial pain of the high cost of translation on top of transcription. "The different languages present a challenge at the level of interviewing when one might need a translator to conduct the interview," said Indira Chowdhury, an oral historian in Bangalore:

> At the level of transcription, it pushes up costs as in addition to a transcriber who would do the transcription in the language of the interview, we would need the services of a translator. In many of our projects, the interviews are done in local languages but if the book is to be written in English, we use what I would call, a transcription in translation so we can incorporate it into the book. This process requires the transcriptionist to know both languages and transcribe a translated version. Naturally, this process sometimes creates complications with permissions from interviewees who may not agree to the translation.[11]

Interviews Conducted in a Narrator's Non-Native Language

Projects working with narrators who are being interviewed in a non-native language need to be careful to get the meaning right, especially if the narrator's language level is not very advanced. Australia-based oral historian Carol McKirdy, author of *Practicing Oral History with Immigrant Narrators*, encounters narrators with all levels of competence in English—from native language level down to those with hard-to-understand accents and poor grammar. In the latter case, she said,

> For these narrators I think transcriptions are inappropriate because the narrator's language has so many errors their intended voice will not be heard. Grammar is highly important because tense (time/when something actually happened) varies in the way it is expressed across languages, for example. Pronouns are confused, prepositions used incorrectly can change someone's intended content entirely, idiomatic language, collocations and phrasal verbs are confused etcetera, etcetera. Also, in my experience, new speakers of English are embarrassed by their English skills and in the release agreements I've been asked to take out any poor grammar. An accurate transcription could be unreadable.[12]

In this case, an interviewer might be able to work with the narrator and a translator to come up with an accurate summary if needed for a research project. But unless the narrator feels at home in the newer language, a true oral history would be better done in the narrator's native language and then translated.

Dialects

The question of how to render dialects is an old one in oral history circles, and probably relevant in all but the tiniest, most homogeneous countries. Let's look at the example of the US. Depending on which scholar you ask, the continental US has eight, 24 or more distinct dialects. These include Chicago Urban, Upper Midwest and Pacific Southwest.[13] But when people mention dialect in the US, they most often are talking about the ones that are most distant from elite academic areas. For example, Boston and Appalachia each has its own dialect. But if a researcher from Harvard is interviewing a narrator from Appalachia, she is unlikely to consider rendering her own speech as "pahk the cah," even while noting the vowel differences in Appalachian phonetics.

This often unconscious elitism is also found in folklore. As an article in the *Journal of the Society of Georgia Archivists* noted:

> To the earliest folklorists, including such notables as the brothers Grimm, not everyone was a part of the folk. Indeed, only the peasants were considered bearers of oral traditions, and folklore was viewed as a mysterious remnant of quaint and curious pagan rituals. This elitist view of the folk, based on a faulty syllogism, established a dichotomy which influenced the definition of folklore for at least a century. The syllogism goes something like this: Only folk possess folklore; the folk is peasantry; and therefore, only the peasantry possess folklore.[14]

Since oral history often tries to rectify injustices by giving voice to people with fewer resources to have their voices heard, a similar dichotomy often happens: the oral historian is like the folklorist, and the narrator like the folk. Dwelling on the language differences between an academic and a person from a group with less social, financial or political power only highlights the gap in education and opportunities, which contradicts the "bottom-up" aims of oral history.

As oral historian Michael Frisch put it:

> There is a class and cultural dimension to the communication of such testimonies, in terms of who is speaking to whom, that renders both literal transcription and passive editing especially problematic. This is because, in our society, every newspaper and magazine contains statements of people of position or power, statements routinely printed with correct syntax and spelling; interviews are selectively edited so that articles or reports always contain coherent statements; readers are similarly used to autobiographical prose in which the established or well-known talk about themselves and their lives in regular words, flowing sentences, and shaped paragraphs. In this context, to encounter the narratives of common people or the working class only in the somewhat torturous prose of 'faithful' transcription ("So I wuz jes', uh, y'know, talkin' t' the foreman, uh, when, y'know...") is to magnify precisely the class distance it is one of the promises of oral history to narrow.[15]

Unless you're a linguist or have some other good reason to wrestle with dialect and accents, don't try to capture phonetic spellings of standard words which a narrator pronounces differently than you would pronounce them yourself. By all means, leave in colorful phrases and alternative grammar, but don't mess with the spellings.

Every place has its own special regional words, which lend a transcript so much life and interest. Depending on what part of Australia you're in, you might call swimwear cossie, togs, bathers, swimmers, boardies or budgie smugglers.[16] Here are just a few examples from different US states:

- Geoduck (large edible clam) Washington
- Glawackus (an imaginary monster) Connecticut
- Jook (a hidden place or isolated stand of trees) Georgia
- Lamb licker (sheep-herder) Montana
- Pully bone (a wishbone) Indiana
- Tunklehead (a fool) Maine
- Whistle pig (a marmot or woodchuck) Idaho.[17]

Difficult Terminology

While the transcriptionists I interviewed for this book all cited poor audio as their biggest challenge, the project managers mentioned special terminology as an obstacle to getting good transcript. Reagan Grau at the National Museum of the Pacific War, said, "One major concern for transcription is the weird geographic nomenclature found in the Pacific: Eniwetok, Kwajalein, Kolombangara, Popondetta, etcetera."[18] Several social scientists mentioned the prolific use of acronyms in their fields tripping up transcriptionists.

Then again, it could be terminology specific to an area. "The vast majority of our interviewees work in health sciences, and often in highly specialized fields that have distinct terminology," said Maija Anderson of Oregon Health & Science University Library:

> Good transcription doesn't mean that the transcriptionist has to be an expert in all that terminology, but she does need attention to detail and critical thinking skills to figure out the terminology, ask questions, or note when we need input from someone knowledgeable.[19]

Again, a proper noun list saves the day. In an ideal world, the project manager will take the time to provide one, and the transcriptionist will diligently seek out correct spellings and add to this list as the project goes on. Transcriptionists can begin with an online search. Ask the project manager to verify as soon as possible if mystery terms come up repeatedly.

Extremely Difficult Speech

Sometimes the speaker will be extremely difficult to understand, no matter how diligently the interviewer sets up the equipment. I've had several projects where the narrators were on their death beds or had been recently intubated and spoke in whispery, scratchy voices. One narrator was interviewed following major throat surgery. I also worked on a disability rights project where one person with a severe speech impediment interviewed another person with a severe speech impediment. In these cases, I often listen way more than three times to each passage. This may be the person's last or only chance to be heard, and the audio circumstances are unlikely to improve. Transcriptionists, if you accept audio like this, it helps to be patient and respectful, and keep in mind your important role in preserving the many voices that make up history.

As a project manager, consider the limitations of the narrator and convey this to the transcriptionist. Understand that dealing with a very difficult recording will potentially slow down the transcriptionist's work flow with other clients. They might not be able to fit your time-consuming interview into their schedule. Graciously accept them opting out if they can't do it. Transcriptionists usually charge a premium for difficult audio but they still take a loss. For example, if a transcriptionist charges 50 percent more for difficult audio and it takes her three times as long to transcribe, she's clearly not covering her time.

Transcriptionist Lois Glewwe recommends transcribing difficult speech from video, if video files are available. When she was working on a project about AIDS, some African doctors interviewed had strong accents. She was able to get video files of those interviews:

> I would run the video in a little tiny window on my computer. I was also hearing the audio through the headphones. But I could look at the person's face and see if that helped me understand. And it does.[20]

Nuances of False Starts

While many projects decree that the transcriptionist should eliminate false starts—and for good reason—it takes focus and a discerning ear to decide when to leave them in. As Jeff Corrigan explains, sometimes an "uh" or "um" has a deeper meaning. He told transcriptionists,

> If they're just filling the space because they're thinking, you can skip that. But if somebody left you on a cliffhanger of, "Oh, hmm, I don't know if I want to tell you that…" well, that's different. There's context behind that.

He advised transcriptionists to thoughtfully consider when to include an um and when to edit out an uh. "Is this meaningful or is this just filler? Because context is important. And you don't want to screw up the context."[21]

Experienced transcriptionists know that it's easy to go on autopilot and type words without focusing on what the narrator is saying. But this example of differentiating between filler and meaning-laden "uhs" is just one example of why it's important to keep your focus. Taking regular breaks or switching between tasks can keep your mind fresh and make it easier to pay attention.

Walking Tour or Photo Show

Oral historians often introduce a visual component to the interview, such as asking narrators to describe mementos around the house, using old photos as memory triggers, or walking through an old structure to discuss the changes over time. This can be very successful when captured on video. The interviewer can zoom in on photos or interesting features of a historic building. But when I'm transcribing an audio interview and the speakers drag out a photo album, I groan aloud. This overused memory stimulant seldom works well on audio recordings. Interviewers are being overly optimistic to think that 20 years from now the photos and the audio will be together.

Here's a typical transcript from such a photo show:

INTERVIEWER: So, who's that?
NARRATOR: Oh, my. Look at Aunt Cathy! Look at those pants. (laughter) [pause] That's over at Clem's place. Oh, that was my bicycle.
INTERVIEWER: Who's this cute kid?
NARRATOR: I don't know. May be a neighbor?

This can go on for ten minutes, 20 minutes, an hour, or more.

Even worse is the walking tour of an old house. This is the kind of thing that's typically found in a box 30 years after the fact, unlabeled and unaccompanied by explanatory information.

UNIDENTIFIED INTERVIEWER: How about the condition of the perimeter as far as rot is concerned? Is there a lot of rot in it?
UNIDENTIFIED NARRATOR: Well, there's not a lot of rot in it, surprisingly enough. The outside board, you don't see it on this side of the house. The other side, you'll see it when we go around, that's buried below ground is starting to decay. And the corner support posts may be the [howling wind obscures voice] point or [moving out of mic range].
UNIDENTIFIED INTERVIEWER: So, a few things that look like they were added. Do you have any idea, like this bathroom?
UNIDENTIFIED NARRATOR 2: I don't know when that was done. [slamming noises, next passage obscured].

Where is this house? Who are these people? Often these walking tours and photo shows are older interviews that some unsuspecting project manager inherits and passes on to the transcriptionist without previewing.

Transcriptionists, if you receive this kind of audio, provide a short sample transcript—a page or two should suffice—to the project manager and let them decide whether it's worth their resources to continue transcription. Perhaps the project manager has a way of tracking down names of the interviewer, the narrators and the location of the house they're discussing. Perhaps it's a house of historic importance. Then she may ask the transcriptionist to proceed. But if the interviews seem useless, the project manager may cut her losses. The transcriptionist should only charge for the amount of transcription completed and a reasonable hourly rate to cover the time spent dealing with the files.

You may wonder how a transcriptionist ends up with a useless box of audio. People are busy. Sometimes a person administering a historical site or small archive comes across a mystery box, perhaps labeled "oral history materials," and naïvely believes that's a guaranteed treasure. In the best scenario, they'd take the time to preview the materials and make an informed decision before sending them out for transcription. But this doesn't always happen.

Profanity

The question of whether or not to transcribe profanity comes up in some projects, and is debated on internet forums. Here are a few views from online commenters:
[These are all individual quotes from different people.]

In research, you should quote them verbatim. Editing, or censoring, swearing is wrongly representing your research subjects and is thus a form of scientific misconduct. If you need to edit the quote for specific audience, you must make it clear that you have done so.

You could use [expletive] if you really feel uncomfortable.

I've also seen on the internet people using 'f*ck' standing for the f-word. Could this be a solution? (I personally find this solution a bit prudish.)

Personally, if I saw an asterisk or similar, I would presume you interviewed them via chat or email, and they actually self-censored. If it were a printed text, I'd think it a part of the edition you used.

If you're quoting someone, quote them as they said it. We're all adults. In the literature world, we quote swear words and other potentially offensive things all the time and no one bats an eye. I've no doubt other fields are the same.

One very strong argument for not censoring is that what we consider obscene is very much time and place dependent.[22]

Many transcription style guides are silent on profanity. Those that address it often disagree. The Walden University Writing Center website advises:

The use of profanity is generally considered an important sign of the speaker's attitude and tone. As such, it should be transcribed. However, if the language is so strong that readers could be offended, then the offensive word could be represented by its first letter followed by a double-dash (——) to represent the missing letters: *d*—— or *f*——. The context would make the meaning clear. The counterexample—the one to avoid—is that of the Nixon White House tapes, which made famous the phrase *expletive deleted*. While it avoids offense, it doesn't distinguish between the use of mild or virulent profanity.[23]

The Historic Columbia River Oral History Project also recognizes the importance of profanity, while seeking to cloak it in the transcript. Its guidelines state, "For the HCRH Oral History Project, profanity should not be included, but should be noted by ellipses (…) and asterisks (★★).

Example: I told him, "No, I'm not going to …★★… do it, it's too dangerous!"[24]

Baylor is straightforward on the matter: "Type exactly as said. Do not abbreviate or alter the words."[25]

Jeff Corrigan ran into the profanity dilemma on one of his first interviews after he started his job of oral historian at the State Historical Society of Missouri. He found that students and volunteers had a more formal view of what should be included in a library collection. "It was a 90-year-old sailor, and he cussed like a sailor. There were cuss words, and words strung together that I had never heard in my life, they were so creative." Corrigan's coworkers tried to talk him into removing profanity from the transcript, insisting that his family would be offended.

Corrigan went to speak with the late sailor's wife. He reported:

She said, "I don't care about that. You know what that means? That means he's an authentic sailor. That's how he was, and that's how I'm going to remember him and that's how all his family is going to remember him." In an hour or two interview, there were something like 256 cuss words. So, they're there. And that was important to me that somebody wouldn't censor that.[26]

The best practice is for oral historians to choose authenticity over respectability. Most wouldn't consider "cleaning up a transcript."

Dangerous or Illegal Conversation

This topic will be discussed more in the "Editing for Libel and Other Legal Concerns" section of Chapter 8. The transcriptionist might notice conversation about illegal activities and inappropriate behavior. Lots of life is inappropriate, so the transcriptionist might just need to slog through, distasteful as she may find some stories. For example, a narrator bragging about his sexual conquests. But if that narrator is naming these conquests, or talking about somebody else's conquests, the transcriptionist should note this in the transcript and give the project manager a heads-up about possible slander or libel. This goes for disclosing any private information about another person. Identifying slanderous passages is not the responsibility of the transcriptionist. But as a good team player, it's considerate to point out something that could potentially damage the program or institution.

Bottom Line

Once you learn the basics of transcription—the software, equipment, a project's style guide—you'll be motoring right along. Until some unexpected situation comes along to stump you. Even if you're a diligent freelancer who prides herself on problem-solving, some transcription situations will require help. Often the project manager can answer the transcriptionist's questions. Or, if you're the project manager, maybe you'll need to contact the interviewer for clarification on difficult passages, or set guidelines about profanity, or seek additional transcriptionists to handle multiple languages, or decide that the poor audio quality means transcribing a particular interview is a waste of project funds. A successful oral history project aims for high-quality transcripts with a consistent style. Especially in the early days of a project, this may mean extra time in communication between transcriptionists, interviewers, narrators, the project manager and other parties to hammer out best policies and to ensure accurate transcripts. Once you have an idea of how to handle these hard but fairly common decisions, new problems will be fewer and farther between. But they will happen. Building an oral history collection is a dynamic process.

Notes

1 John Sheehy, interview with Teresa Bergen, June 20, 2018.
2 Sue Shackles, blog, "Tips and Advice," available at: http://waywithwordsblog.com/2011/11/24/a-career-in-transcribing/ (accessed February 15, 2018).
3 Barb Jardee, email correspondence with Teresa Bergen, May 11, 2018.
4 Mandy Sadan, *Learning to Listen: A Manual for Oral History Projects* (Brighton: Green Centre for Non-Western Art and Culture, 2008).
5 Kim Heikkila, interview with Teresa Bergen, November 15, 2017.
6 Panos Network, *Listening for a Change*, p. 88, available at: http://panosnetwork.org/images/downlads/Listening-for-a-Change-Chap-4.pdf (accessed April 7, 2018).
7 Phuoc Tran, email correspondence with Teresa Bergen, August 2, 2018.
8 Unicode website, available at: www.unicode.org/faq/basic_q.html (accessed August 5, 2018).
9 World Economic Forum, available at: www.weforum.org/agenda/2017/08/these-countries-have-the-most-official-languages/ (accessed August 24, 2018).
10 Mark Wong, email correspondence with Teresa Bergen, August 24, 2018.
11 Indira Chowdhury, email correspondence with Teresa Bergen, August 25, 2018.
12 Carol McKirdy, email correspondence with Teresa Bergen, January 7, 2018.
13 Reid Wilson, "What Dialect Do You Speak? A Map of American English," *Washington Post,* December 2, 2013, available at: www.washingtonpost.com/blogs/govbeat/wp/2013/12/02/what-dialect-to-do-you-speak-a-map-of-american-english/?noredirect=on&utm_term=.f2ed5a2c4fbc (accessed November 24, 2018).
14 Katherine Martin and John Williams, "The Appalachian Oral History Project: Then and Now," *Provenance: Journal of the Society of Georgia Archivists,* 1984, p. 49, available at: https://digitalcommons.kennesaw.edu/provenance/vol2/iss1/5/ (accessed February 18, 2018).
15 Michael Frisch, *A Shared Authority: Essays on the Craft and Meaning of Oral and Public History* (Albany, NY: State University of New York Press, 1990), p. 85.
16 "Linguistics Roadshow," available at: https://lingroadshow.com/resources/englishes-in-australia/vocabulary/mapping-words-around-australia/ (accessed August 11, 2018).

17 Katherine Brooks, "An American Dialect Dictionary Is Dying Out," *Huffington Post*, available at: www.huffingtonpost.com/entry/dictionary-of-american-regional-english_us_599199fee4b08a247275c897, 2017 (accessed February 18, 2018).

18 Reagan Grau, email correspondence with Teresa Bergen, November 8, 2017.

19 Maija Anderson, email correspondence with Teresa Bergen, November 14, 2017.

20 Lois Glewwe, interview with Teresa Bergen, January 15, 2018.

21 Jeff Corrigan, interview with Teresa Bergen, December 18, 2017.

22 Academia Stack Exchange forum, "How to Handle Swear Words in Quote/Transcription?" available at: https://academia.stackexchange.com/questions/79656/how-to-handle-swear-words-in-quote-transcription (accessed February 18, 2018).

23 Tim McIndoo, "Transcribing Audio Files from Interviews and Focus Groups," Walden University Writing Center, July 16, 2012, available at: http://waldenwritingcenter.blogspot.com/2012/07/transcribing-audio-files-from.html (accessed February 18, 2018).

24 Historic Columbia Highway Oral History, "Guide to Transcribing and Summarizing Oral Histories," 2010.

25 Baylor University Institute of Oral History Style Guide, 2018 edition.

26 Corrigan, interview, December 18, 2017.

7

EDITING AND POLISHING THE TRANSCRIPT

Once the transcriptionist finishes the draft, it's time for fact checking, spell-checking and general polishing. These steps create a document that looks good and is useful to researchers. There is no sweeping protocol of who does which of the following tasks. It will depend on the size of the project staff and people's particular strengths and preferences. Transcriptionists often audit transcripts and sometimes index them (see Chapter 3 for indexing). In my experience, transcriptionists are rarely contracted to edit transcripts, although this is well within many transcriptionists' skill sets. All these tasks should be negotiated individually by the project director and the team members. That said, this chapter is aimed more at project directors and individuals who are doing all the steps of their oral history projects than at freelance transcriptionists, unless they are contracted to do these tasks.

This chapter covers editing basics, including:

- auditing transcripts
- editing for style and consistency
- adding clarification
- transcript review by narrator
- editing for ease of reading

Auditing Transcripts

After an interview is transcribed, ideally a person other than the transcriptionist audits the transcript. Auditing means listening to the audio while following along and correcting the text.

Auditing is different than editing because an editor may deal only with the text, never listening to the recording. Though it's a distinct step, auditing is the first step in the editing process because the auditor changes the text as she listens. For example, the guidelines for the Historic Columbia River Highway Oral History Project classifies auditing as a first pass in editing.[1]

The auditor listens carefully to see if she can pick up words the transcriber missed, or catch places where the transcriber misheard words or phrases. Often a different set of ears can pick up missed words and mistranscriptions. The person auditing the transcript will have different life experiences than the transcriptionist, and perhaps will recognize more of the narrator's vocabulary or have an ear for the narrator's regional accent. For example, in one program I work with, the recordings were done in the 1970s, the narrator has a strong German accent and he expounds on early twentieth-century European theories, movements and philosophers that I know nothing about. Fortunately, the program head works miracles with my very rough transcripts, as he knows the narrator's life and work inside out. I'm astounded when I see his audited versions of my work. This is an example of where the right auditor makes all the difference in the world.

Here are a few examples of mistranscriptions that might be caught and fixed at this stage, from Willa Baum's *Transcribing and Editing Oral History*:

> Transcription: They had Larry Baceretti right under the shadow of Harvard.
> Correct: They had Mary Baker Eddy right under the shadow of Harvard.
> Transcription: They used to have the customers sitting up with the dead.
> Correct: They used to have the custom of sitting up with the dead.
> Transcription: They wouldn't send any money. Unless you ask the brother...
> Correct: Who asks anybody? The less you ask, the better.[2]

This third example is way off the mark, and you might think the transcriber was entirely at fault. But between poor acoustics, degraded tapes, accents and positioning the narrator too far from the mic, this kind of stab in the dark for what the narrator might be saying is incredibly common. Otherwise, enormous sections would be transcribed as [unclear].

Depending on program guidelines, the auditing stage may also be the step where you do the following:

- Eliminate false starts and superfluous crutch words.
- Eliminate interruptions, such as asking somebody in the other room about the progress of dinner or unidentified third parties entering to ask when a room will become available.
- Pare down rambling interviewer questions.
- Jot down places that may need further clarification from the narrator.
- Note places that need additional information, such as full names or dates, passages you suspect might be historically inaccurate, and places that don't fit with the style guidelines of a project.

Next Editing Steps

Depending on the oral history project, once a transcript is audited, project staff may conduct several more rounds of editing for different purposes, or one comprehensive edit. We'll look at these purposes separately, while understanding that the approach to editing depends on the expected outcome for the oral history transcripts, and the project's philosophy, goals, staffing, timelines and budgets.

Editing for Style and Consistency

The next pass consists mostly of copy editing and may be done while listening to the audio or simply reading the text. This stage of editing will comply with the style guidelines agreed upon for the project. When I edit a transcript that someone else transcribed, I like to compare the audited version with the audio because often a third set of ears will pick up a few things missed by both the transcriptionist and the auditor. Here is what to look for in this step:

- Layout and format consistent with project specifications for page one heading, headers, footers, tab spacing, font style and size and spacing.
- Correct use of homonyms. Theirs versus there's, write versus right. Even knowledgeable transcriptionists occasionally make this mistake, and the auditor might have missed it, too.
- Rendering of numbers as per your chosen style guide. Again, consistency reigns.
- Capitalization. Many people incorrectly capitalize words to show that someone or something is important. Now's the time to fix that, and to capitalize any words that should have been but weren't.
- Apostrophes. They're small, but mighty. Repair any its/it's travesties, and make sure possessives are used correctly.

Allow for the narrator's flair. As noted by the LSU guidelines,

> Sometimes speakers use words that make sense to you as the listener although they aren't words you can find in the dictionary. If you can spell these words the way they sound, include them as-is.
> Examples:

- There was no other sustenance other than what we could scravenge.
- She caretaked us when we were little children.
- She was swimming in the lake and she drownded.[3]

Adding Clarification

Add clarifications at this time, or note they need to be added. For example, I've been transcribing for an oral history project done in the little town of Brusly,

Louisiana, for going on 20 years now. They started the project for their centennial in 2001 and just kept going. It's a town with fewer than 2,800 citizens, most of them related. They can tell you who lived in just about every house in their neighborhood growing up, the names of their cousins and how far everyone lived from Brusly's pride and joy, a 350-plus year-old oak tree. The main interviewer is a Brusly native. All this closeness means that nicknames and places are thrown around like crazy, confusing outside listeners, including myself as transcriptionist, but full of meaning to the narrator, interviewer, and town residents. I'm hoping that somewhere down the line, a more knowledgeable citizen of Brusly edits my transcripts and fills in the real names of Mutt, Tooky, Fish and Greek.

I've noticed the insider/outsider dilemma a lot in listening to interviews. Outsiders won't know as much, so sometimes their questions will seem either irrelevant or too obvious to narrators. But this can be useful for future researchers. Insiders have the advantage of more local knowledge, but this can mean they don't ask the questions they should, or that the narrator worries about boring them with things they already know, so they talk in a shorthand which researchers might find impenetrable. A wise editor will carefully comb through insider interviews and insert clarifications as necessary.

Here are a few examples of adding clarification to an interview:

- We moved to Jogya [Yogyakarta, Java] in 1987.
- I got a lot out of [John] Mbiti's book about African religion.
- She married my cousin Gordo [Adalberto Martinez].
- That book about the whale, I can't remember the name [*Moby Dick*].
- That was in July [1978], the year before I went to college.
- I'm originally from Chuxiong [Yunnan].
- That was before Cameroon filed the case with the ICJ [International Court of Justice].

Sending the Transcript for Review by the Narrator

Somewhere along the oral history editing process, the project manager sends the transcript to the narrator for review and approval. This is a very important but often touchy step. It's important because the narrator might catch mistranscriptions and uncover inaccuracies in their own accounts. Often a narrator can fill in a missing name or add a necessary clarification to make the transcript more useful for researchers.

There is another reason narrators should see the transcripts before they become available to the public. Some information in them may be just too personal for public access. Kim Heikkila was collecting interviews of women who'd given birth and surrendered their babies at a maternity home for unwed mothers. "These conversations are very personal, they're very intimate," she said.

They're about really hard chapters in these women's lives. Over the course of the interview, I'm able to establish a good rapport with these women, a kind of trusting relationship. And they divulge things that they maybe haven't told anybody else in their life.

Despite understanding the project goals and signing a release form, the transcripts came as a shock:

What came out naturally in the course of an intimate conversation looks different in ink. That is a moment of realization for people sometimes. Probably five of those seven women looked at that transcript and thought, I said what? This is going public to whom? What?!

While the women had understood the project in an abstract way, their perspective changed once they thought about their transcript sitting in the University of Minnesota archive available to the public.

Heikkila renegotiated the releases and placed some restrictions on interviews:

As much as that is a time-consuming process, I think it's a really important one. Because as an oral historian, I want to make sure that I'm respecting my narrators' wishes, and their right to privacy. And without that transcript, without them having the chance to review that transcript, they wouldn't have the opportunity to really understand and set conditions upon their interview materials that they're comfortable with.[4]

At Baylor University, oral historian Steven Sielaff also feels strongly about giving narrators the chance to review transcripts before they are made publicly available:

I always call it an extra ethical layer that we put into this process as far as making things accessible, in that we know we've given the opportunity to every interviewer and interviewee after they conduct an interview to look at transcript, to reorient themselves around the interview, and realize what they said and basically sign off on it another time. I feel a lot better because we have that baked into our process.[5]

The most common reason narrators want to change transcripts is that they're uncomfortable with the way their speech looks on paper. Many oral history projects will encounter narrators who want to recraft the transcript into something that resembles the written word more than the spoken. Narrators from all walks of life may want to refine their prose, but professionals such as physicians, lawyers and judges can be especially adamant. People understandably have concerns over how the transcript represents them to current and future generations.

So how do you best handle the narrator review step? Well, first you have to find the narrator. In projects that have a big backlog, the interview might have taken place many years ago and the narrator may no longer be living or easily found.

If you find a living narrator, send the transcript along with a letter asking the narrator to review the transcript for accuracy and make clarifications, corrections and additions as needed. This cover letter often urges narrators to accept the unpolished spoken quality of the transcript, stressing that spoken language is supposed to sound different from written language. Include a deadline for returning the transcript, and be willing to extend your deadline if necessary. "Deadlines, even flexible ones, are necessary to avoid having transcripts languish in processing limbo," oral historian Elinor Mazé points out.[6]

It is common for a transcript to "disappear" once it gets into the hands of the narrator for review. What's the holdup? Sometimes narrators don't understand what they're supposed to do, or the subjects are sensitive, or reading and writing are hard for them because of age or education. Some narrators might be too busy to review the transcript. Or perhaps they enjoyed the undivided attention of the interviewer over multiple interviews and are reluctant for the process to end.

Best case scenario, the narrator carefully reviews the transcript and makes needed corrections and clarifications. Again, be sure to clearly specify a deadline—I've heard of projects giving as little as two weeks and as long as several months—to review the transcript. If the time expires without the narrator returning the manuscript, you are cleared to proceed through the editing steps without narrator input.

BOX 7.1 SAMPLE LETTER TO NARRATOR ACCOMPANYING TRANSCRIPT

Date
  Address
  XXXXXXXXXXXX
  XXXXXXXXXXXX
  Dear XXXXXXXXX:

Following your interview conducted by XXXXXXXX on XXXXXXX, the recording was transcribed in our office and then the transcript was checked with the recording. Two people have listened to the recording and logged what they heard to the best of their abilities.

In order to prepare the transcript of your interview for access through the online facilities of the Baylor University Libraries, we need some help from you. As you read the enclosed transcript, please pay close attention to spellings of proper names and technical terms, marking corrections on the transcript itself. Where parts of the recording were difficult to hear, the transcriber has left blank lines. If you can determine what was said, please fill in those blanks.

Oral language is seldom as neatly organized as written language. Part of the charm of oral history is that it is unrehearsed and stream of consciousness. Since we will be uploading both the audio file and transcript online, please avoid the temptation of making the transcript read like a polished manuscript with heavy edits. The resulting discrepancies between the audio and transcript would be confusing to the future user.

When you are finished, please place the corrected transcript in the enclosed self-addressed envelope and mail it back to us. Your prompt response will enable us to make this interview available to the public in a timely manner. If we have not received the transcript within **2 months** of the date of this letter, we will assume you have no corrections to make and will proceed to finalize the memoir for access. If you do not wish to review your transcript at all, please contact us immediately.

Thank you for giving your valuable time and effort to oral history. Your story is important!

Cordially,
Michelle Holland
Editor

(courtesy of Baylor University Institute of Oral History)

Incorporating the Narrator's Changes

Once the narrator returns her marked-up manuscript, it's time to incorporate changes large and small. Editing guidelines are usually determined by the interviewing institution. At LSU, an editor makes the judgment call about which of the narrator's changes should be incorporated and which "would take away from the conversational tone of the interview or alter the interviewee's voice and content."[7] In addition to (understandably) wanting to make themselves more coherent, narrators might mistakenly add grammatical errors and misspellings.

Cases of mistranscription are easy to fix. If the transcript reads, "My first job was at the Taco Bell on Oliver Street" and the narrator points out that should really be Tolliver Street, simply replace the word.

Clarifications and misstatements require brackets. If the narrator realizes he said the wrong year, an editor may be tempted to correct it. The problem is that a researcher listening to the original audio will be confused by this discrepancy. A few examples of bracketed corrections or clarifications:

- I was there for Loma Prieta earthquake in 1988 [Shapiro's correction: 1989]
- What's that famous book by Zinn? [Shapiro was speaking about *A People's History of the United States*]
- That was the summer I stayed with [my cousin] Julia.

Some narrators will turn in corrections and additions that double a transcript's size. According to Mazé, Baylor's policy is to incorporate all these changes:

In this case, the changes will result in a document that is much more a written autobiographical memoir than a transcript of an interview, a nearly complete shift of genre. In the institute's view, it is the interviewees' prerogative to do this. However, if interviewees in no way restrict access to the recordings of their interviews, a note in the front matter of the edited and deposited transcripts may inform readers that the transcript differs significantly from those recordings.[8]

Oral historian Sarah Milligan wrestled with conveying to narrators at Oklahoma State University that, while the transcript could be changed, the recording would stay intact. They describe the recording as a performance and the primary document, and the transcript as a supplement where the narrator may add notes and annotations.[9]

In some cases, the transcript may legitimately be the authoritative document. Folklorist Edward Ives takes an alternative view on the audio versus the enhanced transcript:

> [I]f the interviewee does in fact make alterations—deleting passages, adding fuller explanations, correcting sentence structure and the like—then the resultant manuscript becomes the primary document, the tape and transcript merely rough drafts. In this situation, if you want to find out what the informant "said" about something, you would not go to the tape but to the corrected transcript.[10]

Editing for Ease of Reading

Is the primary purpose of the transcript to transcribe the words of the narrator verbatim, or is it an access tool to be made as readable as possible for the researchers? This question sparks many a heated debate among oral historians. Ultimately, the answer is: It depends on the intended end use of the transcript and the resources available for editing. The biggest debate about oral history editing is how much to edit for ease of reading. On the light side, some style guides require removing excessive verbal ticks (you know, I think, kind of), break up run-on sentences, shorten enormous paragraphs, smooth out syntax and make small changes for clarity. Some might fix grammar. (If grammar is altered, this must be done for all speakers, narrators and interviewers alike.)

Some oral historians embrace a more drastic approach to editing. In a typical oral history interview, a narrator might revisit a subject multiple times, either forgetting he'd already covered it or wanting to add something. Baum recommends cutting repetitions that are due to the narrator forgetting she already mentioned something, and leaving in repetitions that show emphasis. Narrators will probably thank you. "We have found that one of the main things older people are afraid of when they are invited to give an oral history is that they will repeat themselves," Baum wrote. [11]

Michael Frisch is well known for a heavy-handed editing approach. He explained:

> Together, these considerations have led me to a position that may seem at first paradoxical: the integrity of a transcript is best protected, in documentary use, by an aggressive editorial approach that does not shrink from substantial manipulation of the text. One must respect the original enough to come to know it deeply, and this knowledge must be the benchmark for measuring the validity of any digest, excerpt or editing. But on this basis, one must also be able to abandon the pretense of literal reproduction, in order to craft the document into a form that will answer to the needs of successful presentation and communication.[12]

Then Frisch gave an example of an edited and unedited transcript, respectively 14 versus 42 pages, to show his technique. Mostly this involves putting like information together, editing out false starts, repetitions and extraneous stuff, to stay true to the original but be easier to read.

Text manipulation means, of course, that the editor is deciding what to leave out and what to highlight. The reader may not even realize that the oral history has been edited, as is the case with many readers of Studs Terkel's books. As American Studies professor Andrea Gustavson pointed out, "Most oral historians today privilege transparency with respect to their methods and attempt to avoid crafting overtly politicized works. Terkel, however, aggressively edited his texts, crafting documentary memories of the past to politicize the present."[13]

Transparency is key. As Francis Good wrote:

> My view is that editorial intervention at any level only becomes problematic when the reader is not given information that explains the process and the source of changes. As a user, I would want to be able to judge for myself if the intervention goes too far for my purposes. We all draw our own line in different places in the sand. There can be legitimate concern about factual accuracy and the completeness of the record, but care is needed not to fall into linguistic imperialism or historical policing. It is a process that attracts highly loaded and subjective descriptions like "appropriate" and "sensitive" which do little to invalidate disquiet about the level of intervention and loss of other kinds of meaning from the oral original.[14]

Best practices are to answer the following questions about an edited transcript. (These are adapted from Good's article.)

- What was the context of the recording?
- What kind of process did the transcript go through?
- Is it a first draft?
- Who checked it and what did they do to it?

- Is there enough information for readers with an interest in language aspects to detect how far they can rely on what they see?
- What system is employed to indicate outright changes in the text from what is heard on tape?
- What information was added by compilers?[15]

If you decide to take a more intense approach to editing, alert readers with a note at the beginning of the transcript. Refer them to the audio if they want to hear the words exactly as the narrator spoke them, if the audio is available.

Bottom Line

Your project's goals will shape your editing process. For example, if you're most interested in capturing the mental processes of your narrators, you'll want to leave in more false starts. Many programs stick with a light edit, removing false starts, correcting mistranscriptions and adding clarifications. This is a common editing choice for established programs, and also a useful approach for any project that is stretched for staff and financial resources.

Some oral historians favor a more aggressive approach to editing. They might rearrange the text to minimize repetitions and make it easier to read. This approach is conducive to writing books that appeal to a wider market than researchers using an archive.

Whether you edit lightly or more drastically, it's important to keep the narrator's way of speaking as true to life as possible to present an accurate portrait. This includes retaining verbal quirks, unusual word order and regional phrases.

Most oral history projects treat narrators as partners and want to ensure the manuscript is acceptable to them before making it available to the public. This means giving narrators a chance to review the transcript and make corrections, deletions and additions. The project determines the best way to incorporate these changes.

Notes

1 Historic Columbia River Highway Oral History Project, "Guide to Transcribing and Summarizing Oral Histories," Oregon Department of Transportation Research Section, 2010, p. 2.
2 Willa Baum, *Transcribing and Editing Oral History* (Nashville, TN: American Association for State and Local History, 1977), p. 37.
3 T. Harry Williams Center for Oral History Editing Guide, p. 7.
4 Kim Heikkila, interview with Teresa Bergen, November 15, 2017.
5 Steven Sielaff, interview with Teresa Bergen, June 29, 2018.
6 Elinor Mazé, "The Uneasy Page: Transcribing and Editing Oral History," in Beth M. Robertson (ed.), *The Oral History Handbook* (Adelaide: Oral History Association of Australia, 2000), p. 264.
7 Williams Center editing guide, p. 8.
8 Mazé, "The Uneasy Page," p. 257.

9 Sarah Milligan, interview with Teresa Bergen, May 11, 2018.
10 Edward D. Ives, *The Tape-Recorded Interview: A Manual for Field Workers in Folklore and Oral History* (Knoxville, TN: University of Tennessee Press, 1980), pp. 74–75.
11 Baum, *Transcribing and Editing Oral History*, p. 47.
12 Michael Frisch, *A Shared Authority: Essays on the Craft and Meaning of Oral and Public History* (Albany, NY: State University of New York Press, 1990), p. 84.
13 Andrea Gustavson, "From 'Observer to Activist': Documentary Memory, Oral History, and Studs Terkel's 'Essence' Narratives," *Journal of American Studies,* 46(1) (February 2012): 105.
14 Francis Good, "Voice, Ear and Text. Words, Meaning and Transcription," in R. Perks and A. Thomson (eds), *The Oral History Reader*, 3rd edn (London: Routledge, 2016), p. 466.
15 Ibid.

8

LEGAL, ETHICAL AND REGULATORY ISSUES

Beyond the task of listening closely and translating words into text, the project manager, transcriptionist and independent oral historian must sometimes wade through legalities and decipher legislation. This chapter covers some of the less obvious issues you might encounter that can affect transcription:

- Editing for libel and other legal concerns
- Sealing and restricting interviews
- Confidentiality
- GDPR legislation
- Sensitive materials
- Online access to interviews
- Institutional Review Boards
- Liability insurance

Editing for Libel and Other Legal Concerns

Sometimes narrators get rolling with their juicy stories, which may include negative statements about people they have known. The editor needs to hone her eye to discern harmless gossip and poetic license from defamation. Lawsuits involving oral history aren't common, but they do happen and there will probably be more due to increased online access to interviews. Laws affecting oral history differ by country. Defamation—or communicating something that may cause harm to someone else— is one important area where oral history meets the law. American legal expert John Neuenschwander, author of *A Guide to Oral History and the Law*, identifies five major categories of defamation:

- committing a crime;
- acting immorally or unethically;
- associating with unsavory people or otherwise acting disgracefully or despicably;
- demonstrating financial irresponsibility or unreliability;
- demonstrating professional incompetency.[1]

Committing a crime is probably the clearest cut of these categories. The others are somewhat open to interpretation, as despicableness is in the eye of the beholder. Bruce Sanford, an authority on defamation, compiled a handy list of red flag words. These include such obviously pejorative terms as booze-hound, coward, deadbeat, double-crosser, incompetent, mobster, scoundrel, seducer, shyster and stool pigeon.[2] However, gay, alcoholic, and atheist also made the list, all terms which many people use to straightforwardly describe themselves. If somebody self-identifies as gay or an atheist, that's not defamation. But if they take offense when you use those terms to describe them, it might be.

It's not defamation if the allegation is true. "Not every shocking statement or characterization is defamatory," Neuenschwander wrote. "You may in fact be able to corroborate the truth of a statement by consulting written sources and even other interviews."[3]

You can't slander or libel a dead person. However, if the injured party started the lawsuit and then died while the case was pending, the lawsuit might outlive the deceased. Also, offended family members occasionally file a lawsuit if they think an oral history has besmirched the reputation of their late relative. "Such lawsuits usually try to get around the rule by filing a civil action for invasion of privacy and/or intentional infliction of emotional distress," according to Neuenschwander. "In only a few rare instances have such lawsuits been successful."[4]

There's a lot more leeway in what people say about public figures than private ones, which is obvious if you've ever gone through a supermarket checkout and seen the tabloid headlines about celebrities. Just think how rich they'd be if they could successfully sue every publication that aired—or fabricated—their dirty laundry. One of the trickier classifications is the "limited-purpose public figure," heretofore private individuals who suddenly rise to public view, usually over an incident or issue. Neuenschwander explains:

> For example, publicity that is given to a heretofore private individual does not by itself turn the person into a limited-purpose public figure. The first question to ask is whether or not there was or is a public controversy. The second question goes to the extent to which the person at issue chose to participate in this public controversy. In other words, did he or she step forward and take a leadership role or seek media attention? Finally, do the alleged defamatory statements relate to his or her actual role in the underlying public controversy or not?[5]

Maintaining narrators' privacy is also a concern. Jennifer Cramer, director of LSU's Williams Center, has removed addresses and Social Security numbers from interviews done in the 1980s.[6] Obviously, narrators don't want that information on the internet, or even in an archive.

Sealing and Restricting Interviews

What if after reviewing a transcript, the narrator decides she doesn't want all or part of her interview released to the public? Or what if you as the editor suspect that certain passages will open your oral history project up to a defamation case?

Despite Neuenschwander's legal warnings, he cautions editors to protect the stories within their interviews. "The historical record is not and should not be something that has been sanitized by its creators and keepers," he wrote. "If, however, you are unable to corroborate the statements in question, then start your damage control by starting first with the least invasive procedure."[7] He recommends sealing possibly defamatory portions of the interview for a designated amount of time—presumably until the people involved are all likely to be dead. (I hear the archivists groaning. While they may agree in theory, managing interviews with restrictions is a nightmare. Some archives don't accept them.) His second course of action is to carefully edit defamatory statements while keeping the historical record mostly intact:

> The last, and least desirable option in terms of being faithful to the historical record, is deletion of the material. This approach is certainly a form of censorship that is anathema to academic freedom and should only be used as a last resort.[8]

Project managers and independent oral historians can discuss options with the narrator, gently making the case for why their contribution is important to the historical record. Sometimes the results may disappoint. Jennifer Cramer at LSU told me:

> I recently had a narrator who did five interviews and came back and restricted every one of them. In perpetuity! I mean, he has the right to deaccession them if he wants to. But I told him I thought they were really good stories, and I thought he should keep them for somebody to read sometime.

Cramer offered to edit out libellous comments, but he refused. Eventually he agreed that one out of five interview sessions could go public 25 years after his death.

This is a difficult position for an oral historian, financially—putting all the staff time and resources into collecting and processing these interviews—and ethically. On the one hand, Cramer said:

I don't want to be a censor. I don't want to be a judge of what's okay. I don't want that responsibility and I don't want to mess up the document. It was told, and if it's not illegal, I'm okay with putting it out there.

On the other, the project must ethically defer to the narrator. "Again, that's why the start to finish transcription is so important," Cramer said. "So that the person who is part of the interview process is your partner every step of the way, and they have a chance to object and restrict anything that they want."[9]

I worked with an independent oral historian on one project dealing with covert ex-CIA operatives where many of the interviews were restricted. The way we dealt with this was to edit the transcript to the narrator's satisfaction and make that available to researchers immediately. We sealed the audio and an unedited transcript for an agreed-upon number of years. This was much easier than having to edit the audio. The oral historian negotiated this arrangement with the archive where the materials now reside.

Projects with the staff and skills may also edit audio. If you're making both an edited transcript and an edited audio file available to users, be sure to go back and adjust the time stamps on the transcript to match the edited audio. Note places in the transcript where passages have been removed. Add a bracketed note, such as [personal information omitted] or [portion restricted per narrator's request].

The Canadian Museum for Human Rights in Winnipeg specializes in sensitive materials. Depending on the project, they've dealt with the need for anonymity several ways. "We have anonymized a handful of interviews," Heather Bidzinski, head of collections, told me in an email. "Some through conducting audio only, some through obscuring video and/or audio, some by restricting the files for internal use only."[10]

LSU's Williams Center has developed a good system for keeping track of edited audio. The original WAV file will not be edited and will have "_restricted" appended to the file name. The digital user copy, an MP3, is edited by a sound engineer, leaving only a second or two of dead air where passages are removed. That version gets "edited user copy" added to its file name.

Confidentiality

Depending on the materials and project, transcriptionists may or may not be asked to sign confidentiality agreements. This is uncommon if you're transcribing for a project that will be accessible to the public as soon as it's processed. I've never had to sign a confidentiality agreement when transcribing for an oral history center housed in a university. But if you transcribe for social scientists, a confidentiality agreement is standard. An individual working on a book or documentary project might also want confidentiality, at least until their book or movie comes out.

Here are some typical requirements in confidentiality statements I've signed:

- Holding in strictest confidence the identification of any individual that could be revealed while transcribing an interview, or in any associated documents.
- Storing all study-related audio files and transcriptions in a secure location on one password-protected computer, accessible to me only.
- Deleting all audio files and transcription texts after they've been delivered to the researcher.
- Deleting all electronic files containing study-related documents from my computer hard drive and any backup devices.
- Not discussing the content of the interviews with anyone besides the research team.
- Acknowledging that I can be held legally liable for any breach in the confidentiality agreement.

I've never had legal trouble with a confidentiality agreement. But I'd caution transcriptionists to change the wording of an agreement to not delete the transcription texts until after getting paid for the work.

The level of confidentiality can seem like overkill in many projects. For example, health researchers affiliated with universities might have to follow a high degree of confidentiality because of their institutional review boards (see more about IRBs below). For example, the researchers might be studying how fitness trackers affect people's everyday habits. They might send me files with anonymized names or, more often, cryptic combinations of letters and numbers, such as TL00062. The steps and calories data will be ho hum to everybody outside of exercise scientists and behavioral researchers, but once you sign the confidentiality statement, you must adhere to the conditions. Bending confidentiality rules is a slippery slope.

Sometimes researchers might insist on some kind of encryption to maintain confidentiality. They might decide that one cloud-based system is safer than another for uploading and downloading information, or they might have faith in the security of their university-based file sharing system. It is the transcriptionist's duty to follow the instructions of the interviewers.

If the transcription involves medical details, you're dealing with an extra level of confidentiality and security. In the US, HIPAA, or the Health Insurance Portability and Accountability Act of 1996, protects people's personal health information and medical records. Researchers in other countries will face other restrictions. Freelance transcriptionists, you might encounter sensitive medical information if you're working for social scientists in health or behavior change research. In general, a few best practices for people working with health information include:

- Using a separate password-protected computer for work.
- Ensure that your wireless connection is encrypted.
- Don't send transcribed files or other patient details over instant messenger.
- Remove personally identifiable information from any files you store on your computer.
- Have up-to-date virus software.

Transcriptionists working with protected medical information need to know the fine points of laws applicable to the country where interviews take place, to make sure they stay in compliance.

It's rare for an oral history project to wind up in court, but it has happened. For example, in 2012, transcripts were at the center of the Boston College Belfast Project litigation. The British government demanded that Boston College turn over oral history transcripts from interviews about the violent conflict in Northern Ireland. Researchers had promised lifelong confidentiality to their narrators—a promise they ultimately couldn't keep. A federal appeals court ruled against them. When you're writing your consent forms and prepping narrators, keep in mind there is no academic privilege of confidentiality, especially if law enforcement gets involved.[11]

GDPR Legislation

In 2018, the General Data Protection Regulation (GDPR) came into effect. While the primary aim was to protect the online privacy of European Union citizens and decrease data breaches, the law has some complicated effects on oral history.

The GDPR applies to any group, individual or organization within the EU and the European Economic Area that collects personal data, including oral history projects. Researchers, whether voluntary or paid, are deemed "data collectors." Personal data is anything that lets people identify an individual. It refers to obvious things, such as name, address and phone number, and also such intangibles as their relationships with other people, their opinions, and the opinions of others about them. Fortunately for oral historians, GDPR Article 89 includes an exemption which allows them to retain personal data for "archiving purposes in the public interest," and for "scientific and historical research purposes." This means that requests to delete or amend archived interviews can be declined. However, narrators may withdraw previous consent for public online access to their interviews.

The GDPR brings up a lot of questions about, and changes to, consent. Notably, EU oral historians will now need to use two consent forms—one before the interview starts, "which includes information about the aims and objectives of the project, what personal data will be collected, where it will be stored, how it will be used, and how the interviewee can contact the project to access their data."[12] The second consent form, completed after the interview, covers copyright and access conditions.[13]

The British Library has deemed its usual consent forms sufficient to cover existing interviews already in the archive. But the status of online interviews is hazier. The GDPR also introduces "special category data," personal data about identifiable living individuals that might cause "substantial damage and distress" to people if released publicly.[14] Topics in this category include religion, philosophy, politics, sex, trade union activities, corporate or industry info, bad behavior, race, ethnicity, war, violence, colonial military activity, health, medicine and gossip—pretty much any interesting story an oral historian might want to record.

The Oral History Society (UK) gives this guidance on sensitive data:

> For new and on-going oral history projects all staff need to be made aware of the kinds of sensitive data that might exist in a typical interview and be encouraged to flag up any such occurrences. The original recording need not be changed in any way if it is only being archived and not accessed. But where any of these occurrences are deemed likely to cause 'substantial damage and distress', then those passages need to be embargoed and muted prior to any public access. The only exception to this would be where the identified third party could be contacted to approve public access. But this could be hugely time-consuming, impractical and is not recommended.[15]

Failure to comply with GDPR has stiff penalties. Organization can be fined up to £20 million—probably more than all the UK's oral history programs' operating budgets combined.[16]

The GDPR may affect other qualitative researchers differently than oral historians. For example, Lindsey Annable reflected on changes the GDPR might require for her UK-based market research firm. One notable aspect of the new regulation is the right to be forgotten, or RTBF for short. "Any respondent will have the right to ask for their data to be removed from the project at any point," Annable explained to me in an email:

> This presents complexities in the context of a group discussion where it will mean isolating and removing an individual's response. Quite how practical this will be if a particular participant has sparked off a new angle of discussion remains to be seen, i.e. would the topic have arisen if the participant hadn't been there? This also means speaker ID will be essential for transcriptions. Whilst this is something perfectly doable, it does add cost. It also requires far more effort on the side of the transcriber to identify correctly each individual voice particularly if they are only working with audio.[17]

Sensitive Materials

"Sensitive materials" is a subjective term. Depending on the people involved, some materials could prove sensitive to the researchers, the narrator, the transcriptionist and/or members of the general public. A couple of times oral historians have cautioned me that narrators use curse words or describe raunchy situations which their former transcriptionist found troubling. Of course, just like the trigger warnings employed by university professors, there's a long list of what different individuals will find sensitive, and you can't always guess ahead of time.

"Every now and again, we will reach out to someone to double check to make sure they're okay with us putting sensitive stuff online," said oral historian Jennifer Cramer. The collection she oversees at Louisiana State University includes a very raw set of oral histories collected from Vietnam vets in the 1970s, soon after they came back from war. I indexed this collection myself in the 1990s, and was struck by how upfront these young men had been. Most had not yet married, reproduced or embarked on a serious career path. "You can say, 'I shot up all this heroin and I went every day to get a hooker when I was in Vietnam.' Like you can't really libel yourself, right?" Cramer said. "That's not legally our problem. But maybe you said that when you were 17 and now you're 70." Since she can't contact everybody in the collection, she said, "We'll make efforts to put a summary up instead of the transcription. And just make it harder for people to get."[18]

Cramer has also experienced the opposite situation. LSU's Williams Center interviewed one closeted gay man in the 1990s who has since come out and become very well known. When the Williams Center started putting all their interviews online, Cramer contacted him. "In 1993, when he was interviewed, that was not a possibility. Like the idea of typing your name in and five seconds later being able to find all this intimate information about you." So Cramer asked if the narrator wanted to restrict certain portions of the interview available online. This is a considerate and compassionate thing to do, even if you're not legally compelled to do so.

Sometimes an oral historian might make the executive decision to restrict some information without asking the narrator. Jeff Corrigan censored one thing in his nine and a half years at the State Historical Society of Missouri. A narrator called an identifiable African-American person a derogatory word and made other negative statements about him. Corrigan worried about putting the transcripts online and the man's children or grandchildren stumbling upon it. "I would love for the world to know, if that's how the person wants the world to remember them, that they're a horribly racist bigot." But ultimately he chose to protect the descendants of the maligned man, and the historical society, as the statement was both foul and libelous.[19]

When John Sheehy was interviewing a former Reed College student for the school's oral history project, he learned why one noted professor had left so suddenly—he'd impregnated the woman Sheehy was interviewing. "Sometimes these memories would come up and they hadn't thought about them for 30, 40 years and they'd be really upset," he said. "I was there to talk about Reed history, not to go into somebody's deep personal history."[20] These are the kind of cases where transcripts may end up sealed or restricted.

Online Access to Interviews

The preceding sections on GDPR and sensitive materials both bring up questions of online access to interviews. This issue surfaces in many phases of the oral history process. Interviewers and narrators might find themselves self-censoring because they anticipate widespread access to their stories. Transcriptionists might flag sections of interviews as sensitive, if asked to do so by the project manager. Editors may question whether interviews could open them up to lawsuits. When reviewing transcripts, narrators may request that parts to be sealed or redacted. Even after a narrator's death, family members may contact institutions and ask for interviews to be taken offline.

"There is no question but that placing an oral history on the web is different from earlier forms of distribution, even published books," wrote oral historian Sherna Berger Gluck.

> Indeed, it is a quantum leap, and the resulting public scrutiny raises issues that we must still consider, regardless of the narrator's agreement and/or intent. In fact, consequences of both the personal and political implications of web distribution and the potential for unintended uses by others might even make us reconsider how we conduct our interviews.[21]

As oral historian Kelly Anderson summed up online access to oral histories, "The material no longer feels like an archival document with any kind of gatekeeper but rather a trove of personal information available to the masses."[22]

Many oral historians have experienced a narrator asking to have a transcript removed from easy online access. Elinor Mazé, retired from BUIOH, wrote about a narrator who decided more than a decade after the interview that she'd said things that might be hurtful to a family member and damage her career:

> But in those years, our Institute was still depositing bound volumes in the archive downstairs, accessible only by appointment with the archivist, and the world would know about an interview only by a very brief, bare-bones record in our university library's online catalog. Our agreement forms, however, did give us copyright to the material and made it explicit that we would make it publicly available. What caused her to reconsider her donation of her story to us, apparently, was the enlarging of context, both geographically and temporally, in which her interview was presented. She had discovered her interview more or less inadvertently in a Google search and realized her family members and her employer could easily do the same.[23]

So institutions must strike a balance between revisionism and being sensitive to narrators' feelings about what's online. This is a wider cultural issue than just oral history. For example, in my freelance writing, people I write about sometimes want to make changes to articles I write for websites after the fact. Sometimes this is legitimate, such as correcting an incorrect statistic. But sometimes one person at an organization told me one thing, but a higher-up doesn't like that wording and contacts my editor or me requesting a revision. Not only are revisions time-consuming, whether for an oral history archive or an online publication, but they can make the truth overly fluid. An interview captures what a person says and thinks at a specific time. Already, one person's version will be different than another who experienced the same event. But if each person provides multiple revised versions of the same event, truth gets squishier and squishier.

Mazé notes:

Some European archivists, for example, have reacted cautiously to popular moves to restrict access to some kinds of information, or to make it easier for those who wish to do so to delete information that they do not want made available. Revisionism can be, and certainly has been, a dangerous practice, in service to tyranny of many kinds. That individuals might, either of their own volition or under duress, be able to change their stories to serve repressive political ends, is a prospect that should give pause to historians as well as the archivists who care for the primary resources so indispensable to the best practices of their endeavor."[24]

Even seemingly innocuous things can be of interest to the right researcher. Mazé noted one interviewer and narrator who worked together to expurgate a passage that troubled the narrator after the interview, leaving the rest of the text intact and accessible. While the interviewer thought the part they cut out was unimportant, Mazé noticed that it closely echoed a passage in an unrelated interview by a different narrator:

> The pair of comments, separated as they were by time and immediate context, seemed to me to suggest a possibly fruitful line of inquiry into an aspect of the broader topic both of these interviewees were addressing—in both cases, the difficulties and challenges facing women who chose careers in the institutions of conservative, evangelical Christian religious groups.

She pointed out:

> Perhaps it was a connection of interest only to me, but are not such epiphanies concerning possible larger meaning and unexpected connection the essence of work in history? Is this not really why we collect interviews in the first place, as well as all the other primary sources we so treasure, and admire the work of those who bring fresh perspectives and insight to those sources? Relevance is always relative.[25]

Sometimes the solution is to keep oral histories intact in archives but not make everything available online. Oral historian Mary Larson wrote:

> If oral history is to survive as a meaningful and scholarly endeavor, there still must be room in the profession for controversial or sensitive interviews that would never become part of the archival record if widespread dissemination were a part of the plan. There are also heritage collections in repositories around the world that have unclear legal rights, or thoughtful archives that are concerned for other reasons about their ethical rights to put materials online, but most have still found ways to make their materials discoverable and available.[26]

One way to do this is to take an exhibit versus a repository approach online. A center could present excerpts of interviews online, while sensitive parts could be reserved for serious researchers rather than casual internet surfers.

Institutional Review Boards

I first became aware of IRBs and how they affected social scientists differently from oral historians in 2005 when I was reviewing a book for the *Oral History Review*. My editor asked me to find out where the interviews were housed. I tracked down the author, who told me she'd destroyed the recordings. While the book was interview-based, the author was a social scientist, not an oral historian. I was shocked to learn this is fairly standard practice.

Nowadays, I transcribe for social scientists nearly as often as I do oral historians, but the two groups are almost opposite in their aims. Oral historians usually chronicle an individual's life, diligently checking back with the narrator afterwards to make sure everything is correct, editing and archiving the interview under the individual's name, and preserving and migrating recordings in climate-controlled archives. Social scientists usually collect anonymized interviews, analyze and draw conclusions from the interviews in aggregate, then destroy all the recordings. This drawing of conclusions is what IRBs consider *generalizable knowledge,* and it's what usually separates projects that need IRB approval from those that are exempt.

What's called an institutional review board in the US is called a research ethics committee in Canada. Many countries, including Japan and Australia, follow similar models. In Europe, ethics committees work regionally, reviewing research done in certain geographic areas. As a department of the National Archives of Singapore, the Oral History Centre is accountable to the Ministry of Communications and Information and the National Library Board, and receives guidance from the National Archives Advisory Committee, which is composed of academics and professionals, including historians and legal officers.[27] We don't have the space or need to go into each in detail, but transcriptionists should be aware of protocols, and project managers will need a nuanced understanding of whichever version operates in their country.[28]

In the US, institutional review boards were originally intended to protect subjects of biomedical and behavioral research, and apply to any research that receives support from the US government. Their reach has expanded beyond scientific research. As oral historian Linda Shopes explains, "Increasingly throughout the 1990s and early 2000s, researchers affiliated with colleges and universities have been required to submit protocols for oral history interviewing projects to their campus Institutional Review Board (IRB) prior to conducting any interviews." IRBs claimed authority over oral history because their regulations included interaction with human subjects as one of the research modes subject to review, Shopes said.

> Interviewers have been asked to submit detailed questionnaires in advance of an interview; to maintain narrator anonymity, despite an interviewee's

willingness to be identified; and to destroy tapes and transcripts after the research project is completed. Clearly these practices violate fundamental principles of oral history.[29]

The official OHA position on IRBs is that oral history be explicitly excluded from review by institutional review boards (IRBs), since oral history already has its own code of ethics, including the principle of informed consent.[30]

Sarah Milligan surveyed other institutions when working with Oklahoma State University's IRB Board on its oral history regulations. She found that many IRBs had cut and pasted the same confusing language when setting their policies, using examples of oral histories of Holocaust survivors and Negro League baseball players being excerpted for museum exhibits or archived, respectively. In an online search, I found a couple dozen universities using the same exact language. "So it's arbitrary," said Milligan.

> I mean, you can interview a Holocaust survivor as long as you're going to let their conclusions stand for themselves in an exhibit feature? Great. But you can't interview a Negro baseball player if you're going to deposit it in an archives, but you could if you were going to deposit it in a museum.

Because of the work involved in going through the IRB process, many people are discouraged from depositing their work in an archive. This frustrates oral historians, who aim to preserve interviews and make them accessible, and directly contradicts OHA's best practices of depositing interviews in a repository with an infrastructure for long-term preservation and discovery.

At the beginning of an oral history project, researchers might not know where it's going to lead, so it's difficult to determine whether going through the IRB approval process is necessary. Milligan counsels students embarking on research to check in with their IRB if they're unsure.[31]

American oral historians have been trying to get a blanket exemption from IRB approval for many years. But at the time of writing, an expected exemption at the national level from the Office for Human Research Protections has been delayed.

All this background is more than the contract transcriptionist needs to know, but explains why the protocols may differ between projects. However, if you're overseeing transcription in-house, you'll need to know more about compliance with whatever ethics committee rules your university. At Oklahoma State University, Milligan said, the Oklahoma Oral History Research Program's IRB protocol, like that of many academic oral history programs, states they'll interview, transcribe, edit and allow the narrator a review and comment period of the interviews before providing public access:

> If we do, for example, 100 interviews a year, we cannot keep up. We can transcribe them, but we can't edit them, right? And get them back and get approval within a year. We're running on about a year and a half from the

time we do an interview to the time it goes out. Which is frustrating if you're working with communities or classrooms because they may actually want to use that material in the project they're trying to work on with a more immediate timeline. So it causes problems in some instances.

If your IRB protocol calls for transcription, you can't just substitute a quicker and more cost-effective index.

Qualitative researchers should be sure to write consent forms broadly. As the University of Wisconsin *IRB Insider* newsletter pointed out:

> The IRB has had a flood of student researchers who have realized part way through the study that they need to employ a professional transcription service to aid in transcribing audio files. Again, if consent forms are written very narrowly (e.g., "Only the PI and student researcher will *ever* access the audio file.") then submitting a Change of Protocol to add a transcription service will be problematic, resulting in the need to revise the consent form and, possibly, to reconsent previous participants.
>
> Examples of appropriately broad consent form text:
> "Data may be shared with other collaborators for future research purposes."
> 'Audio recordings will be transcribed by approved personnel."[32]

Liability Insurance

In my many years of transcribing for major institutions, I've filled out an array of paperwork and signed many types of forms. The worst mistake I ever made form-wise was signing something with a liability insurance clause. I've only run across this once, but will include it briefly in case any other transcribers encounter a similar contract, or if you're a project manager preparing the contract yourself and subject to bureaucratic pressures.

I had agreed to transcribe a project for a state historical society. They sent me a 15-page contract written by the state attorney. By the seventh page my eyes had glazed over—which is not an excuse that will stand up in court—and I somehow missed the part requiring me to take out a policy for one million dollars in liability insurance. In retrospect I think this contract was used by the state for people in many capacities, most of which were likelier to do a million dollars' worth of damage. Anyway, I signed it. And then realized I had to get this million-dollar insurance policy. I consoled myself that the historical society had agreed to give me a certain amount of work that promised job security for the next several months, even though paying for the insurance policy meant I'd wind up with a pay cut. Unfortunately, I later realized that "guarantee" of work was a note in the email, and wasn't written into the contract. So I wound up shelling out about five hundred dollars for a useless policy, then getting less work than promised. Ouch.

A year or so later, the same historical society asked me to do more work on this project. It was an interesting set of interviews on women's history, so I wanted to continue. I told them I needed to raise my rates significantly to cover renewing my million-dollar insurance policy. Miraculously, the society decided that clause could be removed from the new contract.

Moral of the story? Obviously, read the contract. But beyond that, negotiate. I was younger at the time, and intimidated by this mountainous state contract. If I'd had more patience and confidence, I would have read the contract more closely, noticed the million-dollar policy, and attempted to negotiate my way out of it in the first place. Also, I could have asked them to guarantee a minimum amount of work in the contract.

Bottom Line

Transcriptionists only need a passing knowledge of the issues covered in this chapter. But project managers and one-person oral history operations should familiarize themselves with any relevant protocols and regulations.

Though lawsuits involving oral history are uncommon, it's important to review a transcript with an eye toward defamation. If you find passages that reek of libel, fact check to see if they're true, or find a way to edit them out while leaving the interview as true to the historical record as possible. Sealing or restricting interviews is a last resort but may be necessary in some cases.

Regulations such as the GDPR and IRBs are frustrating and tedious to try to understand. But if you fall under their jurisdictions, protect yourself by taking the time to learn how they apply to your project.

Online access has drastically changed how researchers and even casual web surfers encounter oral history interviews. Intimate information about our neighbors, employees, bosses and families are just a click away. This rapid change will probably continue, forcing everybody in the oral history world to keep on top of new regulatory developments.

Useful Documents

Confidentiality form in Appendix 7.

Notes

1 John Neuenschwander, *A Guide to Oral History and the Law* (Oxford: Oxford University Press, 2014), p. 47.
2 Ibid., p. 48.
3 Ibid., p. 50.
4 Ibid., p. 40.
5 Ibid., p. 44.
6 Jennifer Cramer. interview with Teresa Bergen, January 23, 2018.
7 Neuenschwander, *A Guide to Oral History and the Law*, p. 50.
8 Ibid., p. 50.
9 Cramer interview, January 23, 2018.
10 Heather Bidzinski, email correspondence with Teresa Bergen, July 24, 2018.

11 Scott Jaschik, "Confidentiality Right Rejected," *Inside Higher Ed*, July 9, 2012, available at: www.insidehighered.com/news/2012/07/09/appeals-court-rejects-researchers-bid-protect-oral-history-confidentiality (accessed February 12, 2019).

12 Oral History Society, "Data Protection for Oral Historians and Organisations Holding Oral History Interviews," available at: www.ohs.org.uk/advice/data-protection/ (accessed May 26, 2018).

13 Ibid.

14 Ibid.

15 Ibid.

16 GDPR FAQs, available at: www.eugdpr.org/gdpr-faqs.html (accessed May 26, 2018).

17 Lindsey Annable, email correspondence with Teresa Bergen, December 8, 2017.

18 Cramer interview, January 23, 2018.

19 Jeff Corrigan, interview with Teresa Bergen, December 18, 2017.

20 John Sheehy, interview with Teresa Bergen, June 20, 2018.

21 Sherna Berger Gluck, "Refocusing on Orality/Aurality in the Digital Age," in D.A. Boyd and M. Larsen (eds.), *Oral History and Digital Humanities* (Basingstoke: Palgrave/Macmillan, 2014), p. 43.

22 Ibid.

23 Elinor Mazé, "Deconstruction Without Destruction," in D.A. Boyd and M. Larsen (eds.), *Oral History and Digital Humanities* (Basingstoke: Palgrave/Macmillan, 2014), p. 150.

24 Ibid., pp. 153–154.

25 Ibid., pp. 150–151.

26 Mary Larson, "We All Begin with a Story," in D.A. Boyd and M. Larsen (eds.), *Oral History and Digital Humanities* (Basingstoke: Palgrave/Macmillan, 2014), p. 162.

27 Mark Wong, email correspondence with Teresa Bergen, August 24, 2018.

28 Joseph Millum, "Canada's New Ethical Guidelines for Research with Humans: A Critique and Comparison with the United States," *Canada Medical Association Journal*, 184(6) (2012): 657–661, available at: www.ncbi.nlm.nih.gov/pmc/articles/PMC3314036/ (accessed August 15, 2018).

29 Linda Shopes, "Legal and Ethical Issues in Oral History," in T.L. Charlton, L.E. Myers and R. Sharpless (eds.), *Handbook of Oral History* (Lanham, MD: Altamira Press, 2006), p. 149.

30 Information about IRBs, Oral History Association, available at: www.oralhistory.org/information-about-irbs/ (accessed November 13, 2018).

31 Sarah Milligan, interview with Teresa Bergen, May 11, 2018.

32 *IRB Insider*, University of Wisconsin Knowledge Base, available at: https://kb.wisc.edu/sbsedirbs/63136 (accessed July 22, 2018).

9

THE HUMAN SIDE OF TRANSCRIPTION

Most of our discussion of transcription so far has been about the equipment, software, protocols, style guides and other practical aspects of the work. However, it's important for everybody on the project team to remember that the transcriptionist is not an extension of her keyboard; she's a human being. In this chapter we'll delve into how transcribing interviews affects the transcriptionist on emotional and physical levels. We'll cover:

- Secondary trauma
- Self-care for the transcriptionist
- Work/life balance and the home office
- Differing abilities
- Transcriptionist/narrator relationship
- Transcriptionist/oral historian or project relationship

Secondary Trauma

If a stranger has ever told you a sad story and you either cried or felt like crying, you won't be surprised by the results of the scientific studies I'm about to mention. You may even wonder why they needed to be conducted. Of course, researchers study just about everything, including the effects of undertaking qualitative research on the researcher. An Australian grounded theory analysis of 30 public health researchers looked at how they dealt with the emotions stirred up by their work:

> While being empathetic, it is often difficult not to get drawn into the emotion, especially when face-to-face with another person who is experiencing emotion. Some researchers do not attempt to hold back, or manage their emotions during the interview, instead preferring to become part of the

experience themselves. Many reported occasions when they were emotionally overwhelmed during the research, stating that this was often directly attributable to the participants becoming emotional.[1]

The study went on to conclude that researchers working with particularly traumatic material may be subject to vicarious traumatization. This concept has been applied to counselors and therapists, but may be equally valid for other human service workers, including qualitative researchers

You don't need to be face-to-face to experience strong emotions in a qualitative interview. One could even argue that it's easier to be face-to-face with somebody telling a sad story than to be all alone listening to the raw recording. The researcher may be upset by the interview in person, and may even cry along with the narrator. But moments of connection with the narrator can be cathartic or bonding. The transcriptionist, on the other hand, feels these same feelings while all alone, unseen, unknown by the narrator, and possibly bound by a confidentiality agreement to not discuss the interview contents.

So I was excited to come across a tiny body of work—more like a little toe than a whole body—exploring the effects on the transcriptionist of transcribing difficult materials.

In the abstract of a 1997 article "Beyond Textual Perfection: Transcribers as Vulnerable Persons," the researchers state, "Primarily women, transcribers are essentially invisible persons, paid to serve as nameless, faceless technicians even though they participate in a transformative auditory experience."[2]

A more recent article by UK researchers Nikki Kiyimba and Michelle O'Reilly builds on this idea, examining four key issues concerning transcriptionists and the research process:

- Transcriptionists tend to be invisible workers.
- Listening to data may emotionally impact transcriptionists.
- Transcriptionists may be limited in access to appropriate support.
- Limited formal attention is given to this group.[3]

The article states:

Transcription has often been viewed as a mundane task ... and one with little status .... For this reason it has typically been assumed that transcriptionists are unaffected by the process ... This may be the reason why very little research has been conducted on the impact of listening to qualitative data on transcriptionists. The transcriptionist, however, is a human being, not simply an extension of the recording equipment, and transcriptionist safety is important and should not be overlooked.

I especially like (1) that the writers feel the need to clarify that transcriptionists are human; and (2) that they to attribute this observation to an official source.

Furthermore, "We argue that the process of translating auditory files into written text inevitably influences the human conduit that is not immune to thoughts, feelings, memories, and reactions to this auditory stimulus." Yes, it's true. We human conduits think, feel, and react to the interviews we hear and transcribe. They make the less obvious point that *hearing* an interview is more intense than *reading* a transcript.

Table 9.1 summarizes some of their findings:[4]

TABLE 9.1 Emotional distress and impact on the transcriptionist

Category	Description	Selected examples of quotations
Being affected	Transcriptionists talked about the effects that repeated listening to the participants' narratives had on them	That has affected me You couldn't help being affected by it It had quite an impact on me It does play on your mind quite a lot It's very upsetting
Being emotional	Transcriptionists talked about the emotions that they felt during the transcription process	I've heard things that have been upsetting I did actually feel quite moved that she was suffering
Being worried	Transcriptionists expressed some concern for the participants whose voices they were hearing and reported being worried about them	They were upset, yes, it was them that were upset and I was worried I do worry about people, I've had some nightmares I was sufficiently concerned about what she said
Being stressed	Transcriptionists reported feeling stressed on occasion by the transcription process	It's stressful You could end up having a mental breakdown
Being shocked	Transcriptionists reported that there were occasions whereby they felt shocked by things they were hearing	Some things were quite shocking It surprises me a lot of the time You do hear things that are a bit astonishing
Being tired	Transcriptionists reported some of the physical pressures they experienced by their job	It's quite tiring transcribing
Being angry	Transcriptionists reported feeling annoyed or angry with some of the content they were hearing on the recording	Slightly grating, slightly jarring I feel slightly annoyed It does stir up some rage in me

I have often laughed out loud at stories narrators told, and cried from sadness or just being moved by a poignant memory. Most interviews that I transcribe are within a usual range of emotion that's not difficult to deal with. But every once in a while, I've had an interview that really threw me. The most memorable was listening to a long interview where a woman described the experience her sister had with a male partner who turned abusive and stalked her when she tried to break up. I had a few of those judgmental feelings uninformed people often have about stalkers, like, why didn't she try harder to leave him? And I also missed the obvious—why was her sister telling the story? Why didn't this abused woman speak up for herself? It hit me hard when I finally learned that the woman couldn't tell her own story because, after a long terror campaign, her stalker ultimately killed her. Her surviving sister wanted to ensure her sister's story wouldn't be completely forgotten and maybe people—at least one ignorant transcriptionist, for sure—could learn from it. Hearing this extremely personal, detailed story in the voice of somebody who lost her sister in such a horrible way had me bawling. Ten years later, writing this still brings tears and some of the feeling back. This is the kind of thing the researchers are talking about when they mention vicarious traumatization or secondary traumatic stress.

I've also worked with a series of interviews about US intelligence agents who participated in black ops—secret, illegal military operations that the government denies ordering. Some were so horrific that the agents had moral turning points that rearranged their minds and in some cases made them drop out of society. For example, kidnapping Brazilian street kids and transporting them to bomb-testing sites to see how the explosions would affect them. Also, many stories of torture and pushing people out of helicopters. A daily dose of this sort of thing leads to nightmares, an ugly perspective on the world, and/or desensitization.

Transcriptionist Barb Jardee had a jarring experience working with materials from a cult:

> I worked on a project, previewing about 65 hours of recordings made by a nutcase religious leader whose followers committed suicide at his urging. I sampled snippets of each recording, making extensive notes of what I'd heard. The client had me transcribe about five hours' worth, and that was all. It was heartbreaking to listen to the recording made by a couple of kids who had found the tape recorder left unattended. They were just goofing around, singing a few popular songs. They said nothing that I would consider valuable in trying to learn more about this group. Broke my heart to realize that those kids didn't survive to see their teen years. Made me value the kids in my life even more. I hug them now every chance I get.[5]

Kim Etherington, a professor and psychotherapist in the UK, details her research involving a transcriptionist in her article "Working with Traumatic Stories: From Transcriber to Witness." Etherington herself experienced vicarious traumatization while transcribing her interviews on sexual abuse while working on her PhD in the early 1990s. So she realized that her more recent work on the desperate lives of drug addicts was affecting the woman she'd hired to transcribe her interviews. She decided to record some interviews with "Annie," the pseudonym she gave her transcriptionist, to understand how the audio affected her.[6]

Listening to the intense experiences of addiction changed Annie. She was unable to get some images of one narrator out of her head:

> I had a picture of her being a very helpless person, prone, because she said he kicked her and he jumped on her stomach, and I just had visions of this poor drug-addled woman who ... was half not aware of what was happening, but very much aware of the fact that she was pregnant, that there was a life in there, and this man just kicking her and jumping on her stomach and I just kept thinking, God that's absolutely dreadful. How did she survive? How did the baby survive?

Annie summed up her transcription experience as, "It's like watching a particularly horrifying film that you weren't prepared for, and the thing staying with you afterwards."

On the other hand, Annie was thrilled and astonished when the narrator's story had a happy ending:

> And for her to have dragged herself out of that when her self-esteem was so low, after having a violent partner and all the drug abuse and everything, I don't know where she found the willpower to do that because I'm not sure I could, and by the time I finished I was almost standing on my chair clapping, you know?

Etherington concluded that while Annie was not yet vicariously traumatized, she was heading in that direction. She realized that instead of just delivering audio to Annie and receiving a finished transcript, Annie would benefit from briefing in advance about the interview content, and a chance to debrief afterwards.

Collecting the voices of people who have been through harrowing times is important work, as is transcribing these voices. The transcriptionist is left with both nightmares and benefits. Jardee values her children more. Annie and I have more compassion for people whose lives spiral out of control from drugs, domestic violence and bad fortune. I would not trade my transcription experience. To outsiders, it looks like I'm sitting in a chair, typing, doing grunt work that researchers don't want to do themselves. To me, I'm slipping into other people's skins, living a thousand lives, with the traumas and triumphs therein.

The secondary stress on transcriptionists study found:

> Transcriptionists' accounts included descriptions about their lack of control and feeling of helplessness to help either the individuals on the recording or the researchers in what they regarded as worrying situations. This seemed to indicate that although transcriptionists were perceived to be on the periphery of the research process, in reality they were affected by the emotional content of the data. The lack of attention paid to the role of the transcriptionists means that they remain marginalised not only from the products of their work, but

also there is little recognition of the emotional labour associated with their productivity.[7]

Helplessness was a recurrent theme, as was a sense of personal engagement with these unknown voices on the audio. "When listening to concerning narratives, transcriptionists expressed feeling trapped between a natural emotional response of worry and the real constraints of participant anonymity and physical distance."[8]

So what's a transcriptionist to do? If you're transcribing your own research, you'll need to find self-care methods to avoid secondary trauma. But at least you know exactly what you're getting into. If you're a contract transcriptionist like me, and you get an email from somebody asking if you want to work on their project, you might want to get more information. Researchers often ask me to work on projects without telling me a thing about the content, as though what I agree to spend 100 hours listening to would make no difference. A simple inquiry could save you some grief, such as answering an email with, "I'm interested in working with you. Could you tell me a little bit more about your research?" This is especially important if you have hot button topics in your own life. For example, if you're a survivor of sexual abuse you may not want to spend your workdays reliving your trauma by listening to a series of interviews on the same topic. Because transcribing is like living in somebody else's head. The narrator's voice is going through headphones and directly into your brain, where it can trigger memories and nightmares. We truly are human conduits. Even if you grow desensitized, it's still burrowing into your subconscious.

Even if the material is not traumatic, individuals find certain topics difficult. Transcriber Susan Nicholls, who works for the British Library, told me, "The most difficult subject matter I can recall was a surgeon describing a complicated operation in very graphic detail. I'm quite squeamish when it comes to medical matters."[9] As somebody who is squeamish about eyes, I can relate to that. I once stumbled into an ophthalmology project.

In some cases, transcriptionists may decide doing a project is worth the possible trauma. Author and transcriptionist Phuoc Tran told me:

> I have a mixed feeling when interviewing boat people. I am a boat person myself and these are memories of days gone by which I don't want to relive again, I don't and will not refresh these thoughts again. But on another hand I am eager to preserve our history by sharing my sea journey in search for freedom whenever I have the opportunity, and to read and transcribe other refugees' haunted memories. By all means, one should have the guts and the courage to share his/her hardship, his/her stories and pass them on to the younger generations and the mainstream.[10]

Transcription can also inspire new ideas, expand your perspective, increase your empathy for other humans and take you in unforeseen directions. Transcribing a project about unwed mothers who gave up their babies for adoption enhanced

Lois Glewwe's perception of her own childhood—because she had known those babies personally.

> My parents took in foster children when I was young. So we had over 37 kids over the time that I was growing up, and most of them were babies who were born to unwed mothers. And I never saw it from the other side. I only saw it from the babies'.[11]

Transcription is kind of like food – what you listen to intently becomes part of you, and you'll absorb that energy. Instead of the old saying, "You are what you eat," for transcriptionists, it's "You are what you hear."

Self-Care for the Transcriptionist

Every job has its occupational hazards. for transcriptionists, these include:

- isolation;
- detrimental health effects of a sedentary lifestyle;
- repetitive strain and carpal tunnel risk;
- listening fatigue;
- emotional distress from listening to traumatic interviews;
- failing to ever change out of pajamas or sweat pants.

To have a balanced life, transcriptionists need to counteract these hazards. I'm guessing that most people who devote themselves to transcription are at least a tad introverted, or they wouldn't be able to endure the many hours of solitude required by the job. But even introverts need some interaction, whether that be time with family, friends, a partner, club, church, sports team, or other type of community.

Transcriptionist Sue Shackles recommends finding support online:

> It can sometimes feel as though you're the only person in the world who's sitting there banging keys and struggling through difficult accents. Forums help you to become part of a wider transcription community and realize that we all have days where we'd rather watch paint dry than transcribe one…more… focus…group! Sometimes just venting your frustration to people who really get it – unlike our families – can be enough to help you get over the tough parts.[12]

Barb Jardee keeps a notebook of her letters of recommendation, notes of appreciation, cartoons depicting transcription or recording, and magazine and journal articles on how to do oral history. "On my down days when I have no work on my desk, I like to leaf through that notebook and read what people have said about my work. That generally perks me up." This is a good idea for breaking the isolation and feeling more connected. Stepping back and acknowledging that we are doing our part to preserve history and make it accessible to scholars reminds me of the meaning in what can feel like very humble work.

Before I met my husband, I lived with just my cat for a few years. Although my cat was excellent company, I made sure to schedule some lunches with friends, exercise classes, and to participate in organizations to offset the time alone. This ties in with the occupational hazard of deteriorating fashion sense, i.e., never changing out of bath-robes or loungewear. This may seem like a silly problem, but I find it psychologically demoralizing when I fail to get dressed just because I'm spending much of the day at home. I associate the all-day pajama look with sickness, depression and slovenliness.

Too much transcription can have severe physical effects, especially if you don't have an ergonomic setup. Any desk job leads to too much sedentary time. According to the Mayo Clinic website:

> Research has linked sitting for long periods of time with a number of health concerns. They include obesity and a cluster of conditions—increased blood pressure, high blood sugar, excess body fat around the waist and abnormal cholesterol levels—that make up metabolic syndrome. Too much sitting overall and prolonged periods of sitting also seem to increase the risk of death from cardiovascular disease and cancer.[13]

If you use a foot pedal, your position will be even more limited. Add in the con-stant small finger and wrist movements of transcription and you have a recipe for carpal tunnel or repetitive strain. A few things that will offset these physical pro-blems include:

- frequent breaks to stand up and stretch;
- yoga;
- walking around the block every hour or two or doing anything outdoors;
- cardiovascular exercise, such as running, brisk walking, hiking, biking, swim-ming, etc.;
- using a standing desk;
- massage.

I like to start my day with a little yoga stretching, then take a break around noon to go to spinning or boot camp class, or take a run. Then, after lunch, I'm ready to sit down again. My dog comes into my home office and stares at me every few hours to remind me to take a walk. Transcriptionist Barb Jardee also relies on prompts from pets:

> I find the best way to avoid physical problems from transcribing is to have a pet that needs/wants to go in or outdoors often. Getting up and moving around every 45–60 minutes has been very helpful—even if it does sometimes break my concentration.[14]

Susan Nicholls said yoga classes help her avoid physical complications from transcription.[15]

Susan Hutton bought an ergonomic keyboard after developing arm pains from transcription. "Relief was felt immediately, and the pains haven't returned," she said. She also credits an ergonomic chair with helping her escape back issues associated with keyboard work.[16]

Changing positions also helps. I have both a desktop and laptop computer. I like to switch between sitting at my desk, the couch, the bed and the patio. Barb Jardee prefers typing with her laptop in her lap, which she said has helped stave off carpal tunnel syndrome so far.

Listening fatigue is a transcription side effect I wouldn't have anticipated. I get cranky when I have to strain to hear, whether it's somebody talking to me, an announcement on an intercom or the TV not turned up loud enough. It's like my ears equate intense listening with earning my living, and are annoyed if they have to work so hard for nothing.

Jardee worries that spending so many years with earbuds inserted in her ears has had a detrimental effect on her hearing. She's also had concerns about her eyes. "Long before I started freelancing, I applied for a transcription job with the local sheriff's office," she said. "I went through a lot of paperwork and an interview, then we got to the typing test. They were still using black screens with green lettering. I knew that would ruin my eyes, so I just said no thank you and walked out." To live a healthy life, everybody needs to know when to prioritize their body over a job. But this is especially true of freelancers, who lack the workplace protections of employees and may feel financially driven to take every scrap of work that comes their way.

Work/Life Balance and the Home Office

Disclaimer: I am not an expert on this, as I tend to work long and erratic hours. My husband works swing shift and has two weekdays off, the dog and cat need refereeing and the house is small. Thank goodness I have a home office with a door that closes, but sometimes that doesn't seem enough. I need locks, barricades and blackout shades so nobody can try to talk to me through the window from the backyard.

Every person who works from a home office—not just transcriptionists—faces some version of this. Kids are loud, dogs bark, spouses are underfoot. Even if you live alone, there's a strong temptation to multitask with household chores, like putting a load of laundry in while transcribing. And there will still be interruptions from postal deliveries or random people with clipboards knocking on the door.

Transcriber Sue Shackles is admirably disciplined about her work, staying in her home office during her set working hours and only taking planned breaks:

> To me, there's no difference between going out of the house to work, and going to work in the office. I wouldn't be doing laundry, or cleaning house,

or watching TV if I were working outside of the home, so for me, the same rules apply. My family knows that if they call me during the day, their calls will go straight to voicemail, and I'll call them back when I have the time. This is my job. It's not my hobby.[17]

She confines work to her home office, rather than transcribing at the kitchen table, to draw a clear boundary between work and personal life.

Freelancers may face the problem of not knowing when to say no, especially if they experience some lean months of work. There's always more to be done, whether it's working on a current transcription job, trying to solicit new business or improving your skills. But there's more to life than screens and typing. Taking breaks—whether for an hour or an occasional week—provides a crucial change of pace for mind and body.

"As a freelancer, I get to work half days—and I can decide which 12 hours that is!" Jardee said:

Seriously, I like being able to do other activities in the middle of the day, but that also means I may be working late at night sometimes. I do only answer clients' phone calls and e-mails during office hours (8–5), figuring if I'm working nights and weekends, it's because I have something that needs to get done, and I don't need interruptions (except from the pets, as mentioned above). I absolutely refuse to work on Sundays—I need at least one day away from work to rest and recharge.

Differing Abilities

One common estimate is that it takes the average researcher up to eight hours to transcribe one hour of audio. Professional transcriptionists are faster than this. But people with physical disabilities can be much slower. Public history graduate student Grant Stoner wrote a post for the Oral History Association blog on his struggles with transcription. Since he was diagnosed with Spinal Muscular Atrophy Type II when only 13 months old, his entire academic career has featured such high-tech innovations as an electric wheelchair and speech-to-text programs, and low-tech assistance like help from friends.

Stoner tried using Dragon NaturallySpeaking speech-to-text software:

After all, I had read that voice recognition programs, while not entirely successful, were accurate enough to create a decent transcription. With my professor agreeing to my plan, I borrowed the appropriate equipment, and set out to create a modified transcription. After returning home, I simply activated the software, positioned the microphone toward my speakers, and turned on the recording.

This is the result:

"All 616 so first question what do you dislike and the individual the only Mount Washington my father would it is so applied to it quite a while will but I really want to stay home and precinct on was the campus like very welcoming verys the student union with just a cross place that was really nice the ball all that was your starting to have been possible names that this that was a witness agreed by non-as far as I think that was it wasn't so much the buildings and everything is it was the intellectual."

Despite a lifetime of workarounds, transcription flummoxed him. "Within an hour, the software was only capable of producing 99 words, none of which formed a cohesive sentence. My plan had spectacularly failed."

After an additional attempt to train the software to differentiate between two voices, Stoner's professor intervened and found another student to transcribe the interview.

I do not write this post to complain about my transcription woes, but rather to comment on this aspect of inaccessibility within the oral history field. Oral historians who require assistive technology need to be aware of the pitfalls of voice recognition transcription. Speech-to-text may seem like a panacea to the obstacle of transcription, but it is far from perfect, and will not solve the issue of transcription for those of us with accessibility needs.

For now, Stoner and other oral historians with similar disabilities need to out-source transcription to another student, researcher or professional. "I am hopeful that my university continues to invite me to conduct more oral history interviews; I just won't be the one to transcribe them."[18]

Transcriber/Narrator Relationship

Unless the interviewer transcribes her own interviews, there is generally no rela-tionship between the transcriptionist and the narrator. Once I transcribed an interview where the narrator was a friend's mother who happened to be part of a project I worked on. And I may also have met, in passing, a few narrators at an exhibition based on a project they were part of. But usually the only relationship between the transcriptionist and the narrator is in the transcriptionist's head.

This makes for a strange non-relationship between the narrator and the tran-scriber. The transcriptionist may spend many hours with a narrator's voice deep in her ear canals, the words burrowing into her brain. There's an intimate feel to being alone with somebody's voice literally in my head, since my earbuds are shoved inside my ears. As I transcribe I have grown so fond of some narrators that I feel like I know them. I've found myself reflecting on their wisdom, wanting to tell them my own stories, and sometimes arguing with them in my head. Once or twice I've had a strong urge to email them. (Of course I didn't; I am a profes-sional.) Some interviewers seem dear, some I deem ignorant, bigoted or conceited. All this judging, agreeing, disagreeing, considering their point of view, and most don't even know I exist. And I don't just mean me personally—many probably assume that the interviewer will do the transcription, if they think about it at all. Interviewers often say, "When I transcribe this," making the transcriptionist even more invisible. It's a strange role to fill, like the unheard ghost in the room that says, "Hey, you want to know what I think?" while the interviewer and narrator continue chatting. This is not a job for somebody who needs a lot of attention.

In my research on the subject, I came across one article that explored the narrator/transcriptionist relationship in a surprising way, as discussed above in the section on "Secondary Trauma." When professor and psychotherapist Kim Etherington was researching her paper "Working with Traumatic Stories: From Transcriber to Witness," she recorded her transcriber's reactions to listening to the story of a woman suffering from drug addiction. The transcriber was moved and impressed by what the narrator had gone through, and that the narrator eventually changed her ways and left the drugs behind. Etherington suspected it might prove therapeutic for the narrator to hear the transcriptionist's reactions to the interview. Once this was cleared by all parties, Etherington played the recording for the narrator. This exercise turned out well—the transcriber got the chance to share her feelings and the narrator was gratified that telling her harrowing story had helped at least one person better understand addiction.[19] But this is a highly unusual situation, and would not be generally useful or appropriate.

Transcriber/Oral Historian or Project Relationship

Relationships between transcriptionists and oral history projects vary widely. For many years, I've attended the annual meeting of the Oral History Association. By serving on committees, attending sessions, reviewing books and media for the *Oral History Review* and networking with oral history professionals, I've attempted to position myself as someone who is intelligent and knowledgeable about oral history, not a mere typing automaton. This has resulted in close friendships with oral historians. But I also transcribe for people who have heard of me by word of mouth, whom I never meet in person.

Some people value personal connections between oral historian and transcriptionist, while others are neutral. Transcriptionist Lois Glewwe said she enjoys her work more when she knows the people she's working with.[20] Several times I've been excited to meet oral historians in person at a history conference after working with them only through email. Some return my enthusiasm. But I've also been met with a confused look as to why I bothered to seek them out.

Documentary filmmaker Victoria Greene prefers feeling a connection with people on her project, whether they're transcribing interviews or wielding a camera:

> Because if you're interested and invested in a project, and you have a relationship, well, it's going to usually generate more success. To me, when you have relationships with the individuals that work on the project with you, it

generally is more harmonious and everybody works harder and does a better job.[21]

Transcriptionist Barb Jardee counts oral historians among her friends, but is mostly neutral about having personal relationships with her clients:

> I've been working for some folks for over 20 years, and we've never met face-to-face. I'm often surprised when I see them on a documentary, or in Facebook photos, and they don't look anything like I have imagined them from their voices. I do work for some folks in town, or certainly within easy driving distance, but I discourage in-person meetings. If my fingers aren't on the keyboard, transcribing, I'm not earning any money. Blunt, but true.[22]

I don't think it makes any difference to the quality of my work whether I know people involved with a project, but I enjoy the team feeling I occasionally get. The secondary stress study mentioned above found that transcriptionists occupy a space on the periphery. "They all expressed views regarding the 'invisibility' of their role in the process, and they saw themselves as relatively marginal to the research team." That study urged researchers to consider transcriptionists a more integral part of the research team, and to offer them both briefing and debriefing opportunities.[23]

While that study focused on transcriptionists' unmet emotional needs, researchers have an additional impetus for involving transcriptionists. Often we're the people who listen to the interviews more deeply than anybody else. We're certainly listening more closely than the interviewer, at least while they're conducting the interview, who is often half-focused on choosing a follow-up question. It always floors me how researchers don't make better use of transcriptionists. While transcribing, I could easily highlight coherent sound bites for their museum listening station, or note down topic areas for a book they're writing. This time-saving help is very affordable—the price could be the simple flattery of treating a transcriptionist as an intelligent human rather than a machine.

As for debriefing, in my 20 years of transcription, I can only remember this happening a couple of times. When I worked on the CIA covert operations project, I had many conversations about the material with the oral historian collecting the stories, who was extremely diligent about the well-being of her colleagues. So even though I became desensitized enough to cope with the difficult material, the researcher was very conscious of the effects of the stories and was supportive of all involved, especially the narrators. Another time, a researcher asked to interview me and tape my reactions to a series of interviews I'd transcribed. This wasn't traumatic material, but I appreciated being included and having my observations valued. In this case, she thought to ask me after I sent her a newspaper clipping that seemed relevant to her research. I'd worked with her for several years at this point and never had a conversation about her research. It was as if once I sent her the clipping, it occurred to her that the human conduit *could* think, and might have useful insights. She was apologetic about not realizing this sooner.

I've heard many interviewing techniques over the years, and I almost never comment except to occasionally say something positive when an interviewer is especially skillful. However, I once worked on an ongoing social science project that was interviewing immigrant youth on many aspects of their lives. I noticed one middle-aged interviewer gave them a lot of feedback, such as saying that was good when they reported church attendance, or commenting on their family relations. I was almost positive that her interjections were affecting the narrators' answers. After much deliberation, I emailed the principal investigator about my concerns. She sent me a neutral reply. I don't know what the outcome was, but I felt that since they were still interviewing and I was probably the only person so far to listen to the interviews, I should speak up before the interviewer skewed any more data. However, on another project, I stayed quiet when the white interviewer told an African-American man that he should focus on the positive instead of recounting some particularly heinous race-based incidents. In this case, unfortunately, the interviewer was the head of the project and the person who had hired me.

Some researchers prefer the human conduit remain mute. I worked on one project that required me to email 13 different researchers six transcripts at a time on certain preset dates over a three-month period. Instead of clogging their email boxes, delaying delivery, and having to keep track of the schedule, I made what I considered a reasonable suggestion of loading the files into a file sharing site and inviting the researchers to share the folder. Twelve of the 13 researchers stayed mute—I felt they were recoiling as if the couch had spoken. "We will continue with the planned method," eventually came the terse reply from the thirteenth.

I have also encountered patronizing attitudes when I say I do transcription. Several times oral historians have said, "Oh, that's important, too." At one Oral History Association meeting, I attended a presentation called "Finding People to Do the Dirty Work: Tips on Hiring and Managing Transcriptionists."[24] I'm sure this was meant to be cute, but I doubt someone titling their presentation that way expects transcriptionists to be in the room as fellow organization members of equal stature. As transcriptionist Susan Hutton put it, "Unfortunately many people practise hierarchy, and place transcribers on the bottom rung."[25]

Once I visited an archive in Cambodia with a remarkable oral history project. I introduced myself, excited to meet Cambodians whom I considered to be working in the same field. The man looked confused by my presence and said, "Oh, we have students to do that." He did not perceive me as a colleague.

Project managers, if you value your transcriptionists, let them know. Consider asking them for their perspective on your research. Or simply recognize their contribution by including them in book acknowledgments or the credits of a documentary. Inviting the transcriptionist to a museum opening of an oral history-based exhibit is a gracious and much-appreciated gesture. Once, a researcher bought me a plane ticket to Louisiana so I could participate in the seminar based on the research I'd transcribed. This is way above and beyond what I'd ever expect, and few projects would have those funds, but I was moved and grateful to be acknowledged in such a grand fashion.

Bottom Line

Yes, it's true. Research has proven that the human conduit both thinks and feels. This means that the project manager should prep the transcriptionist if sending potentially trauma-inducing materials. Debriefing may be in order, especially if the transcriptionist has signed a confidentiality agreement prohibiting her from discussing the harrowing tales she's heard with anybody outside the research team.

The flip side of the human conduit's sentience is that she may have valuable insights and ideas to offer the project. Project managers could suggest a conversation where the transcriptionist gives her perspective on the research. Often she's listened to the interviews more closely than anybody else.

Transcriptionists need to take care of themselves. Even if the interviews are free of traumatic content, sitting and typing for extended periods take a toll on the body. The transcriptionist needs breaks from the desk, movement and time spent outside. Isolation is also detrimental. Social interaction needs to balance time alone typing.

There's a wide variety of relationships between transcriptionists and the projects with which they work, ranging from close friendships to brief emails between people who never meet face-to-face. When possible, project managers should include transcriptionists as part of the research team and find ways to recognize their contribution to the project.

Notes

1 Virginia Dickson-Swift, Erica L. James, Sandra Kippen, and Pranee Liamputtong, "Researching Sensitive Topics: Qualitative Research as Emotion Work," *Qualitative Research*; 9(61) (2009): 65. doi:10.1177/1468794108098031.
2 David Gregory, Cynthia Russell, and Linda Phillips, "Beyond Textual Perfection: Transcribers As Vulnerable Persons," *Qualitative Health Research*, 7(2) (1997): 294–300.
3 Nikki Kiyimba and Michelle O'Reilly, "An Exploration of the Possibility for Secondary Traumatic Stress Among Transcriptionists: A Grounded Theory Approach," *Qualitative Research in Psychology*, 13(10: (2016): 92–108. doi:10.1080/14780887.2015.1106630.
4 Ibid.
5 Barb Jardee, email correspondence with Teresa Bergen, May 11, 2018.
6 Kim Etherington, "Working with Traumatic Stories: From Transcriber to Witness," *International Journal of Social Research Methodology*, 10(2) (2007): 85–97, doi:10.1080/13645570701334001.
7 Ibid.
8 Ibid.
9 Susan Nicholls, email correspondence with Teresa Bergen, December 9, 2018.
10 Phuoc Tran, email correspondence with Teresa Bergen, August 2, 2018.
11 Lois Glewwe, interview with Teresa Bergen, January 15, 2018.
12 Sue Shackles blog, available at: http://waywithwordsblog.com/2011/11/24/a-career-in-transcribing/ (accessed February 10, 2018).
13 Mayo Clinic, "What Are the Risks of Sitting Too Much?," available at: www.mayoclinic.org/healthy-lifestyle/adult-health/expert-answers/sitting/faq-20058005 (accessed July 27, 2018).
14 Barb Jardee, email correspondence with Teresa Bergen, May 11, 2018.
15 Susan Nicholls, email correspondence with Teresa Bergen, December 9, 2018.

16 Susan Hutton, email correspondence with Teresa Bergen, December 9, 2018.
17 Sue Shackles, blog, "A Career in Transcribing?," November 24, 2011, available at: http://waywithwordsblog.com/2011/11/24/a-career-in-transcribing (accessed February 13, 2019).
18 Grant Stoner, "Transcribing Woes of Disabled Oral Historians," available at: http://ora lhistoryreview.org/oral-history/transcribing-woes-of-disabled-oral-historians/ (accessed February 13, 2019).
19 Etherington, "Working with Traumatic Stories."
20 Lois Glewwe, interview with Teresa Bergen, January 15, 2018.
21 Victoria Greene, interview with Teresa Bergen, November 18, 2017.
22 Barb Jardee, email correspondence with Teresa Bergen, May 4, 2018.
23 Kiyimba and O'Reilly, "An Exploration of the Possibility for Secondary Traumatic Stress Among Transcriptionists."
24 OHA annual meeting, Montreal, October 2018.
25 Susan Hutton, email correspondence with Teresa Bergen, December 9, 2018.

10

USING TRANSCRIPTS FOR RESEARCH

Once the transcripts are processed by an archive, they're usually ready for researchers to use (unless they're restricted, see Chapter 8). Some researchers may retain exclusive access while writing a book or creating a documentary film, then later deposit the interviews in an archive where they're available to the general public.

This chapter presents the ways people use oral history transcripts for their own research, or locate, access and interpret that done by others. These topics could easily comprise their own book.[1] I offer a sample of the ways oral history is used, the kinds of people using collections and their ways of organizing information gleaned from transcripts.

Here are some of the issues we'll consider:

- Why researchers may or may not prefer transcripts
- Oral history consumers
- Using your own collected oral histories for research vs. other people's
- How people find oral histories to use in their research
- Accessing oral history transcripts
- Organizing transcripts for research
- How museum curators decide which parts of a transcript to use
- Citing oral history interviews
- Interpreting oral history
- How social scientists code qualitative interviews

Why Researchers May or May Not Prefer Transcripts

Douglas Boyd lamented:

As an oral historian, I would like to assume that people working with oral history in an archival setting would be drawn, first, to the recorded audio and video. As an archivist, however, experience has shown that it is idealistic and naïve to think users can effectively discover specific information in interviews without the assistance of a transcript or an index.[2]

Scholars, like everybody else these days, are busy. And listening to recordings takes a long time. Boyd went on:

Even in today's digital context, users and researchers of oral histories in archival settings largely prefer the transcript as an access point. In the typical reference encounter I still hear on a regular basis "Just send me the transcript," or a surprised, "Oh, it's not transcribed?"

My other informants corroborate this experience. Australian oral historian Francis Good told me:

Over 21 years of experience at the archives I worked in, I can vouch that the search room users preferred transcripts wherever they were available. Requests for audio recordings of interviews were by far in the minority.[3]

Oral historian Kim Heikkila agreed that transcripts are hugely important, because few people would be willing to listen to a two-hour recording or watch a two-hour video. And you can't skim audio the way you can text.

"Researchers will not use interviews that are not transcribed unless, like I said, it's a family member or a radio program," Jeff Corrigan said of his time as oral historian at the State Historical Society of Missouri:

Or if they absolutely had to have it, and it was so important to their research, and this is the only way to get it. Other than that, no one would touch an interview that wasn't transcribed. They want it to be a Word document or pdf that they can keyword search and not read it all and just get through it.[4]

Of course, podcasters and documentary filmmakers fall into the exception category, as do linguists and family members of narrators. These folks will all need to listen to audio, not just read transcripts. But even in some of these cases, transcripts are valuable.

At Baylor, the online audio is stored as MP3s to take up less space and be streamable. But if a researcher needs higher quality audio for a documentary, the institute can grant them access to WAV preservation files via an online shared folder.

Some repositories with older collections have transcripts only, since it used to be the practice to discard the recording after the transcript was complete. Of Baylor University's 4,000 online transcribed interviews, the audio is available on only 3,000. Most of the unavailable audio are the institute's early interviews from the 1970s, which were recorded exclusively on reel-to-reel tape. "We're still in the process of digitizing," said Sielaff. Occasionally a family member requests the audio. "It might be genealogical research for some of these," Sielaff said:

> We'll hear from grandsons or granddaughters who found their grandfather or grandmother's interview in our collection. And then of course they're over the moon if the audio's there or I can digitize the audio for them so they can actually hear their voice again.

Sometimes researchers listened to clips of audio to verify a transcript. Corrigan encountered scholars who found parts in the transcript that seemed out of character for the people they were researching, so wanted to check to make sure the transcriptionist had heard it right. He was sometimes disappointed by researchers' refusal to listen to some of the untranscribed interviews he deemed relevant. "They just wouldn't do it, even if I made a compelling argument." He put their reluctance down to time constraints and a strong focus on text.[5]

When author John Sheehy was writing his book *Comrades of the Quest* about Reed College, he often consulted the original recordings:

> Sometimes I wanted to get a flavor of the personality that was being interviewed. You can sort of pick that up on the transcript, but it's fascinating sometimes to hear the actual voices. Sometimes to get their speaking voice and to make sure I was editing and staying true to their voice and their expression, I would go back and try to get a sense of what their voice was like.[6]

The Reed project included many group interviews, occasionally with up to 40 people present. Since the transcriptionist couldn't keep track of that many voices, Sheehy sometimes went back to try to figure out the speaker of particularly interesting quotes.

Corrigan thought a lot of context was lost by keyword searching, rather than reading an entire transcript. "When you're doing that, you're assuming that you know the words that the individual would use. Lots of people talk about topics, and never use the actual word."

Transcription quality varies. Corrigan felt confident about the transcriptions he hired out to professional transcriptionists, which were then audited and edited in-house. "But a lot of projects that were donated by groups, or school groups, or student classes and things, you take a risk if you solely go by that transcript." In the case of iffy transcription, researchers are wise to listen to the audio.

Oral History Consumers

Oral history has moved increasingly into the mainstream. StoryCorps, which has helped ordinary people record more than 65,000 conversations since 2003, has been one of the driving forces. Many oral historians resent StoryCorps because the short conversations it records don't fit their definition of oral history. At the Oral

History Association meeting in Pittsburgh in 2008, oral historians lined up to grill keynote speaker and StoryCorps founder David Isay. Emotions ran high as oral historians angrily questioned his right to use the term "oral history" for his project, and one woman unleashed her resentment that StoryCorps racks up the grants while her own small project goes unfunded.[7] However, for better or worse, StoryCorps has undeniably raised the profile of the term "oral history."

Now the use of oral history as a methodology and descriptor has moved way beyond academics. Post-StoryCorps mainstream book titles include *The Daily Show (The Book): An Oral History as Told by John Stewart, the Correspondents, Staff and Guests; Louder than Hell: The Definitive Oral History of Metal; As If!: The Oral History of Clueless, as Told by Amy Heckerling and the Cast and Crew;* and *World War Z: An Oral History of the Zombie War.* Journalists for mainstream magazines have also adopted oral history, with *Rolling Stone* doing an oral history of the Allman Brothers, and *New York* magazine using oral history to investigate allegations against Bill Cosby.[8]

Despite this widespread popular use of oral history methodology—or at least a watered-down version, purists would say—most people using archives to do in-depth research are likely to be scholars working on academic projects or researchers writing books and articles. They might also be documentary filmmakers, broadcast journalists, podcasters or people interested in genealogy. At Oklahoma State University, Juliana Nykolaiszyn, assistant head of digital resources and discovery services, said disciplines using their oral history collections include history, sociology, gender and women's studies, geography, English, linguistics, education, art, art history, agricultural communications, ESL and theater, as well as grade school and college students. Since so much is accessed online, OSU lacks granular statistics. Often they only know a particular researcher is using the collection because they receive an additional request, or a thank you note.[9]

Since 1971, Baylor University Institute for Oral History (BUIOH) has actively encouraged faculty members to do oral history research by offering fellowships. Faculty research fellows interview individuals in their fields of interest, then use this information in papers and books. The institute benefits by keeping the interviews by the fellows as part of its collection. "So we're probably an outlier here in that it's almost like we're instigating these things," said Steven Sielaff. Without the institute's incentive, some of these scholars would probably never have thought to include oral history methodology in their research:

> We have a lot of projects with people on campus from any number of disciplines. They're interested in interviewing someone else in their field, or it could be someone who's a mentor to them, or someone who was the first to do this thing, or to come up with this methodology. They're interested in interviewing them and getting that story.[10]

BUIOH also holds an annual regional history fair on campus. Many middle school and high school students use the institute's collections for their projects, especially if they're focusing on local history.

Like Nykolaiszyn in Oklahoma, the question of who, exactly, is using Baylor's collection is one that Sielaff puzzles over. "It's probably the minority of individuals that are using our collection that we actually hear from. I think probably most collection managers would tell us that." Google Analytics and CONTENTdm data only reveal so much. "A lot of times, like in my top ten or top five, I'll see a particular interview pop up there, and sometimes across multiple months," Sielaff said:

> Someone or some group is accessing this multiple times, obviously doing research on it. But I have no idea who that person is, or what that organization is, or why they're using it or what they might be ultimately creating.

The institute has a message on its "Search Our Collection" page that clearly states, "Please note that if you wish to use material from our collection for either scholarly or for-profit publication, you must first contact us and be granted permission, as BUIOH holds copyright over all content found online."[11] Most of the people who contact Sielaff about using the collection are faculty either at Baylor or at other universities. Sielaff isn't sure if this is because they're the main users, or if it's because they're likelier to respect copyright. He struggles between wanting to know more about users and striving to preserve access. "Some people have authority walls on their online collections where you have to sign your life away in order to view the collection," he said.

> I don't necessarily want to do that. I want people to actually be able to access things. Because usually if people are confronted with something like that, their first inclination is to close out that window and go somewhere else.

Oral history can inform the work of people far from academia. During her time managing the museum at the Santa Monica Mountains National Recreation Area, Linda Valois found oral history a practical way to gather information about the area. For her research on homesteaders in the Santa Monica Mountains, Valois discovered it was faster to ask people first, then look up the land records and old newspaper articles. "One individual I interviewed also knew how people were connected. Looking at land records does not necessarily show relationships. People remember who brother, sister, cousins, and friends were." Valois used oral history transcripts for information on past trails, homesteaders, and mountain activities, which she wove into her interpretive talks.[12]

Using Your Own Collected Oral Histories for Research vs. Other People's

Researchers run the gamut, from people who want to conduct all the oral histories themselves, to those wholly relying on research gathered by other people. I understand the impulse to want to do primary research and add to the general pool of knowledge, which seems fresher than using existing resources. On the other hand, as somebody who has spent a great deal of her life typing interviews, I'm a champion of dredging the archives for treasure. I suspect that many hours of the audio I've transcribed are lying dormant in collections, just waiting for a researcher to discover them and give them their chance to shine.

London-based writer David Katz, author of *Solid Foundation: An Oral History of Reggae* and other reggae-centric books, is on the do-everything-yourself side of the spectrum. "I almost always conduct my own interviews," he told me.

> In very rare instances, I may have used some content where someone else did an interview with someone who died before I had the chance to meet them. But that is rare, and if so, it would only be a very brief extract used by me.

For him, meeting and interviewing people are central to his work. "It can be hard for people to open up at first if they don't know you personally, but usually the whole process is a fascinating joy." Not only does he conduct all his own interviews, he also transcribes them himself:

> I find that the process of doing the transcription helps me to store the information in a more complete way. Plus, memory can play tricks on you, so it is useful to listen back to everything in full during that process.[13]

John Sheehy worked on a giant oral history project commemorating the centennial of Reed College in Portland, Oregon. He conducted perhaps two dozen of the 400 interview sessions that eventually turned into his book, *Comrades of the Quest*. Since he was predominantly working with other people's interviews, I asked him if he ever got frustrated with shortcomings in the transcripts. "Yes. I was constantly screaming," he said, laughing. "And I was screaming at my own self, too, looking at my own transcripts." Sheehy was often frustrated by interviewers sticking too closely to their prepared questions, and missing the opportunity for an interesting follow-up. He also encountered transcripts where the interviewer knew either too much or too little. If the interviewer and the narrator knew each other too well, they'd talk in shorthand, he said, and leave out all the relevant background. "They'll mention things, and say, 'Oh, yeah, yeah. You know about that.'"

On the other hand, knowing too little about the subject led to missed opportunities. "It's not the first question, really, that's important in oral history, it's the follow-up question." Sheehy said. "If you couldn't go that second question, you didn't really get beyond the superficial with people. And that was the frustrating part."[14] To complete the research for his book, Sheehy often had to follow up with narrators and conduct short spot interviews to fill in missing information and plug narrative holes. Of course, this is a luxury available only when narrators are still living.

How People Find Oral Histories to Use in Their Research

How do people know that a certain archive has a certain collection? Unfortunately, this is not as easy as it should be. One of the biggest problems in finding oral histories is that they aren't catalogued or made available in any consistent way, and many are not tagged with the term "oral history." Most researchers begin with an online search, but even then, oral histories may be buried in the list of results, or not come up at all. For example, a search on "religious cults," will retrieve many pages of irrelevant hits, before finding the oral histories. The search term "religious cults oral histories" will bring you quickly to such promising sites as the British Library's "Oral Histories of Religion and Belief" and the University of Leeds' "Community Religions Project," but will fail to display others that weren't tagged clearly.

In our digital world, it's easy to forget that not all oral history collections are online. "Cultural heritage institutions and repositories with limited funding may not be able to provide a mechanism for discovery. This makes it difficult for researchers to access this content—because they are often unaware it exists," Nykolaiszyn said.[15] Whether online or available only in-house, oral history collections present cataloging challenges to archivists, especially if they include additional artifacts.

> Transcripts are just one piece of the puzzle for us, so a discovery platform has to be able to incorporate all components we hope to include with a collection (transcript, photos, a/v) with ease. Outside of having a transcript, metadata also becomes important with online access, so we try to also include subject, keyword, spatial, and temporal information (for example) to assist with discovery.[16]

Baylor Institute strategically plans its metadata to maximize search potential. Once a month, its collection gets exported to WorldCat, the world's largest network of library content and services. WorldCat allows people to simultaneously search for items at local libraries and thousands of far-flung libraries around the world. Sielaff plans to continue improving transcript metadata, creating more thematic, category-based metadata fields to make it easier to find interviews by topic rather than by the narrator's name.

I tested how easy it was to find oral histories from Baylor's collection in WorldCat. First I went to the Baylor site and pulled up a transcript at random. I chose the term "Burton Texas," as that was a town I'd never heard of. Then I went into WorldCat and typed "Burton Texas." That was too broad, bringing up every person with the surname Burton that had anything remotely to do with Texas. But when I typed "Burton Texas oral history," Baylor's collections popped right up on the first page.

Baylor also launched a Waco history app with clips about local historical events and people. "We have a link back to the full interview," said Sielaff. "So that's another entry point into our collection."

Accessing Oral History Transcripts

As research materials have moved online, access has become much easier. I get a little nostalgic for my days researching in the 1990s, sitting in the deep silence of special collections libraries, my eyes straining over a microfiche machine. But would I really want to go back to that? Of course not. The internet makes finding oral histories and other research materials approximately a million times easier.

Still, oral history access is far from standardized. Some institutions make research unbelievably easy. For example, if you want to read a transcript from the Oral History Center at UC Berkeley's Bancroft Library, you need only go to a drop-down menu of the oral history collections, pick or search an interview within a collection, agree to the terms of a disclaimer, and pull up the transcript.

Despite the move to loading materials online, Steven Sielaff said the results of his 2017 Metadata Task Force survey revealed that there are still plenty of oral history centers and programs that remain reading room-based.

> We're a freestanding institute. We work with libraries a lot, but we're not beholden necessarily to their systems, and we're not beholden to their regulations. I think a lot of oral history programs, because they're caught up in that library or archival environment, that depending on kind of how twenty-first century their library and archive are depends on how accessible their materials are.[17]

Accessing some collections may require several steps. Let's say a researcher wanted to listen to interviews conducted in the early 1990s as part of the Player Queens Oral History Project, a series of interviews with New Zealand women who transitioned from amateur to professional acting. The researcher could locate online a list of narrator names, dates the interviews were recorded and the duration of the tapes, and the fact that an abstract is available for each interview—not a transcript. Since this collection is restricted, the researcher would then have to acquire written permission from the donor. "Once permission has been granted, a digitised copy will be provided which can only be accessed in the Katherine Mansfield Reading Room," the site says. "Please contact library staff to schedule an appointment or for more details."[18] As a further obstacle, any public use would also require permission from the narrator. This is a case where the researcher can identify the *existence* of an interview without actually being able to read it online. If the researcher really needs to see the transcript, a trip to New Zealand will be necessary to access the recording the old-fashioned way.

Researchers wanting to access the Archive for Justice, part of the South African History Archive (SAHA), also need to take more steps than just clicking. They must register on the site, which involves setting a password and agreeing to copyright policies. Once researchers identify the material they want to see, they can email the SAHA archivists a detailed request stating the collection name, number and archival item. The researcher and archivist then agree on an appointment time.

Since many of the archive's materials are housed off-site, it can take up to three working days to retrieve them.[19]

Why is there so much disparity in the ease of accessing oral history collections? Sometimes the sensitive nature of materials inspires archivists or narrators to limit access. But often it's due to limited money and staff time. These records do not organize themselves. Some overworked archivist or oral historian is behind their presence on the web.

Troy Reeves, at the University of Wisconsin, told me in late 2017:

> Our website hasn't been updated in a while. But our website does have a list now of most of the people who've been interviewed. And then we also have audio and the summary documents online for probably about half our interviews through the UW Madison Digital Repository.

If an interview isn't online, a researcher emails Reeves—or, if they email the general archives email address, it gets forwarded to him. Reeves then grants the researcher access for a few weeks so he or she can download audio and any summary document, if available, from the cloud.

> So no one has to come here. And most of what we do as an oral history program, either people find out that we have an interview online, and they just access it without even contacting us, or they contact us and we give them access to the interview.[20]

Reeves has also tried the unusual approach of crowdsourcing, or, in this case, scholar-sourcing transcripts. When he knows scholars are listening to and transcribing interviews, he's asked them to send their drafts. "But again, I think what happens is a lot of times people underestimate how hard it is to transcribe," he said. So, far this approach has only been productive a couple of times.[21]

At Louisiana State University, scholars have several ways to access oral history interviews. Access is free if they visit the special collections reading room, or they can order audio and/or a transcript for a small fee. Williams Center director Jennifer Cramer said she hopes that soon all the cataloged oral history collections will be available online for free. She often waives fees for students. "And definitely, relatives get them free. So if they're digging around and they find an interview with their grandpa, I'm not charging them for that."[22]

Organizing Transcripts for Research

Whether using transcripts for a book, article, film or museum exhibit, researchers face the challenge of organizing materials. This is another topic that could fill an entire book, or a series of books, as it seems every researcher develops his or her own procedures. We'll look at three different approaches that writers have used to organize their book projects—one is simple, one more technological, one more intellectual.

Dirk Vogel worked on his oral history-based book *Skateboarding Is Not a Fashion* for eight years. "It was the most challenging project I ever worked on, mainly because of its size. The final book clocks in at 632 pages and a bit over 130,000 words—and that's just the finished product," Vogel wrote on his website. He interviewed nearly 100 skateboard personalities, with each transcript running 5,000–15,000 words in length. "They were our storytelling gold and I was grateful for every single skate legend we had a chance to sit down with," Vogel wrote:

> But as the interview transcripts folder on my iMac grew in size, one major fear began gnawing at me: What if I collected this golden quote that would be perfect for a chapter in the book, this magic storytelling moment that ties it all together—but forgot that I even had it because I lost track of the transcripts on my hard drive?[23]

His simple solution? Hashtags. As if Vogel was writing the world's longest tweet, he hashtagged all the topics and angles that fit into the rough chapter structure. "Sometimes I used multiple hashtags to mark a juicy quote."

For example, he'd mark a potentially usable quote like this:

#hairstyles #1980s #tonyhawkhair

"The Tony Hawk hair flap, with the hair dyed and shaved on the side and the front of the hair flapping out. That's what we saw in the videos and that's what we mimicked."

After years of research, when it finally came time to write, Vogel could do a desktop search on his Apple Macintosh for a term, such as #tonyhawkhair, in his interview transcript folder. This would pull up all the transcripts that mentioned Hawk's hairdo. From there, he'd go into each transcript and do a Control + F to find the quotes containing that hashtag. This is a simple solution that's available to most computer users without extra software.

Researchers who prefer using specialized software can choose from an ever-changing parade of solutions. Technology writer Nicholas Carlson used the note-taking app Evernote to organize his research for his book, *Marissa Mayer and the Fight to Save Yahoo!*

> I'd be on the phone with someone and taking notes and recording a call, and then transcribe the interview straight into Evernote. By May 2013, I had hundreds of Evernote notes in a file called "Yahoo Book Notes." From May to the beginning of July, my life was lived totally in Evernote.

It took him two months to go through the transcripts, breaking them down into sentence-long sections. But using Evernote's labeling functions kept his data so organized that the writing phase only took him six weeks to draft a 93,000-word book. Disclaimer: This is not recommended for the average writer.[24]

John Sheehy used a highly intellectual method of organizing material for his book, in keeping with the subject matter. *Comrades of the Quest* tells the story of Reed College, a small liberal arts institution known for its academic rigor. First, he found a book he admired to use as a model —*Comrades and Chicken Ranchers*, an oral history-based book about radical Jewish chicken ranchers who settled around Petaluma, California, in the 1920s.

To track 400 interviews with approximately 1,400 participants (a mix of one-on-one and large group interviews), Sheehy relied on what he calls "a book org sheet" (more on that a little later) and an integral map. Ken Wilber, a writer on transpersonal psychology, developed the integral map which guided the project. It uses a four-quadrant grid to divide personal experience into the interior (I), interior (we), exterior individual (it) and exterior collective (its) (Figure 10.1).

In Reed's case, the interior side meant:

> We wanted testimonials from the students and their personal experience on campus, in their social and intellectual realms. And then we also wanted kind of the group experience that they experienced in the group and also the values of the college personally. What that meant to them.

The exterior individual involved things like academic rigor, academic hurdles and curriculum design. The final quadrant included the overall system design of the

Interior - Subjective	Exterior – Objective
I PERSONAL EXPERIENCE: "I value …" Core Value: Intellectual Freedom This quadrant addresses the individual's intention, and their personal and educational development. It deals with subjective feelings that people experience in the community, and the emotional bonds they form to the college. Personal exploration in the social and intellectual realms is key here.	**It** GOALS & PERFORMANCE MEASURES: Behaviors that will lead to higher performance. Core Value: Academic Rigor This quadrant addresses the curriculum design (humanities, course requirements), the academic hurdles (junior qual, thesis, orals), and the pedagogy of the faculty. This is the realm of modeling and direct transmission from professor to student.
We CULTURAL EXPERIENCE: "We value …" Core Value: Democratic Governance This quadrant addresses the collective world view of Reed, passed down through myth, story, and rituals. It encompasses the egalitarian values, spirit of inquiry, honor principle, nonconformity, and an unwritten rules and beliefs that form an esprit de corps among community members. This is the realm of Olde Reed.	**Its** SOCIAL SYSTEM: the organizational design and system of policies and procedures that determine the institution's high performance. This quadrant addresses Reed's system design, including innovations such as an emphasis on teaching instead of research, the lack of intercollegiate sports and fraternities, faculty and student governance, small conferences, 10-to-1 student/faculty ratio, non-disclosure of grades, four divisions, etc. This is the realm of distinction to the outside world, of Reed's iconoclastic nature.

FIGURE 10.1 Reed Community: integral map

college, and its policies and procedures. "So if a person talked about how did you come to Reed, that was very much their first person experience. Or their first impression of coming on the campus. That would be in the I story," Sheehy explained:

> Renn Fayre and what that was like, we'd categorize that story in the We section. That was the cultural experience. If we wanted to talk about their senior thesis, and how they went through that process with the faculty and their faculty advisor, that went into the It column. And the larger distinctions of Reed, about what was it like not having sports on campus, or no fraternities or sororities, how did you deal with that, or how was that distinctive, it went into the Its column.

Within each quadrant, Sheehy and his co-editors organized distinct topics, such as stories about the college mascot, literary societies, food and theater on campus. They mostly worked by hand, cutting and pasting in Word, since they had too many volunteers to train in a more efficient project management tool.

The Reed project also relied on Sheehy's so-called book org sheet. This was a timeline based on Dr. Ichak Adizes' corporate lifecycle, which delineates distinct phases in an organization's lifespan.[25] Sheehy divided Reed College's life thus far into five stages corresponding to roughly 20-year blocks. Then he could arrange all the integral map topics chronologically (Box 10.1).

This was an awful lot of work. But Sheehy was committed to capturing the entire experience of Reed College:

> I didn't want it just to be stories about college students partying and having a good time. I wanted to show the evolution of the organization, and also the impact of history on the times, too, as they were reflected in the school.[26]

BOX 10.1 REED ORAL HISTORY PROJECT BOOK ORG

Chronological Structure: divide into 4–6 sections based on sociological arcs over time. Within each section, present the four quadrant model:

I: Reed Experience
We: Reed Community
It: Faculty, Curriculum
Its: Institutional History

The sections: Foster's ideal in practice in community across time (Table 10.2).

TABLE 10.2 Development

	Stage		
Date	Adizes stage		
1911–1920	The Foundation	Forming	Infancy
1920–1944	The Golden Years	Storming	Toddler
1945–1965 (the national college)	Rise of Individualism	Norming	Go-go
1966–1988 (challenge to vision)	Expansion and contraction	Storming	Adolescence
1989–2011	The maturity of the vision	Performing	Prime

How Museum Curators Decide Which Parts of a Transcript to Use

Confronted with many audio hours and hundreds or thousands of pages of transcripts, researchers winnow the stories down to a meaningful end product, whether that's an exhibit, book, film or audio tour. Now we'll turn our attention from authors to museum curators preparing museum exhibits that feature oral history. However, authors and filmmakers working with transcripts employ a similar process of discernment when deciding which experts to use in their work.

Greek researchers Andromache Gazi and Irene Nakou have studied the use of oral history in museums. They note:

> The original context is usually domestic and intimate and the narrator is typically addressing just one person, the interviewer. Normally, the interviewees are not fully cognizant that they may also be addressing a wider, possibly international, audience or even posterity.

Researchers must comb through the audio and transcripts to find coherent, relevant, self-contained segments that will have meaning to their museum audience. This is similar to a documentary filmmaker's decision-making process when choosing excerpts. As a further challenge, museum staff must transfer a personal one-to-one communication to an impersonal public forum like a museum exhibition.[27] The preferred way to do this is by setting up listening stations with video or audio. Providing earphones makes the experience more intimate for the museum visitor, and cuts down on noise pollution for people looking at other displays.

The Museum for Human Rights in Winnipeg, Manitoba, Canada, sets exhibits up for success by pre-project planning. "The intent, approach, and messaging of an exhibit are typically defined ahead of the oral history interview," Jodi Giesbrecht, manager of research and curation, told me in an email interview:

> We usually have an idea of the kind of excerpt we would like to support the messaging, though also adapt this according to the dynamics and the flow of

the interview itself. Oftentimes, an interviewee will provide perspectives or stories that we had not anticipated but that would nevertheless make for a very powerful excerpt. In these cases, we adjust the intended messaging of the exhibit if appropriate to ensure the voice of the interviewee is communicated in a way that is authentic to the interview.

Connecting visitors to stories is everything for a museum with more stories than artifacts. So they select their excerpts very carefully. "Excerpts are satisfying when they convey a personal story or new insight to the audience," Giesbrecht continued:

> Stories that are relatable, with which visitors can empathize, tend to resonate well. Conversely, stories that are wholly different from a visitor's own personal experience also resonate well when they provide insight into an entirely different way of being or kind of experience that is unfamiliar.

She added that the honesty and authenticity of oral history help visitors feel a personal, empathetic connection.[28]

Practical considerations also dictate how museum exhibits turn out. Reagan Grau at the National Museum of the Pacific War faced budgetary and content issues when installing oral history kiosks into the museum's galleries. The original plan to include a kiosk in the Japanese-American internment gallery was cut when he realized they didn't have enough good interview content. He also decided to combine Iwo Jima with Okinawa, which are housed in adjoining galleries. "In the end, we settled for the kiosks that we felt were major war events and that we had enough content in the collection to help tell the story adequately."[29]

Museums may have collected oral histories, but lack the funds for high-tech listening stations. When anthropologist Olga Orlic was curating an exhibit on weaving for the Ethnographic Museum of Istria, she used a low-budget way of presenting conversations with weavers. "Their statements which I found essential and important were written down and stacked on the wall or a part of the exhibit, to talk about objects or photos."[30]

Citing Oral History Interviews

Oral history centers are often generous about use. Jennifer Cramer, director of the T. Harry Williams Center for Oral History, said they don't charge for use in documentaries or other projects. "We usually just ask that they send a copy of the book, the radio show, etc." Since the collection is online, she realizes she has little control over use, anyway. "We just want to make sure that the proper citations are on there."[31]

Baylor doesn't charge researchers, either. If interviews are online, Steven Sielaff said, they have to be free to use, since they're beyond Baylor's control:

Unless I put up an authority wall, I can't dictate who's using our collection online once we put it online. So I can't differentiate between a person who works for a nonprofit or who works for a corporation. So because of that, everything that we do have online, people have signed releases that it can be used.

Again, all he asks is a proper citation.[32]

But what is a proper citation? Different oral history programs use different formats. Here we will defer to Baylor, an authority on oral history style. Baylor accounts for various scenarios, including whether you're citing the materials in notes or in a bibliography, and what format was used on recordings:

Examples of notes (N) and bibliographic forms (B):

For recordings

(N) 1. Albert Harry Reed, interview by Stephen Sloan, October 9, 2007, in Waco, Texas, compact disc, Institute for Oral History, Baylor University, Waco, TX.

(B) Reed, Albert Harry. Interview by Stephen Sloan. October 9, 2007, in Waco, Texas. Compact disc. Institute for Oral History, Baylor University, Waco, TX.

For online transcripts

(N) 2. Lonnie Belle Hodges, interview by Vivienne Malone-Mayes, August 30, 1990, in Waco, Texas, transcript, Baylor University Institute for Oral History, Waco, TX, available online at http://digitalcollections.baylor.edu/cdm/ref/collection/buioh/id/5361.

(B) Hodges, Lonnie Belle. Interview by Vivienne Malone-Mayes. August 30, 1990, in Waco, Texas. Transcript. Baylor University Institute for Oral History, Waco, TX. http://digitalcollections.baylor.edu/cdm/ref/collection/buioh/id/5361   (accessed June 10, 2014).

For print transcripts deposited in an archive

(N) 3. Abner Anglin Hyden, "Oral Memoirs of Abner Anglin Hyden," interview by Lois E. Myers on January 20, 1998, in Waco, Texas (Waco, TX: Baylor University Institute for Oral History, 2001), 22.

(B) Hyden, Abner Anglin. "Oral Memoirs of Abner Anglin Hyden." Interviewed by Lois E. Myers on six occasions from 20 January to 19 August, 1998, in Waco, Texas. Baylor University Institute for Oral History, Waco, TX.

If you're publishing your research, be sure that your citations conform to whatever style your book or journal publisher requires. If there are no guidelines, use Baylor's format.

Some researchers use software to manage citations. They can save, format, organize and share citations from article databases, library catalogs and other online places. This extremely handy software lets them easily pump out reference lists or bibliographies in whichever style format a given publication desires. Zotero, Mendeley and Endnote are currently popular programs, but this is an ever-changing landscape and will vary from country to country. "Your specific work environment may dictate your choice—e.g. are you joining a lab where something else is already in use?" the Columbia University Libraries website asks. "Do you expect a lot of collaborative work in which it might be useful to share citation libraries on the same platform?"[33] If so, check with colleagues to see which program they are using.

It's courteous to provide a copy of your book or article or DVD to the archive if possible. If it's beyond your means to provide this, at least let them know that this new interpretation of their collection exists. It's to your benefit, too. Since so many institutions are on social media these days, they may very well help you promote it.

Interpreting Oral History

Once the interviews are transcribed, edited, approved by the narrator and deposited in an archive, they're ripe for interpretation by scholars, journalists, genealogists and the general public. Interpretation is another giant subject which warrants its own book. As anybody who's ever taken a literature class knows, what seems like a text with a straightforward message to you often means something entirely different to another reader. Let's look at some basic issues in interpreting oral history.

Before we even get to scholars putting their spin on things, what about the veracity of the testimony? Is it truth or tall tales? For a folklorist gathering stories, this might not matter. But a historian or biographer must weigh the accuracy of the narrator.

Oral historian Linda Shopes gives some useful baseline tips. First, the researcher attempts to assess the reliability of the narrator, taking into consideration the narrator's mental state both at the time of events described and during the interview, and his personal stake in his version of events:

> The veracity of what is said in an interview can be gauged by comparing it both with other interviews on the same subject and with related documentary evidence. If the interview jibes with other evidence, if it builds upon or supplements this evidence in a logical and meaningful way, one can assume a certain level of veracity in the account. If, however, it conflicts with other evidence or is incompatible with it, the historian needs to account for the disparities: Were different interviewees differently situated in relationship to the events under discussion? Might they have different agendas, leading them to tell different versions of the same story? Might the written sources be biased or limited in a particular way? Might intervening events—for example, ideological shifts between the time of the events under discussion and the time of the interview or subsequent popular cultural accounts of these events—have influenced later memories?[34]

So triangulation is necessary. Some aspects are easy to ferret out, such as when a narrator falsely recalls reading a book before it was published or seeing a play before it was produced. Some are more difficult, such as narrators remembering themselves in ways that will ease their consciences, such as being kinder, more patient, unselfish or less racist.

The researcher must also take time to understand the content, especially when dealing with narrators from a different country, class, region, race, ethnicity, religion or subculture. Language, expressions and shared beliefs are key to understanding interviews.

Writer David Katz, who has written extensively on Jamaican music, sometimes faces challenges interpreting his interviews. "Especially when the speaker has a strong use of Jamaican patois. Sometimes it can be difficult to comprehend the full meaning of poetic language and slang terms."[35]

Researchers should try to face their own agendas. The fastest way of sucking life out of a good story is to impose an agenda upon it. When I was in graduate school, I had a literature professor who insisted on comparing every book we read to Christ's journey. No matter what kind of interesting or innovative scenes, characters or ideas the author invented, this professor contrived to highlight similarities to Jesus. In the same way, when a researcher sets out with the mindset that his book is about oppression, or triumph, or any other single topic, it flattens out the nuances of a life story.

Aspersions are sometimes cast upon research projects after the fact by other scholars who believe the interviews should have been interpreted differently. A PhD candidate recently told me that her dissertation was rejected because her committee thought the Latino narrators in her interviews had been too positive about their experiences. The committee demanded that she rewrite it, adding in more calamity and oppression.

An article by London doctor and researcher Julia Bailey showed just how malleable a simple recorded conversation can be:

> Researchers' methodological assumptions and disciplinary backgrounds influence what are considered relevant data and how data should be analysed. To take an example, talk between hospital consultants and medical students could be studied in many different ways: the transcript of a teaching session could be analysed thematically, coding the content (topics) of talk. Analysis could also look at the way that developing an identity as a doctor involves learning to use language in particular ways, for example, using medical terminology in genres such as the 'case history'. The same data could be analysed to explore the construction of 'truth' in medicine: for example, a doctor saying 'the patient's blood pressure is 120/80' frames this statement as an objective, quantifiable, scientific truth. In contrast, formulating a patient's medical history with statements such as 'she reports a pain in the left leg' or 'she denies alcohol use' frames the patient's account as less trustworthy than the doctor's observations. The aims of a project and methodological assumptions have implications for the form and content of transcripts since different features of data will be of analytic interest.[36]

John Sheehy was determined to let people tell their own stories when writing *Comrades of the Quest.*

> I looked at so many oral histories from academics who would write a long interpretation and then have, like, two paragraphs from an oral history in it. And then go on and on and interpret that again. I'd be, like, oh my God!

Instead of interpreting the stories himself, Sheehy let the narrators speak. "I transposed excerpts from one person against another," he said. "So someone would tell a story of something that had happened. And then I'd put right after that a story from somebody else describing the same event from a different perspective." He included narrators who were brutally honest, and those who recounted tales more carefully:

> I really wanted to have a chorus telling the story. And I wanted to feature different kinds of voices in each of them. So people could see that this person's experience was probably different from that person's experience, because of the nature of the person them self. The person was really captured in these stories.[37]

Some scholars experiment with using poetic forms to interpret oral history. Lorina Barker turned to free verse after being disappointed with verbatim transcripts. An Aboriginal Australian from Weilmoringle, New South Wales, Barker had participated in other people's research. She felt that the transcripts of her own words made her sound silly and ignorant, and were embarrassing and often boring to read. When she started interviewing other Aboriginal people for her own research, she wanted to be sure they were more satisfied with the end product than she had been. She wrote:

> For the Aboriginal participants in my research, the verbatim transcript is not the only, or the most appropriate, form of converting the recorded interview to print form. Free verse is used as an alternative in an attempt to retain the speech mannerisms: the "rhythm and rhetorical style," tone and accents of the speaker. Also, within the context of this research the utilisation of free verse is intended to be less intimidating than a verbatim transcript.[38]

Barker devised a process for converting voice into free verse. First, she types a verbatim transcript. Next she removes her questions and responses so the interviewer voice doesn't interrupt the flow of the story. "I then arrange the narrator's words on the page by using lines and space to convey the narrator's speech mannerisms: when they have paused, have gone silent or have changed topics." Barker's method pushes the boundaries of oral history interpretation in a bold and intriguing direction.

How Social Scientists Code Qualitative Interviews

Another technique commonly used in qualitative research, though less so among oral historians, is coding interviews either manually or electronically. As Johnny Saldaña explains in *The Coding Manual for Qualitative Researchers*, "A code in qualitative inquiry is most often a word or short phrase that symbolically assigns a summative, salient, essence-capturing, and/or evocative attribute for a portion of language-based or visual data."[39] He describes coding as "the transitional process between data collection and more extensive data analysis."[40] More than labels, codes are links between data and ideas. Like editing, a researcher starts with rough coding and finesses it through the project until it's as illuminating as possible.

As we saw in the example above about the different ways one could interpret a talk between hospital consultants and medical students, data codes and terms used will depend on the perspective and aims of the researcher. Saldaña gives a couple of different examples from interview transcripts focusing on education. This first is a high school senior describing a teacher. Codes are the words in all caps.

He cares about me. He has never 1 SENSE OF SELF-WORTH
told me but he does. 2 He's always 2 STABILITY
been there for me, even when my parents
were not. He's one of the few things that
I hold as a constant in my life. So it's nice.
3 I really feel comfortable around him. 3 "COMFORTABLE"

This second except is from an interview with a mother describing her son's troubles in school, using more colloquial coding terms.

1 My son, Barry, went through a really 1 MIDDLE-SCHOOL HELL
    tough time about, probably started the end
    of fifth grade and went into sixth grade.
2 When he was growing up young in 2 TEACHER'S PET
    school he was a people-pleaser and
    his teachers loved him to death.
3 Two boys in particular that he chose to 3 BAD INFLUENCES
    try to emulate, wouldn't, were not very
    good for him. 4 They were very critical of 4 TWEEN ANGST
    him, they put him down all the time,
    and he kind of just took that and really
    kind of internalized it, I think, for a
    long time.[41]

Manual coding involves printing out transcripts, then using pencils and highlighters to plan your strategy. Electronic coding requires CAQDAS—Computer Assisted Qualitative Data Analysis Software programs. Saldaña recommends

learning manual coding basics before moving to CAQDAS, as the focus on technology may divert attention from developing important analytical skills. He wrote:

> There is something about manipulating qualitative data on paper and writing
> codes in pencil that give you more control over and ownership of the work.
> Perhaps this advice stems from my admitted lack of technological expertise and
> old-fashioned ways of working that have become part of my "codus"
> operandi.[42]

Sharon Kruse prefers manual coding. "Old school—printouts, markers, and post-
its," the academic director and professor of education at Washington State University, Vancouver, said in an email. "For me that's the best way to interact with
the material. Maybe I've never invested the time to learn software well, but each
time I've tried to use it, it always leaves me cold." She generally codes in two
ways:

> First I use the literature/theoretical frame on which the questions were origin-
> ally created. I look for ways that the answers confirm, extend, or refute prior
> work in the field. That way, I've checked off the obvious ideas that are present
> in the text. Then I look to the interview from a fresh perspective looking for
> new themes/words/phrases/ideas that are present. I work to create big buckets
> of thinking (e.g., bigger constructs like access or equity) and then work to find
> the details that flesh out how participants are using those ideas. Finally, I look
> for a coherent full narrative from abstract to coda to explore the structure of the
> ways stories are told.[43]

Alexis Waldron, now a human performance specialist for the US Forest Service,
learned to use NVivo coding software in graduate school in 2007. But coding
software doesn't do all the work for you. It still depends on human choices. "With
the transcripts, first I printed them all out and I had another person that helped me
code them, make sure that what I was seeing is the thing they were seeing,"
Waldron told me. After she'd chosen her codes, she entered them in NVivo:

> Then after they were coded into those themes, then I went back through
> them again to say okay, what's being said in this theme? How are people
> describing it? What words are they using and what phrases might be really
> quintessential in capturing that theme?

When she determined sub-themes emerging, she re-coded as necessary.[44]

In oral history, keywords can act like codes for search purposes, and are a useful
tool for narrowing down to specific subjects within a large group of interview
transcripts, similar to the hashtag method mentioned above. In an article for the
Iranian Journal of Nursing and Midwifery Research, Mohammad reza Firouzkouhi and
Ali Zargham-Boroujeni made a case for using coding to assess the accuracy of oral

history. They applied coding to a project about nursing practice during the Iran–Iraq War. "Historians believe that using theories and models creates bias toward the investigations," they wrote. "If this is true, how do novice researchers become familiar with robust techniques and processes of inquiry required in research?" They developed a four-stage method "to clarify the data obtained by the researcher through oral history interviews." Their analysis stages were:

- Data gathering through interviews with the oral witness and first-level coding.
- Second-level coding and determining the sub-categories.
- Third-level coding and determining the main categories.
- Connecting the main categories to each other and writing the narrative.

First-level coding reflects the researcher's first impressions of an interview. The authors give this example:

> [I]n some military operations like Kheibar, 1985, the conditions were such that we worked for three days nonstop due to the excessive number of wounded. There was no time to rest, eat or pray properly. I remember that the young doctors and nurses couldn't resist and just lay on the floor next to the patient's bed. Code: nonstop nursing activities

In the next stages, codes are reviewed and refined and subcategories emerge. The researchers check the validity of the codes with the participants. Eventually, the researchers establish the veracity of an oral history interview and use the codes to draw their best conclusions.[45]

Qualitative research expert Valerie Janesick finds that coding informs the direction of her subsequent interviews. Reviewing transcripts is a crucial part of her process. "The three themes which struck me in the first interview were used to construct most of the questions for the second interview," she wrote of a research project in her field of education and leadership.[46] She warns against trying to rush through coding transcripts:

> I sometimes found my mind wandering and would have to return to a portion of the transcript that I had already read. I realized that marking text must be done over time, giving myself breaks when needed. This is not something to plough through, because it will not be done well.[47]

Reading the transcript also helped Janesick improve her interviewing skills:

> To begin, I did not do a good job of asking probing questions in the first interview. In reading the transcript, I was amazed at how I bumbled through the follow-ups. I know this is a skill that takes lots of practice, but reading the transcript of how I handled these questions has made me re-focus on the importance of this skill.[48]

Bottom Line

Scholars need to be able to find transcripts in order to use them for research. The most accessible collections are available online. Some collections are partially online, while others still require traveling to reading rooms. Ideally, scholars will have access to both a transcript and the audio. While many researchers prefer the convenience of skimming through a printed document or using Control + F to search for their desired terms in a pdf or Word document, nothing replaces hearing the person speak for himself or herself. The voice gives the flavor of the personality, and listening helps scholars stay true to the narrator's unique voice. It's also important to listen to the audio if you have any doubt about the transcript's accuracy, especially if you're quoting the narrator on a sensitive subject.

Researchers are idiosyncratic. They will devise their own way to organize and interpret oral history materials, whether this means turning them into poetry or coding them with software. When excerpting transcripts, researchers are usually looking for a good—and optimally succinct— story well told, that adds knowledge or emotional impact to their project.

Narrators, collections and institutions deserve proper credit. Just because a transcript is online doesn't mean it's everybody's property. Crediting a transcript shows respect for its creators and processors. Researchers should get permission when necessary, and let the collection know about the finished product, whether a book, exhibit or film.

Notes

1 Oh, there is a book. See *Curating Oral Histories* by Nancy MacKay (London: Routledge, 2015).
2 Douglas Boyd, "I Just Want to Click on It to Listen," in D.A. Boyd and M. Larsen (eds.), *Oral History and Digital Humanities* (Basingstoke: Palgrave Macmillan, 2014), p. 84.
3 Francis Good, email correspondence with Teresa Bergen, July 22, 2018.
4 Jeff Corrigan, interview with Teresa Bergen, December 18, 2017.
5 Ibid.
6 John Sheehy, interview with Teresa Bergen, June 20, 2018.
7 I witnessed this exchange. It wasn't pretty, and I apologized to Mr. Isay afterwards for the poor behavior of my fellow OHA members.
8 Keith O'Brien, "The Power of Oral History as Journalism," available at: http://niema nstoryboard.org/stories/the-opposite-of-writing/ (accessed June 12, 2018).
9 Juliana Nykolaiszyn, email correspondence with Teresa Bergen, July 13, 2018.
10 Steven Sielaff, interview with Teresa Bergen, June 29, 2018.
11 Available at: https://www.baylor.edu/oralhistory/index.php?id=931703 (accessed July 1, 2018).
12 Linda Valois, email correspondence with Teresa Bergen, June 4, 2018.
13 David Katz, email correspondence with Teresa Bergen, June 26, 2018.
14 Sheehy interview, June 20, 2018.
15 Nykolaiszyn correspondence, July 13, 2018.
16 Ibid.
17 Sielaff interview, June 26, 2018.
18 National Library of New Zealand website, available at: https://natlib.govt.nz/records/ 35838354?search%5Bi%5D%5Bsubject%5D=Women&search%5Bpath%5D=items&sea rch%5Btext%5D=oral+histories (accessed June 17, 2018).

19 South African History Archive website, available at: www.saha.org.za/collections/oral_
history.htm (accessed June 17, 2018).

20 Troy Reeves, interview with Teresa Bergen, December 11, 2017.

21 Ibid.

22 Jennifer Cramer, interview with Teresa Bergen, January 23, 2018.

23 Dirk Vogel, "This Is How I Organized Large Interview Transcript Files with Hashtags,"
January 22, 2018, available at: http://dirkwriter.com/this-is-how-i-organized-large-in
terview-transcript-files-with-hashtags/ (accessed February 13, 2019).

24 Evernote website, available at: https://blog.evernote.com/blog/2015/01/18/wri
te-93000-word-book-evernote/ (accessed July 2, 2018).

25 Adizes Institute Worldwide, "Adizes Corporate Lifecyle," available at: http://adizes.
com/lifecycle/ (accessed February 13, 2019).

26 Sheehy interview, June 20, 2018.

27 Andromache Gazi and Irene Nakou (eds.) "Museums and Education – Oral History,"
2015, MuseumEdu 2, available at: http://museumedulab.ece.uth.gr/main/el/node/417
(accessed February 13, 2019).

28 Jodi Giesbrecht, email correspondence with Teresa Bergen, July 24, 2018.

29 Reagan Grau, email correspondence with Teresa Bergen, November 28, 2016.

30 Olga Orlic, "How to Present Oral History at a Museum Exhibition?" Paper presented at
the conference "Can Oral History Make Objects Speak?," Nafplio, Greece. October
18–21, 2005.

31 Jennifer Cramer, interview with Teresa Bergen, January 23, 2018.

32 Steven Sielaff, interview with Teresa Bergen, June 26, 2018.

33 Columbia University Libraries, "Research and Citation Management," available at: http
s://library.columbia.edu/research/citation-management.html (accessed February 13, 2019).

34 Linda Shopes, "What Is Oral History?," available at: http://historymatters.gmu.edu/m
se/oral/oral.pdf (accessed July 7, 2018).

35 Katz, email correspondence, June 26, 2018.

36 Julia Bailey, "First Steps in Qualitative Data Analysis Transcribing," *Family Practice*, 25(2)
(2008): 127–131, available at: https://academic.oup.com/fampra/article/25/2/127/
497632 (accessed July 7, 2018).

37 John Sheehy, interview with Teresa Bergen, June 20, 2018.

38 Lorina Barker, "Using Poetry to Capture the Aboriginal Voice in Oral History Transcripts," in *Passionate Histories: Myth, Memory and Indigenous Australia* (The Australian
National University E Press, 2010), available at: http://press-files.anu.edu.au/downloa
ds/press/p70821/pdf/ch0935.pdf (accessed July 7, 2018).

39 Johnny Saldaña, *The Coding Manual for Qualitative Researchers* (London: SAGE, 2009), p. 3.

40 Ibid., p. 4.

41 Ibid., p. 4.

42 Ibid., p. 22.

43 Sharon Kruse, email correspondence with Teresa Bergen, December 18, 2017.

44 Alexis Waldron, interview with Teresa Bergen, January 5, 2018..

45 Mohammad reza Firouzkouhi and Ali Zargham-Boroujeni, "Data Analysis in Oral History: A New Approach in Historical Research," *Iranian Journal of Nursing and Midwifery
Research*, March–April (2015): 161–164.

46 Valerie Janesick, *Oral History for the Qualitative Researcher* (New York; Guilford Press,
20100, p. 155.

47 Ibid., p. 172.

48 Ibid., p. 171.

EPILOGUE

As I knew going into this project, processing interviews from audio to transcripts is a very time-consuming and exacting process. Budget is a major limiting factor. But doing my research, I was impressed by the creative ways people find to fund the work they really care about, whether it's crowdsourcing volunteer transcriptionists or hosting a spaghetti dinner and wine auction.

Projects have to make tough decisions about their priorities. There's a lot that project managers can do to make the process go more smoothly, such as being realistic about the size and scope of a project, and communicating with the transcriptionist and other research team members. Some projects will conclude that they can make do with indexes rather than complete transcripts. My research underlines that planning is key. Otherwise, you wind up with that untranscribed box of mystery tapes—or the modern equivalent, MP3 files on forgotten thumb drives—that's been corroding in the basement for decades.

Sooner or later, automated voice-to-text technology may well take over much of transcription. I expect this will be the case for other types of interviews first. I already know magazine writers who record many interviews and conversations and get them automatically transcribed for a small fee. Usually, they need only the gist of the conversation, and will choose a few significant quotes for their articles. Hopefully they go back and listen to these quotations to ensure the software got them right.

But for oral history transcripts, which researchers count on to be highly accurate, human transcriptionists will last longer. Will I, the transcriptionist, eventually become obsolete? As technology gets more dependable, I expect transcriptionists might move into auditor roles, with computers doing the first pass, at least for top quality audio. Problematic recordings will probably always require human ears to decipher.

It's possible that instead of bringing transcriptionists less work, technology will generate more, but of a different kind. If computers take over transcription and transcriptionists become auditors, editors and fact checkers, oral history projects may flourish. Since transcription is usually the biggest project cost, programs may be able to record, process and preserve more high-quality oral history, which the AI transcriptionist /human auditor duo will turn around faster.

Smartphones and other inexpensive recording devices are making it easier than ever to capture people's stories through oral history methodology. So while developers continue to improve speech-to-text, the interviews are pouring in. I'll keep my fingers on the keyboard.

LIST OF INTERVIEWEES

Maija Anderson, former director of library operations, Oregon Health & Science University, USA

Lindsey Annable, director, Free Spirit Consulting Ltd, London, UK

Jenna Bain, digital projects leader, State Library of New South Wales, Australia

David Beorlegui, oral historian, University of the Basque Country, Spain

Heather Bidzinski, head of collections, Canadian Museum for Human Rights, Winnipeg, Manitoba, Canada

Jennifer Campbell, owner of Heritage Memoirs, Cobourg, Ontario, Canada

Indira Chowdhury, founder-director of the Centre for Public History at the Srishti Institute of Art, Design and Technology, Bangalore, India

Jeff Corrigan, former oral historian for the State Historical Society of Missouri, USA

Jennifer Cramer, director, T. Harry Williams Center for Oral History, Louisiana State University, USA

Jodi Giesbrecht, manager of research and curation, Canadian Museum for Human Rights in Winnipeg, Manitoba, Canada

Lois Glewwe, author and transcriptionist, Saint Paul, Minnesota, USA

Francis Good, retired manager of the Northern Territory Archive's Oral History Unit, Australia

Mary Contini Gordon, researcher and author, Arizona, USA

Reagan Grau, chief archivist and director of collections at the National Museum of the Pacific War in Fredericksburg, Texas, USA

Victoria Greene, documentary filmmaker, New Orleans, Louisiana, USA

Kim Heikkila, author, educator, owner/president of Spotlight Oral History, Minneapolis, USA

Susan Hutton, freelance proofreader and transcriptionist for British Library and other projects, Somerset, UK

Barb Jardee, owner, Jardee Transcription, USA

David Katz, author, London, UK

Sharon Kruse, academic director, Washington State University, College of Education, USA

Almut Leh, historian and research fellow at the Institute for History and Biography at the University of Hagen, Germany

Carol McKirdy, oral historian and adult educator, proprietor of History Herstory, Australia

Sarah Milligan, head of the Oklahoma Oral History Research Program, USA

Susan Nicholls, transcriptionist, British Library, UK

Juliana Nykolaiszyn, assistant head of digital resources and discovery services, Oklahoma State University, USA

Troy Reeves, director, University of Wisconsin, Madison Oral History Program, USA

Carol Roberts, owner of Hawkesbury Valley Heritage Tours, New South Wales, Australia

Jami Roskamp, curator, The History Center at the Linn County Historical Society, Cedar Rapids, Iowa, USA

John Sheehy, author, Penngrove, California, USA

Steven Sielaff, senior editor and collections manager, Baylor University Institute of Oral History, Waco, Texas, USA

Trần Thị Minh Phước, author, oral historian and bilingual Vietnamese/English transcriptionist, Minnesota, USA

Linda Valois, former park ranger and manager of the museum collection at the Santa Monica Mountains Recreation Area, National Park Service, USA

Alexis Waldron, human performance specialist, US Forest Service, Big Bend, Texas, USA

Mark Wong, senior oral history specialist, Oral History Centre, National Archives of Singapore

Sun Yi, documentary filmmaker, China

RESOURCES

Here's how to find some of the resources mentioned in this book.

Style Guides

- Baylor University Institute for Oral History Style Guide: A Quick Reference for Editing Oral History Transcripts: www.baylor.edu/oralhistory/doc.php/14142.pdf
- Guide to Transcribing and Summarizing Oral Histories: Historic Columbia River Highway Oral History: www.oregon.gov/ODOT/Programs/ResearchDocuments/guide_to_transcribing_and_summarizing_oral_histories.pdf
- Learning to Listen: A Manual for Oral History Projects: www.burmalibrary.org/docs21/Sadan-2008-learning_to_listen-en-tpo.pdf

Transcription Services

- Audio Transcription Center: https://audiotranscriptioncenter.com/
- Teresa Bergen, oral history and other qualitative research transcription, indexing and editing, USA: teresa.bergen@gmail.com
- Lois Glewwe, oral history transcription, USA, 651-457-3403: lglewwe@hotmail.com
- GoTranscript: https://gotranscript.com/
- Susan Hutton, professional proofreading and transcription, UK, 00 44 01823 275132: susan@susan-hutton.com
- Barb Jardee, Jardee Transcription, 520-325-6121: barbjardee@msn.com, www.jardeetranscription.com
- Trần Thị Minh Phước, oral historian and Vietnamese/English transcriber: Ptran9tm@gmail.com

Software

- Audacity digital audio editing and recording software: www.audacityteam. org/
- Breevy text expansion program: https://breevy.en.softonic.com/
- Dragon Naturally Speaking voice-to-text software: www.nuance.com/dragon. html
- Evernote note taking app: https://evernote.com/
- Express Scribe transcription software: www.nch.com.au/scribe/index.html
- Fraunhofer IAIS audio mining system (in German): www.iais.fraunhofer.de/ de/geschaeftsfelder/content-technologies-and-services/uebersicht/AudioMin ing.html
- GearPlayer transcription software: www.transcriptiongear.com/gearpla yer-4-transcription-software.html
- GoTranscript: https://gotranscript.com/
- InterClipper Audio: www.interclipper.com/
- NVivo coding software: www.qsrinternational.com/nvivo/nvivo-products
- Oral History Metadata Synchronizer (OHMS): www.oralhistoryonline.org/ help/release/
- PhraseExpress text expansion program: www.phraseexpress.com/
- Pop Up Archive searchable audio technology: www.crunchbase.com/organiza tion/pop-up-archiveTranscribe voice-to-text software: https://transcribe.wrea lly.com/
- Trint voice-to text software: https://trint.com/

Other

- Amplify–crowdsourced transcription project of New South Wales: http s://amplify.sl.nsw.gov.au/
- Randforce Associates oral history collection management and indexing tools: www.randforce.com/

APPENDIX 1: SAMPLE TRANSCRIPT

Narrator: Nancy Drew
Interviewer: Trixie Belden
Date: May 1, 1970
Transcribed by: Teresa Bergen

TRIXIE BELDEN: Today is May 1, 1970, and Trixie Belden is interviewing Nancy Drew in her home town of River Heights. Nancy, thanks for agreeing to be interviewed this morning.

NANCY DREW: My pleasure, Trixie.

BELDEN: I'd like to start with some background information. When and where were you born?

DREW: Well, as you mentioned, I'm from River Heights. I was born here in 1914. Yes, a long time ago. (laughs)

BELDEN: Tell me a little about your childhood and your parents.

DREW: It was an idyllic childhood, really, when I was very young. My father, Carson Drew, was an attorney. My mother took wonderful care of me. But it all changed when I was ten. (sighs) My mother died.

BELDEN: I'm so sorry.

DREW: If it wasn't for Hannah Gruen, our housekeeper, I don't know what I would have done. And my friends Bess and George. I had to grow up fast. [pause]

BELDEN: So, Nancy, when did you get interested in detective work?

DREW: I just stumbled into it as a teenager. (laughs) Mysterious things always seemed to happen around me. And I had the talents and resources. I studied psychology in high school, and my upbringing included learning lots of useful skills, like driving at a young age, and marksmanship, giving first aid, swimming, riding horses and piloting boats. Yes, back then I was up for just about anything.

BELDEN: What were you like back then, personality-wise?

DREW: I was often criticized for being outspoken. Some people said it was because my mother wasn't around to make me more demure. But I've always had a strong sense of right and wrong, and had the courage of my convictions. I stay cool under pressure and I don't have any patience for people who lie, cheat, steal or are generally unkind. I learned all about the law growing up with my father, and have never respected people who don't respect the law.

BELDEN: As a girl detective who came along a few years after you, I always looked up to you. You were so good at everything! And you traveled to more exotic places than I did. Tell me about some of the locales your cases took you to.

APPENDIX 2: PROPER NOUN LIST

[For a fictional person living in Portland, Oregon]

Celilo Falls
Clackamas Street
Clatskanie
Couch Street
Deschutes River
EPCC [East Portland Community Center]
Equi, Dr. Marie
Failing Street
Going Street
Klickitat
Meier & Frank
Multnomah County
Pittock, Henry Lewis
Scott, Harvey
Sleater-Kinney
Terwilliger Curves
Umatilla
Unthank Park
Wallowa Mountains
Willamette River
Yachats

APPENDIX 3: TRANSCRIPTION PREFERENCE LIST

Directions for typist

Do you have the ability to receive documents via e-mail?

No _____ Yes _____ e-mail address:

Do you require a printed document? (additional charge)

No _____ Yes _____

We will keep your documents on backup for one year. It is recommended that you back up your documents as well.

Software and layout

Documents are saved in Microsoft Word.

The page format used to determine page counts for billing is based on one-inch margins all around, left justified, double spacing, no indents, 10 characters per inch, no footers or page numbers, 27 lines per page. Thanks to the wonder of word processing and computers, however, you may have whatever parameters you like for your documents. Please indicate your preferences below.

Margins: Top _____" Bottom _____" Left _____" Right _____"
Spacing: Single _____ 1.5_____ Double _____ Other (specify) _____

Times New Roman, point size 12, is one option. Other type styles are available, please let me know if you have a favorite you'd like me to use. MS Word default is Calibri 11 point.

A centered footer, showing narrator/interviewee's name, date of interview, draft #, and page # is recommended:

John Doe, X/XX/2011, Draft 1, Page X

How should speakers be identified? By last name, or by initials? Other?
   After the speaker is identified, do you want the text indented,

   like this?

Or should the text return to the left margin,
   like this?

Spellings and styles

- The vernacular for "yes" should be spelled

  yeah or yah or ya or some other way? _____

- The grunt that is understood to mean "yes" should be spelled

  uh-huh or some other way? _____

- The grunt that is understood to mean "no" should be spelled

  uh-uh or unt-uh or some other way? _____

- Shall I retain the flavor of the narrator's speech by reflecting such mannerisms as dropping the final "g" in a word, as in "fallin', walkin', or startin'"? Should I retain speech mannerisms as "gonna" for "going to," and "gotta" for "got to" or "have to," or should I clean this up and use the more correct forms?
- Em dashes—will be used, with no spaces before or after, to indicate a mid-sentence change of subject. If software requires, double dashes may be used.
- When the speaker says "Summer of '42," shall I provide the missing digits, "Summer of 1942," or use the abbreviated form? Even if using the abbreviated form, it is recommended that on the first mention, the century-specific date be included in square brackets, "Summer of '42 [1942]."
- When talking about a decade, the fifties or the '50s
- When a person trails off without finishing their thought, do you prefer ellipsis points.... Or do you prefer an em dash followed by a period—. ?

- All numbers less than one hundred will be spelled out. Years, addresses, temperatures, and the like will appear in numeral form. A person's age will always be spelled out, avoiding assumption of a typo.
- Abbreviations: One or two letters, with periods, no spaces. Three or more letters, no periods, no spaces.

U.S. or USA or UNICEF

Or whatever your preference.
When abbreviating a person's first two names, do you want a space between the initials, or not?

B. H. Jardee (with space) or B.H. Jardee (no space)

- How should emphasized words be indicated? By <u>underline</u>, or ALL CAPITALS, or **bold**, or *italics*, or some other way? If you choose to use ALL CAPITALS, how should the word "I" be emphasized?
- Titles of books, magazines, newspapers, lawsuits, and the names of ships, trains, and aircraft, will be *italicized*.
- Titles of TV shows, movies, plays, songs, and paintings will appear "in quotes."
- When a speaker spells a name or word it will appear in ALL CAPS with hyphens in between, J-A-R-D-E-E. Or would you prefer that I use the spelling as given, but not bother with T-Y-P-I-N-G it out?
- Brief interjections in a discussion can appear in the text of the main speaker, without going to a new line:

"I attended the seminar (Jardee: So did I!) to learn all I could about oral history transcription."

- Non-English words will appear in *italics*, unless they have become anglicized (i.e., café, gringo, habeas corpus, gesundheit).
- Capitalization: The army, the air force, the navy, the marine corps. The U.S. Marine Corps, the French Army, the Israeli Air Force, McHale's Navy.

Really, really big numbers

25 million or twenty-five million or 25,000,000

The majority of the printed text I see uses the first option, because readers tend to get confused when they see a string of zeros—especially if it gets up to billions and trillions. Numbers one through ten, when mentioned with millions, billions, etc. will be spelled out.

And what about when it's dollars? $25 million or twenty-five million dollars or $25,000,000?

Percentages

> 50% or 50 percent or fifty percent

Please indicate your preference. Numbers one through ten, when mentioned with percentages, will be spelled out.

Time

Spelled out "five o'clock" (if it's on the hour) but numerals "5:20" or "5:45" if the minutes are mentioned. If the speaker says "five or five-thirty" it will appear as "5:00 or 5:30."

If the person says "a.m." or "p.m." after mentioning the time, numerals will be used, "5:00 a.m." Do you prefer A.M. and P.M. (capitals), or a.m. and p.m. (lower case)?

Odds 'n Ends

Which spelling do you prefer?

> okay or O.K.

How shall I spell the shortened version of "until"?

> 'til or till

If the narrator mentions an acronym that commonly appears in print with an ampersand, how shall I type it?

> AT&T or A T & T or A T and T

Centuries: different options?

> 21st century or twenty-first century

Shall I spell out "et cetera" or use the abbreviation "etc."?

I'm always open to suggestions, so if you notice something on the transcript that you'd like to have appear differently on future transcripts, or if you have suggestions for changes/additions to this list, please let me know.

A lot of these items may seem nit-picky, but I'm hoping to save my clients precious time in proofreading. I like to get things right the first time.

This list is not copyrighted. Feel free to photocopy it, amend it, employ it to your benefit. You are obliged, however, to share it freely with others, as it has been shared with you.

Courtesy of Barb Jardee. Revised May 4, 2018

APPENDIX 4: SAMPLE CONTRACT

Note: If somebody sends you a contract, it will probably never be this simple. But if somebody asks you to provide one, here's where you can start. Both parties might want to add further stipulations, but this clearly covers absolute basics.

Contract for transcription

Agreement between [name of individual, institution or organization] and [name of transcriptionist]

[Institution] will send [x] hours of audio interviews in [mp3, wav or whatever] format by [date]. The transcriptionist will furnish electronic copies of transcriptions within [x amount of time] of receiving materials. The completed transcript must be accurately typed using [Microsoft Word, Pages, etc.] using the transcription template provided by [institution].

[Institution] shall pay vendor compensation of [transcription fee per hour, page or however billed] for all work and services. Total compensation is not to exceed [amount of money]. [Institution] will pay the transcriptionist within [amount of time] of receiving deliverables. This contract may be amended, as long as both parties agree, over the course of the project.

_____

Signature of transcriptionist, date

_____

Signature of project manager, date

APPENDIX 5: INDEX FROM UNIVERSITY OF WISCONSIN, MADISON (WORD PROCESSING)

UNIVERSITY OF WISCONSIN-MADISON ARCHIVES

ORAL HISTORY PROJECT

Interview #436
ABRAHAM, NANCY M.
ABRAHAM, Nancy M. (1934–)

Undergraduate and Graduate Student; Staff; Assistant Director of Summer Sessions; Associate Director of Special Students; Associate Director of Inter-College Programs; Associate Dean of Summer Sessions and Inter-College Programs

At UW: 1954–1955; 1959–1989
Interviewed: 1993
Interviewer: Barry Teicher
Indexed (time code) by: Haochen Wang
Length: 3 hours, 14 minutes

Early childhood and education; Undergraduate work; Office of high school relations; Graduate work; Summer sessions; Director Clay Schoenfeld; Dean's Council; Office of special students; Budget; Protest on campus; Facilities; Bicentennial festival; Enrichment and enhancement programs; Dean Harland Samson's emphasis on enrollment management, budget reduction, upgrading facilities, streamlining and enhancing creativity; Committee work; Summer sessions service organizations; Mental illness organizations; Other interests and activities.

First Interview Session (October 14, 1993): Tapes 1–2

00:00:1 NA came from a blue-collar family in Sheboygan, Wisconsin. She loved school while she was growing up.

00:01:47 She mentions two teachers who influenced her. NA's wonderful first grade teacher made an impression on her at an early age. In high school, she enjoyed all courses she took in the college track. Her history teacher/debate and forensics coach also had quite an impact on her. He was very demanding and taught students to question without fear. He recruited her for the debate and forensics team, participation which she regards as one of the single most important learning experiences in her life. This involvement helped her to overcome her shyness and required she do research on debate topics, an activity she enjoyed. McCarthyism was one of the topics she remembers.

00:06:10 Promising students were encouraged into the college track by principals and teachers. None of NA's relatives had gone to college, so there was no expectation that she would. Her father did not see any reason for her to go because the assumption was that she would just get married. She proceeded to check into scholarship opportunities on her own.

00:08:12 She applied to Stout Institute because she was interested in foods, design, and clothing, and she was admitted. Her family accepted the announcement that she was going.

00:09:12 Her teachers in Sheboygan encouraged her to pursue higher education.

00:10:18 She paid for her education at Stout, which she attended in 1953/54, from money she earned, scholarships, and a small windfall from her parents. She did well academically while she was there, taking both general and specific courses.

00:13:46 NA came to UW her sophomore year, after she married, and continued in the home economics program. She became pregnant that year. The Student Health Center was not equipped to deal with pregnant women because there were not many of them on campus in the early 1950s. She was determined not to drop any courses, and professors were quite accommodating of her situation.

00:18:43 NA did not attend university from 1955 to 1960. She had in the meantime been divorced, so she re-enrolled in 1960 so she could to make a decent living for herself and her son. Her eligibility for a National Defense Loan was questioned on the grounds that a large portion of her budget was designated for child care. She spent two hard years working half-time, attending UW full-time, and caring for her son. She studied home economics and education.

00:21:57 NA continued to work in the medical school two years after she got her B.A. She initially did clerical work in the State Historical Society. She then transferred to a similar position in the Medical School Business, Registrar's, and Dean's Office.

00:25:11 Rita Youmans, a professor of home economics instructor, instilled in students a responsibility to give back when they receive. NA managed to get a dispensation to do independent work instead of living at the Home Management House, a "lab" for home economics students.

00:27:13 NA had James Lipham as a professor while an undergraduate in the School of Education. UW was relatively flexible in granting her "special dispensations." She did abstracts of research reports for a professor in the School of Education to secure her final credit toward her B.A.

00:29:28 There were not large numbers of returning students in the early 1960s. NA's experience was different than that of regular students. She did not have free time to become involved in extracurricular activities.

00:31:19 End of side.

APPENDIX 6: INDEX FROM UNIVERSITY OF WISCONSIN, MADISON (SPREADSHEET)

(reformatted to fit on page)

Name	Session Date	Time Start	Time Stop	Summary
Kevin Reilly	1/11/2016	0:00:00	0:00:29	Interview's Introduction & Sound Check
	1/11/2016	0:00:29	0:02:55	Competency Based Degree Programs? Kevin Reilly (KR) called this an innovation he took up towards the end of his tenure. He offered an overview of this effort, which intended to give Wisconsin adults with college credits a way for them to get additional credits towards a degree from their work experience.
	1/11/2016	0:02:55	0:08:05	More on Competency Based. While tried before in small portions, this UW System stood as the first large effort. KR spoke here about how he proposed this program to the faculty affected
	1/11/2016	0:08:05	0:11:29	KR continued with the Competency Based Degree Program idea, focusing here on how it benefitted the adults involved in it. And continued discussing it, noting how he reminded folks that these adults could do this program and take traditional courses too, meaning it stood not as an "either/or" idea.

Name	Session Date	Time Start	Time Stop	Summary
	1/11/2016	0:11:29	0:16:05	How did KR promote this effort? Primarily through UW Extension. He noted that he and Governor Walker also flew around the state to promote it. When asked if it started to work before he left, KR noted they started small, on purpose. And that he asked Aaron Brower to lead it (and why he did so). KR recalled (although he wasn't sure) that it started with 5 degree programs and grew to 8 before he left.
	1/11/2016	0:16:05	0:25:58	What things didn't go well? Since KR led Extension or System for 14 years, there was plenty of things that didn't do well. KR started with one mentioned in an editorial written at the time of his retirement [**2.8.16 email addition:** The editorial was in the *Wisconsin State Journal*, not the *Journal Sentinel*], the attempt to create a new HR/Payroll system. KR talked about how he moved forward with this effort and how he and others started to see the vendor's proposed creation wouldn't work for them.
	1/11/2016	0:25:58	0:30:01	More on HR/Payroll System issues. KR talked here about the complexity of a large university system's payroll, including how it can be different from a large corporation's payroll. He also talked here about deciding to switch vendors, and although there were bumps (none specifically mentioned) with the 2nd vendor, the lessons learned from the 1st vendor and the 2nd vendor's results led to a new HR/Payroll System.
	1/11/2016	0:30:01	0:34:18	Any other things that didn't go well? KR offered one more example: the issue made out of the System's cash reserves. KR offered an overview of this issue, including why the System carried the reserves, why the Governor and Legislature made it an issue, and how this issue led the System to have far fewer reserves to deal with the current (2014–2016) budget cuts.

APPENDIX 7: CONFIDENTIALITY AGREEMENT FOR USE WITH TRANSCRIPTION SERVICES

Research Study Title: [insert your study title here]

1. I, _____ transcriptionist, agree to maintain full confidentiality of all research data received from the research team related to this research study.
2. I will hold in strictest confidence the identity of any individual that may be revealed during the transcription of interviews or in any associated documents.
3. I will not make copies of any audio-recordings, video-recordings, or other research data, unless specifically requested to do so by the researcher.
4. I will not provide the research data to any third parties without the client's consent.
5. I will store all study-related data in a safe, secure location as long as they are in my possession. All video and audio recordings will be stored in an encrypted format.
6. All data provided or created for purposes of this agreement, including any back-up records, will be returned to the research team or permanently deleted. When I have received confirmation that the transcription work I performed has been satisfactorily completed, any of the research data that remains with me will be returned to the research team or destroyed, pursuant to the instructions of the research team.
7. I understand that [name of university or organization] has the right to take legal action against any breach of confidentiality that occurs in my handling of the research data.

Transcriber's name (printed)_____

Transcriber's signature_____

Date _____

INDEX

Entries in **bold** denote tables; entries in *italics* denote figures.

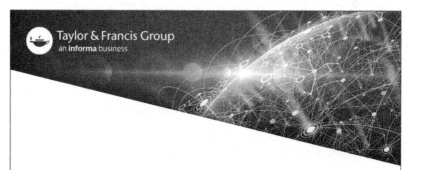

Printed in Great Britain
by Amazon

39119667R00130